# Impact Work

Guillaume Dumont

# Impact Work

## An Ethnographic Journey into the Making of Impact Entrepreneurship

palgrave
macmillan

Guillaume Dumont
emlyon Business School
Ecully, France

ISBN 978-3-031-64660-7 ISBN 978-3-031-64661-4 (eBook)
https://doi.org/10.1007/978-3-031-64661-4



This Palgrave Macmillan imprint is published by the registered company Springer Nature Switzerland AG.
The registered company address is: Gewerbestrasse 11, 6330 Cham, Switzerland

# Acknowledgments

First and foremost, I am grateful to the co-founders of Seal, especially Sofia, for letting me observe and participate in the day-to-day running of the social impact accelerator. This book would not have been possible without her initial interest, curiosity, and willingness to have me around, taking notes, and asking questions. I extend this gratitude to the team, with whom I spent 18 months sharing work and life experiences as I tried to learn the tricks of impact entrepreneurship. I am also grateful to all the entrepreneurs, mentors, impact investors, and corporate partners for sharing their views and experiences with me. Ethnographic fieldwork is always a life-changing experience because of those we meet. This project was no exception. Although the analysis presented in this book does not necessarily represent their views and has been anonymized for confidentiality reasons, I hope that I have been able to capture a taste of their energy as well as their dilemmas as we shared this journey.

Economically speaking, this fieldwork was made possible by a Juan de la Cierva post-doctoral fellowship at the Centre d'Estudis Sociològics sobre la Vida Quotidiana i el Treball (QUIT) at the Universitat Autònoma de Barcelona (grant no. 2015 FJCI-2015-24139). Joan Miquel Verd Pericàs has been unwavering in supporting my application, advising me to move away from my previous research topic and to pivot in a genuinely entrepreneurial fashion. I am incredibly grateful for his suggestions and continuous support during fieldwork. Isabel Hernández provided the much-needed administrative support to survive the Catalan and Spanish bureaucracy. I am thankful for the encouragement of other team members, particularly Alejandro Godino Pons and Oscar Molina Romero. At the Department of Economics, David Urbano and Alex Prieto were very helpful during my time there.

During the second year of my fieldwork, Fabrizio Ferraro welcomed me at IESE Business School as a visiting scholar. He was an invaluable interlocutor as I learned to make sense of management research. His insights were influential in the preparation of Chap. 6. At IESE, I am also very grateful to Alice Mascena Barbosa, fellow fieldworker and co-author, with whom I shared many of my questions and doubts about fieldwork. It is rare for ethnographers to conduct fieldwork in the same setting. The opportunity to share and contrast our views about Seal was significant in shaping and revisiting some of the arguments presented in this book.

Since the fall of 2019, my colleagues at Emlyon Business School and the opportunities to workshop my writing have been vital as I revisited and improved many of the arguments presented in this book. I am particularly grateful to David Courpasson, Frédéric Delmar, and Grégoire Croidieu, who, each in their own way, have been influential in developing my work. I extend this to my positivist and quantitative friend, Ahmed Nofal. I have been lucky to receive feedback from other scholars at various stages of this project, including Benjamin Huybrechts, Lisa Butcher, Jean Clark, Christof Brandtner, Valérie Arnhold, and Saulo Dubard Barbosa. I am also grateful to the students who signed up for my impact entrepreneurship course and challenged some of my arguments.

Earlier versions of two chapters have appeared elsewhere. Parts of Chap. 3 appear in the *Journal of Contemporary Ethnography*. Parts of Chap. 6 appear in *Entrepreneurship Theory and Practice*. I am grateful for permission to use these materials and am indebted to the reviewers and editors for their feedback. Likewise, at Palgrave Macmillan, I wish to thank Elizabeth for being my editor and the external reviewers for their constructive and developmental feedback at the inception and during the final steps of this project. Finally, thank you to Hallie Wells for the copy-editing work and insightful language suggestions as well as to Lídia Pitarch for her careful final read of the manuscript.

# Contents

CHAPTER 1

# The Social World of Impact

You're impact entrepreneurs. You're here to have an impact!

To emphasize his words, Jorge was making eye contact with each of the dozen entrepreneurs staring at him intensely. Eyes sparkling, his excitement was palpable as he launched the boot camp of the acceleration program run by Seal, a social impact accelerator helping entrepreneurs create ventures with social and commercial goals. As usual, Jorge's tone was almost religious as he extolled the virtues of impact entrepreneurship. Sofia and Lola, with whom he created Seal in 2013, were standing proudly at his right. Smiling enthusiastically, they nodded at the end of Jorge's speech to support his words. Their blue suits and heels exuded a formal, business-like style that contrasted with Jorge's Nike sneakers, blue jeans, and grey polo shirt, which signaled a relaxed look *à la* Steve Jobs.

Although not directly visible on their faces, Jorge, Sofia, and Lola's enthusiasm was riddled with doubts. Specifically, they doubted the entrepreneurs' capability to transform their ideas into impact enterprises. Helping them in this process was the heart of Seal's mission, but it was not straightforward. In front of them, entrepreneurs were pinned to their seats, full of optimism and aspiration. Fancy black business suits were rare, mostly the prerogative of those working in the health industry or with financial training. Indeed, for most participants a more casual blue or white suit seemed to do the job perfectly. Grey hair was not uncommon,


G. Dumont, *Impact Work*,
https://doi.org/10.1007/978-3-031-64661-4_1

and many entrepreneurs looked like seasoned workers, contrasting with the popular portrait of the 23-year-old technological entrepreneur fresh out of school.

To insiders, this scene is typical for a boot camp at a business accelerator, an organization envisioned to help entrepreneurs grow their ideas into viable businesses. Entrepreneurs are thrilled by the prospect of starting the program, and the staff is thrilled for the program to start after long weeks of efforts to create the cohort and coordinate with the dozens of external speakers and mentors who will work with the entrepreneurs. After a warm and inspirational welcome from the operating directors, entrepreneurs are introduced to the activities explicitly designed to help them develop their ventures. Mentors played a vital role in this task, and Jorge strongly insisted on their excellence. After trying to make entrepreneurs feel privileged to be in attendance, he gently shared explicit guidelines about the behavior expected from them and the core values structuring the culture of impact entrepreneurship.

At the end of his speech we remained silent, meditating on his final words. Smiling at Jorge, Sofia opened the floor to questions. My closest neighbor, Lisa, timidly raised a hand. The 32-year-old worked as a cardiovascular researcher at the research institute of a leading medical school. She explained that her goal at Seal was “to gain business skills” and learn how to turn her academic excellence into a venture to access funding. For now, these two points were still unclear to her. She asked timidly, uneasy and apologetic, “Excuse my ignorance, I do not want to sound stupid … but what do you mean by MVP?” Her question made me feel better. I was not the only novice around. Sofia smiled and answered, “A Minimum Viable Product. Don’t worry, we’ll talk about this very soon!” Her tone was reassuring, and she added proudly, “In fact, there is a before and an after your time at Seal!”

At that point, however, most of us had not fully realized what Jorge, Lola, and Sofia, expected from us, nor what exactly she meant by a before and an after. It was not until Jorge reiterated what would become his favorite opening sentence that our expectations got clearer. Still in his religious tone, he reiterated, “You’re impact entrepreneurs.” Jorge was becoming truly emotional. His reply expressed a strong faith in the skills of those in the room to reach for the stars. “Being an impact entrepreneur is great. You’re here to accomplish great things, to change the way the economy works, to change how we do business. The world needs you.” In other words, it was not only the entrepreneurs themselves who would undertake a transformative process. Because of this process, the world would become a better place for all of us.

This narrative foregrounding the social nature of entrepreneurs' endeavors and their unique traits was everywhere. It would become the recurrent element underpinning the entire boot camp and, eventually, the three months acceleration training. Jorge soon continued, "Your social goal is what makes you different from others. You have a vision, a vision that is different from traditional entrepreneurs because it's embedded in social goals; this is why you stand out from the masses. But you're also real entrepreneurs! At Seal, we don't want people who want to live off nothing. You must have a sustainable business model to make a change, a real change. Many will tell you that this is not possible. But don't listen to them. They're wrong. Being an impact entrepreneur is worth a try! Many people are now expecting impact entrepreneurs to lead change. Investors, companies, consumers, and governments want to help you; they want to give you money! Do you know what this means for you? It means that developing an impact enterprise has become a commercial advantage!"

## Impact Entrepreneurship

This book is about impact entrepreneurship, a growing phenomenon guided by an explicit promise that creates the possibility for an alternative type of organization—the impact enterprise—to achieve social and environmental goals while being economically profitable. Impact entrepreneurship is one of several recent manifestations of the boost in popularity of the term "impact," which has now penetrated public policies and private initiatives. Nowadays, it is hard to talk about matters as diverse as community building, production processes, digital health, research outputs, investing practices, work regulations, commercial fishing, or the automobile industry without considering impact, at least on the surface. While such considerations have, arguably, always existed, we are at a time when states, foundations, corporations, and private investors, throw money into initiatives of different kinds because of their explicit promise to have a positive impact on society. Within this newly popularized impact economy, research institutes and consultancy firms design and sell labels, certificates, and training programs, increasingly supported by new governmental regulations requiring impact accountability.

Entrepreneurship is one instance where we see clear evidence of this trend, most notably in the emergence and consolidation of social entrepreneurship. Yet, in this book, I deliberately use the term "impact entrepreneurship" to capture what is, I would argue, one of the multiple contemporary evolutions of social entrepreneurship. Impact and social entrepreneurs share common characteristics. Social entrepreneurship has long been defined as encompassing a broad scope of initiatives to address pressing social and environmental issues. Accordingly, most social entrepreneurs create social enterprises with the primary objective of achieving social and environmental goals rather than generating profit.[1] To some extent, social entrepreneurship as a global phenomenon is still emerging, as are its definitional features,[2] but there is scholarly consensus on the primacy of social value creation as the trigger of venture creation.

This scholarship provides normative arguments around an intrinsic desire to "make this world a better place" fueling social entrepreneurs.[3] By adopting the view that unique personal traits characterize these entrepreneurs, it establishes a causal relationship between compassionate, caring, and altruistic behavior and the creation of a social venture. In doing so, this scholarship presents and glorifies the victorious nature of individuals over the irresistible market forces of capitalism, bringing back human endeavor into a world overly focused on profit. This view carries three important consequences. First, we still know very little on the multi-layered nature of entrepreneurial motivations. Second, the dynamics through which people are socialized to impact entrepreneurship have been overlooked. Third, the new expectations raised by companies, investors, and consumers, about entrepreneurs as the providers of profitable solutions to societal issues are largely unknown.

More broadly, the circumstances under which social entrepreneurship develops have changed. To reflect on this change, as well as move beyond the umbrella of social entrepreneurship, throughout this book I use the term "impact entrepreneurship" to refer to the pursuit of social *and* economic goals through new venture creation. Under this view, this dual pursuit is the primary element shaping the development of innovative solutions to social or environmental problems in a way that is profitable. Certainly, in some instances, the economic dimension may take over its social counterpart, and vice versa. However, this process is iterative and both dimensions should be integrated and located at the heart of new

[1] See Dees (1998), Mair and Martí (2006), Dacin et al. (2010).
[2] See Chliova et al. (2020), Nicholls (2010).
[3] Austin et al. (2006), Mair and Martí (2006).

venture creation. However, this process is not barrier-free but requires creating a new type of entrepreneur whose work is supported by a network of collaborators.

The primary reason motivating this analytical distinction is its empirical relevance. In fact, in his introductory speech to the cohort, Jorge strongly insisted on these aspects, reiterating again and again that change would only happen by achieving social and commercial goals simultaneously. He explained to the entrepreneurs in the room that their endeavors differed from *traditional* but not *commercial* entrepreneurs, in an attempt to avoid downplaying the importance of their endeavors' commercial goals. By claiming that impact entrepreneurship represents the only way to achieve a more sustainable future, Jorge contributes to the diffusion of a morally standardized view where economic profitability is necessary for impact. As they shape entrepreneurial training and development, organizations such as Seal play a pivotal role in the implementation and diffusion of this view.

In speaking of impact entrepreneurship, my goal is not to add more confusion to already complex definitional debates;[4] rather, I hope to better capture one of the most important and novel forms of social entrepreneurship. Indeed, it is important to understand impact entrepreneurship on its own, for a number of reasons. Empirically, while social entrepreneurship originated in a context of resource scarcity to find new ways to compensate for significant decreases in public funding,[5] the current financial, material, and human resources available to entrepreneurs are growing.[6] We face a rise in awareness about the negative potential of existing and new social and environmental transformations. Resultingly, some of these transformations have increasingly been qualified as social and environmental problems that must be addressed. Those taking on this challenge may enjoy reputational benefits,[7] and the legitimacy of their endeavor is supported by a growing track record of successful ventures and impact investing funds that are becoming sustainable and, perhaps more

[4] As with any emergent phenomenon, there has been a great deal of discussion and debate on what social entrepreneurship entails, but also whether we need new theories to explain this phenomenon. See, for example, Bacq and Janssen (2011) and Huybrechts and Nicholls (2012). Recent commentators, however, still point to the fuzzy nature of social entrepreneurship. For example, Chliova et al. (2020).

[5] Barman (2016).

[6] Zahra et al. (2009).

[7] See Bandinelli and Arvidsson (2013), Bacq and Alt (2018).

importantly, profitable.[8] Finally, although limited in size and mainly consisting of wealthy individuals, consumer segments ask for alternatives to existing products, services, and means of production.

What Jorge pointed out eloquently that first morning echoes findings from recent scholarship: These reasons are slowly but steadily making impact entrepreneurship a competitive advantage for those planning to launch an enterprise. [9] Moreover, by framing impact entrepreneurs as individuals attuned to the need to address social and environmental issues in a way that is economically profitable, Jorge elevated the pursuit of impact as one of the most noble and legitimate ways to have a career nowadays. In other words, becoming an impact entrepreneur also provides a reputational advantage.[10] Such benefits, however, do not come without a cost. In fact, working alongside and speaking with entrepreneurs in the acceleration program reveals their struggles to meaningfully acknowledge, understand, and integrate social and economic demands.

The implications of these transformations must be reflected theoretically, raising several important questions: If the notion of impact is polysemic, what happens when new actors with their own agendas, such as corporations, investors, or commercial entrepreneurs, step into the game? How do these actors collaborate when they set out to have an impact? Should their respective imaginaries of impact align to enable collective action? With limited expertise and no track records, how do these actors, alongside impact entrepreneurs, build credible visions of this future? Should the primacy of prosocial intention remain the distinguishing criterion used to draw a line between traditional and impact entrepreneurship if the goal is to improve societal and natural life conditions? What criteria should we use to evaluate impact enterprises? Perhaps more important, how do different people make sense of their social engagement in this phenomenon?

## Impact Work

The challenge of achieving impact through new venture creation is a matter of empirical and theoretical analysis. It asks a critical question: how to make "impact" an endeavor worth pursuing. This challenge is also, and

[8] Hockerts et al. (2022).
[9] See, for example, Muñoz and Kimmitt (2019).
[10] See Tucker et al. (2019).

more broadly, to develop new and more sustainable ways of living. Toward this aim, only a more concrete analysis can determine if the persistent normative views advanced by prior scholarship to capture the initial stages of this phenomenon still possess any traction on the ground. Additionally, and more importantly, only this more concrete analysis can provide fine-grained accounts of what it takes to create impact entrepreneurs and impact enterprises. For now, we know markedly little about this process.

This book provides an ethnographically grounded examination of how impact enterprises come to life, and proposes one overall thesis. Specifically, I argue that impact is not a given property of a venture, nor the sole result of the intrinsic desire to change the world, as is typically claimed by impact entrepreneurs and popularized by practitioners as well as much of the related scholarship. Instead, I posit that impact emerges iteratively from a process of social engagement and negotiation among networks of actors who collectively engage in the performance of entrepreneurial work. Accordingly, impact takes shape through the everyday, mundane processes of its production—what I name "impact work." Throughout the chapters of this book, I uncover what impact work entails and show how it revolves around three fundamental characteristics.

First, impact work is a collective activity. It is no accident that impact entrepreneurship has been depicted and theorized as an individual endeavor. Vital for the development of the discipline of entrepreneurship has been the Schumpeterian view of a visionary entrepreneur who detects opportunities and creates businesses.[11] This longstanding obsession with the naturally gifted entrepreneur has fueled more interest in identifying entrepreneurs' biological characteristics than in uncovering the role of social, cultural, and economic contexts in new venture creation. In impact entrepreneurship specifically, this view has been promoted by leading field organizations such as the Ashoka Foundation, which insisted on that some people are naturally driven by social goals and must be identified and supported.

This view, however, has yet to be nuanced.[12] This is particularly important given that innovative social ideas are constantly in the making and that entrepreneurs can hardly turn these ideas into successful ventures all on their own. Likewise, as with any entrepreneurial project, the production of impact work cannot unfold without cooperation networks between

[11] Schumpeter (1911).
[12] See Montgomery et al. (2012).

impact entrepreneurs and investors, serial entrepreneurs, family members and friends, corporations, intermediary organizations such as business accelerators or incubators, and the like. These actors play a vital role in impact entrepreneurship, but this role remains overlooked and downplayed in most description and analysis of this phenomenon. This book addresses this gap by uncovering the myriad ways that people in networks of collaboration contribute to the development of impact enterprises and the broader phenomenon of impact entrepreneurship.

Second, impact work is a processual activity. Beyond the lack of scholarly consensus on what social impact is,[13] it is typically measured at a specific moment in time and by using different indicators. Yet the production of impact work involves the day-to-day labor of people sharing relatively similar views of the future and following conventions. Relatedly, envisioning impact as a fixed construct resulting from the use of measurement indicators hides the complex and contextual mechanisms that would explain how to achieve change from A to B. Consequently, any approach to impact must also work toward identifying the activities enabling change to explain how change actually happens. Approaching impact work as a processual activity increases knowledge about how to produce the changes captured by indicators. In times when a major struggle is to create indicators and measurement frameworks enabling comparability across ventures, this shift in focus from outcomes to activities has the potential to produce comparable insights.

Third, impact work is fundamentally turned toward the future. Impact work takes place in a context of uncertainty that warrants the creation of shared imaginaries of the future.[14] These future imaginaries are necessary to enable collective action resulting in the production of impact through actors' respective social engagements and negotiations. Indeed, it is not only that our understanding of how impact entrepreneurs will achieve impact is limited, but also that the likelihood of their ventures sustaining and scaling this impact is constantly under threat.[15] By creating shared imaginaries of the future, people build expectations about what this future will look like and how it will eventually unfold. The fact that impact work is geared toward a future in which outcomes are hardly predictable requires

[13] Rawhouser et al. (2019).

[14] The work of Jens Beckert on the role of fictional expectations for the economy is particularly illustrative of this point. See Beckert (2016).

[15] Ebrahim and Rangan (2014).

entrepreneurs to build credible promises of impact and to convince others of their social goals. The actors of the impact economy have elevated intentionality as a shared moral standard and use this standard as a core criterion for building expectations and making decisions. When the output of impact work is unknown and its production a challenging and risky endeavor, uncertainty and intentionality work together to build credible future expectations and promises about impact.

## Theoretical Apparatus

This book, therefore, is about what I like to think of as impact entrepreneurship in the making. It teaches us how those entrepreneurs engaged at Seal learn the tricks of the trade and acquire specific skills related to important questions such as raising capital, creating a theory of change, producing compelling stories, and convincing others of the credibility of their promise to achieve impact through new venture creation.

In developing these ideas, I build on a heterogeneous set of concepts primarily formulated by sociologists and anthropologists. The main reason for this theoretical digression is trivial. If the scholarship on social entrepreneurship has been steadily growing since the late 90s, it has been more concerned with describing the emergence of the phenomenon and tentatively solving definitional problems by using concepts imported primarily from the discipline of entrepreneurship, business ethics, and organization studies, than to describe and analyze what is happening on the ground level. While describing the emergence of a phenomenon is, of course, indispensable for paving the way to future research, it also leaves unexplored the nitty-gritty processes and mechanisms that are central to impact entrepreneurship. In other words, now that the dynamics of social entrepreneurship emergence have been theorized abundantly, we need to capture empirically its numerous current forms. From an anthropological point of view, this requires explaining empirically how a group of people, brought together because of their diverse skills and knowledge, set out to engage in impact work.

Paths toward answering this question can be found, first, in the sociological literature associated with Howard Becker. Becker has long been interested in addressing traditional questions in unconventional, empirically informed ways. He does so by decentering the dominant focus of analysis to instead center his sights on actors and production activities that typically remain unseen.[16] For instance, his seminal work on the world of art production shifts the focus from the taken-for-granted talent and genius of the artist to the networks of cooperation between larger groups of people involved with this artist. Indeed, numerous tasks must be performed to produce any type of artwork, and performing these tasks requires different resources and skills and involves a specific division of labor. This division of labor involves different occupational groups and institutions with varying degrees of importance for creating artworks through their production, distribution, and promotion. However, as widely demonstrated in the creative industries and beyond, artists always reap the most attention.

Becker's approach has proven valuable for revealing the world of backstage cultural production and for bringing the role of invisible actors into light. For instance, in her study of fashion modeling, Ashley Mears[17] shows how much a "look" is the result of people doing things together. Instead of being analyzed as a natural, aesthetic feature of a privileged few grasping all the attention, Mears reveals the routine work and negotiation in which clients, bookers, and models engage to define what having a great "look" means, and how much it is worth. In a similar vein, my work with professional rock climbers moves beyond the picture of physically gifted athletes to reveal the world that props up this picture through the production and communication of an idealized self.[18] By working closely with photographers, filmmakers, team managers, sponsors, and fans, professional climbers perform creative labor to turn their athletic realizations into commodities and, this way, build their value on the sponsoring labor market.

While the analogy between impact entrepreneurship, creative industries, and professional sports might initially be surprising, I believe the similarity with early-stage entrepreneurship is striking. In particular, the hype surrounding a minimal number of highly successful ventures hides an entire world of less successful entrepreneurs and less visible actors contributing in multiple essential ways to producing the social world of impact entrepreneurship. While recent commentaries have consistently pointed to the need to broaden the scope of analysis to document and explain the

[16] Becker provided early insights about his approach in his work on the social worlds of art, further developed in his book *Art Worlds* (1982).

[17] See Mears (2011).

[18] See Dumont (2018).

role of these actors,[19] the gravitational center of most scholarship remains entrepreneurs.[20] Becker's approach, I argue in this book, provides us with valuable theoretical tools to complicate the focus on the lone heroic entrepreneur by integrating a plurality of actors and perspectives into the description and analysis of impact entrepreneurship.

The different chapters of this book break new ground in this direction by theorizing impact entrepreneurship as a production world in which impact work takes place. By bringing in Becker's main analytical tools, the book sheds new light on the networks of actors involved alongside impact entrepreneurs. Impact investors, policymakers, corporate executives, serial entrepreneurs, program managers from entrepreneurship support programs, mentors, and consumers constitute a production world where people perform impact work. Impact work, therefore, is as much the product of their mundane practices and interactions and the specific meanings and values they imbue these with, as it is the constellation of tasks performed by impact entrepreneurs.

In a production world where most activities unfold in collaboration, the constellation of relationships among people requires close consideration. To describe and analyze how the relationships at the heart of impact work emerge, prosper, or fail, I borrow some insights from the sociological work of Viviana Zelizer.[21] I use her concept of "relational work," referring to the work involved in matching relations with appropriate transactions and media of exchange for them to become meaningful.[22] Zelizer's approach moves the study of resource exchange away from an analysis exclusively based on market-based principles and foregrounds the economic rationality of calculating actors. While recognizing that we engage in relationships based on our estimation of their benefits, this approach integrates the fact that we constantly negotiate the content of these relationships shaped by culture, institutions, and power. In short, relationality in economic life is a dynamic process in which meanings, emotions, power asymmetry, and broader organizational forces converge.

Another significant influence for the ideas developed in this book is the anthropological work of Brian Moeran[23] on the production of worth.

[19] See, for instance, Aldrich and Ruef (2018), Clough et al. (2019).

[20] Montgomery et al. (2012).

[21] See Zelizer (2005, 2010).

[22] Block (2012).

[23] Moeran (2013).

Starting from the premise formulated by John Dewey[24] that value is not an inherent property of things nor a mere individual preference, Moeran shows that value is constructed by people and the market[25] in a specific cultural context.[26] Resultingly, the judgments of those engaged in evaluation practices about the properties of a thing assign different values to it, resulting in an "ensemblage of worth."[27] For instance, an artwork is not beautiful *per se* but because of the different values brought to bear in its aesthetic and commercial judgment by those involved in the production and distribution chain. Under their view, an artwork might hold material, symbolic, economic, technical, aesthetic, and use values. Consequently, there are no intrinsic qualities of things beyond the materials from which they are made, and the sum of these different values represents worth.

Particularly interesting for the present analysis is Moeran's central thesis that the traditional dualism between value (economic) and values (e.g., cultural, symbolic, social, technical) does not hold, as things always have multiple values.[28] This thesis, I believe, helps overcome the current theoretical cul-de-sac faced by those examining the conflicts raised by the coexistence of different understandings of what is valuable in organizations. It helps solve the evaluation question by proposing that people agree on the predominance of a single standard providing the normative basis for legitimacy.[29] This thesis also moves away from the oppressive focus on economic value in entrepreneurship research, to encompass the multiple types of values at stake in impact entrepreneurship. This, in turn, makes it possible to show how people create, use, and negotiate competing standards to evaluate performance in impact entrepreneurship, and to imbue the output of their work with different values.

## On Organizational Ethnography

This book confronts some persistent views about impact entrepreneurship by presenting and analyzing events and interactions as I experienced them, or as they were narrated to me, by entrepreneurs themselves as well as impact investors, policymakers, corporate executives, employees of the

[24] Dewey (1939).
[25] See also Lamont (2012), Vatin (2013).
[26] Appadurai (1986).
[27] Moeran (2013).
[28] See also Stark (2011).
[29] See Patriotta et al. (2011), Reinecke et al. (2017).

accelerator, and impact managers. Indeed, any detailed examination of impact entrepreneurship must critically address some of the normative assumptions governing the field. In particular, I see these assumptions causing three methodological shortcomings I attempt to address with this book.

First, the samples created by selecting subjects based on their self-declaration of being an impact entrepreneur fail to question the empirical relevance of this claim. However, taking a critical stance on people's discourses is of fundamental importance.[30] This is particularly the case given the rise in popularity of impact entrepreneurship and the benefits conferred by being categorized as an impact entrepreneur, and more broadly a social entrepreneur. Second, the large data sets gathering self-identified impact entrepreneurs or random samples of students used by most studies cannot accurately capture diversity. In pointing this out I don't want to diminish the contribution of these studies; rather, that although students can express their appetence to become impact entrepreneurs, they cannot seriously relate to the day-to-day running of an impact enterprise. We cannot explain what it means to be an impact entrepreneur by collecting data among people who are not, nor have ever been impact entrepreneurs. Third, not all impact entrepreneurs necessarily consider themselves as such because the analytical categories scholars create do not always match their empirical counterparts.[31]

I believe ethnography provides one powerful way to address these shortcomings. Developed at the beginning of the twentieth century,[32] ethnography involves in-depth immersion in the field under study for a relatively long time. Living and working alongside research participants, ethnographers participate in the practices and interactions at the field site and gain a social role. Only by this means can one develop long-term, trustable bonds with people, who in return develop expectations about one's presence.[33] These bonds enable ethnographers to access intimate bits of others' experiences, supporting the collection of fine-grained data by taking field notes, conducting formal and informal interviews, and gathering secondary data. Hence, ethnography moves away from the posi-

[30] See Becker and Geer (1957).

[31] Delmar and Scott (2004).

[32] See Malinowski (1922).

[33] See, for instance, the seminal book by Adler and Adler (1987) on membership roles in the field.

tivist standpoint dictating most management scholarship, which involves professional distance to avoid "contaminating" the findings.[34] Quite the opposite, ethnography posits that involvement alongside research participants provides social competence of the phenomenon, orientating data collection, analysis, and writing in unique ways.

For this fieldwork, I spent hundreds of days in Seal's offices between May 2017 and December 2018. Fortunately, Jorge, Sofia, and Lola gave me virtually free rein during this time. I could document the work of the program managers of the different acceleration areas, shadow the investment analysts working in the impact investing vehicle, join entrepreneurs during their mentoring and training sessions, or attend meetings with Seal's board and external advisory committee. This freedom was particularly useful for developing an all-around view of the accelerator's varied activities, by witnessing how they were designed and implemented and by collecting the views of those experiencing them. Of course, I was not able to observe everything and document the work of everyone, but this is obviously not the goal here. Ethnography is always partial in its production.[35]

During my work alongside the staff at Seal, I held different roles. While I struggled to make sense of my presence on day one, I gradually became involved in a wide array of tasks, from creating and teaching market research seminars to entrepreneurs, to designing a workshop for corporate partners by the end of my fieldwork. This involvement was crucial for forging trustable bonds with staff members. It also allowed me to progressively gain access to entrepreneurs, mentors, investors, policymakers, and corporate executives. I attended staff members' meetings with mentors, visited their local offices, and followed them to several events on technological entrepreneurship taking place every year in the city. Beyond working hours, I also shared informal gatherings, including dinners, birthday parties, and weekend trips. When observing practices and interactions, I compiled participant observation data in my field diary and complemented this information by conducting about 80 recorded interviews.

Summarizing the above as "hanging around" the accelerator office and chatting with people in an unstructured and opportunistic fashion may be tempting, but is highly misleading. Reliable field notes should be taken during or shortly after the scene. Mine were descriptive and analytical in

[34] Langley and Klag (2019).
[35] Clifford (1986).

that they hinted at aspects emerging as important alongside fieldwork progression.[36] These aspects were incorporated soon after into the fieldwork design and flexibly oriented upcoming data collection. This painstaking and lengthy process resulted in thousands of pages of transcriptions from recorded accounts provided by different sources. Because they were collected over a long time, these notes allowed me to observe recurrence in events and to compare these events in order to move from the anecdotal to the factual in the elaboration of my argument. Rigor, thus, emerged in part as the result of a threefold triangulation juxtaposing data collection tools and information about the same event collected from different sources, and from the same source but in different circumstances.

The ethnographer's traits shape access to a specific setting and people, data collection, and the resulting interpretations. This raises several points of caution. Among these is accounting for positionality by infusing reflexivity in data collection and analysis. As I gradually engaged in the activities at the accelerator and shared intimate moments and everyday struggles with its members, I often caught myself falling back on adopting and naturalizing their views instead of analyzing them. Like my research participants, I praised the promise of impact entrepreneurship and defended it against those who were skeptical that alternative organizations could help make life fairer and more sustainable. If embracing their values and taking their beliefs seriously was critical to achieving immersion, the necessary task of gaining analytical distance was greatly supported by sharing insights from fieldwork with colleagues, as well as with supporters and opponents of impact entrepreneurship. They questioned my initial uncritical view of impact entrepreneurship and helped, implicitly, to contextualize it. My "exit" from the field and, soon after, my relocation to another country helped in this process by introducing some geographical distance.

Finally, suppose ethnography allows for documenting the nitty-gritty details of impact work. In that case, the potential of its findings for explaining social phenomena is too often downplayed by arguing that they are idiosyncratic to a particular setting. Accordingly, one might question the capacity to generalize the lessons from this book. My intention here is not to produce a general theory of impact entrepreneurship. Instead, I hope to build an ethnographic theory of impact work based on an in-depth examination of one of its local manifestations. The organization I studied is one of the many instances where people collaboratively engage about

[36] Emerson et al. (2011).

impact. Further, these organizations in general, and Seal in particular, create a specific type of venture—technological early-stage social impact startups—not representative of all impact initiatives. However, there is every reason to believe that many of the challenges these people face in producing impact recur elsewhere, albeit under different forms. By rendering understandable some of the social meaning people assign into impact, I offer one explanation for how a specific group of people addressed these challenges as they engaged in impact work. I hope, thus, that this book will help demonstrate the promise of ethnography for the study of impact entrepreneurship.

## Outline of the Book

I have written this book with three goals in mind. The first is to provide an ethnographic portrayal of impact entrepreneurship that could help contrast with and provide comparable insights on how people engage with impact in different settings. The second is methodological, as I wish with this book to demonstrate the potential of ethnography for studying impact work and, more broadly, entrepreneurial processes. The third goal is theoretical, as I aim to contribute to a better understanding of impact entrepreneurship by making theoretical propositions explaining some of its underlying processes.

In this book, I argue that impact is not the given property of a venture nor the sole result of entrepreneurs' intrinsic desire to change the world. Instead, the crux of my argument is that impact emerges iteratively from a process of social engagement and negotiation among different actors who participate, in their own way, in this process. Accordingly, to uncover how impact takes shape through the everyday, mundane, and collective processes of its production, this book is structured around ethnographic accounts examining how the actors involved in the work at Seal negotiate impact through specific practices and interactions. These practices and interactions are at the heart of impact work, and these accounts approach their social engagement and negotiation from different vantage points.

I start in Chap. 2 by recounting how Jorge, Sofia, and Lola ideated and launched Seal, guided by the primary aim of helping entrepreneurs turn their ideas into impact enterprises. I delve into the day-to-day running of the organization by describing its three areas of operation. The acceleration area shapes the entrepreneurs' experiences, thoughts, and feelings during the program. The investment area provides funding to entrepreneurs. The inspiration area creates a local ecosystem of impact aficionados. I then examine the funding structure supporting these areas and powerfully shaping the division of labor. Finally, I examine the local definition of impact entrepreneurship informing this process, which Seal promotes to produce a particular perspective among entrepreneurs and collaborators. This will provide the foundation for further analysis of the organization and production of work around impact in the following chapters.

Chapter 3 is about how the staff and corporate partners select entrepreneurs. The different interests and goals of these partners, alongside the lack of shared evaluation criteria, and diverging understandings of what social impact means and why it matters, challenge this process. By following the staff during interviews with short-listed entrepreneurs on selection committees, I uncover what makes an early-stage impact enterprise worth accelerating. I complexify the primacy of social and economic values in impact entrepreneurship to suggest that what makes impact enterprises valuable is eminently plural. I unearth five evaluation criteria: problem-solving capability, maturity, technical innovation, social impact, and network capability. I argue that their interplay informs the worth of a social impact start-up and conveys use, technical, social, and relational values. These values form an "ensemblage of worth," revealing that an impact enterprise has no intrinsic worth; its worth is socially constructed during evaluation.

Chapter 4 uncovers entrepreneurs' experiences during their socialization to impact entrepreneurship by Seal. Entrepreneurs tend to be inclined toward a social or commercial demand, and Seal transforms them into impact entrepreneurs. They must integrate the social with the commercial in developing a new role. With this aim, internal and external mentoring and cohort training provide shared social knowledge and form a nuanced understanding of behavioral expectations, leading to salient adjustments in the entrepreneurs' roles. These socialization activities also enable them to gain the necessary skills to turn their idea into an impact enterprise. I propose the notion of "contradictory role demands" to explain how entrepreneurs gain awareness and gradually integrate these demands. I develop this notion by following the entrepreneurs during their day-to-day routine, combining an examination of their biographies with an investigation of their struggles to either make sense of these demands or quit.

Mentoring is the landmark of these socialization activities, and Chap. 4 focuses on the role of serial entrepreneurs, business angels and investment analysts, policymakers, lawyers, business school professors, and top executives acting as mentors. While they share their experience and invest considerable time in advising entrepreneurs, their interactions do not always lead to resource exchange. This, I propose, requires the construction of a "good match" emerging from a shared understanding of the situation and the media of exchange, as well as overcoming how Seal, as a third party, frames the interaction and redefines initial roles. I develop this argument by uncovering Seal's relational infrastructure cemented by expertise, reputation, and behaviors of "giving back." Mentors are presented as resource holders and redefine entrepreneurial needs according to their subjective experience. Entrepreneurs, by contrast, are resource seekers, but negotiate this role by presenting themselves as resource holders. For the exchange to unfold, entrepreneurs and mentors interpret and accommodate their roles to match the relationship, transaction, and media and negotiate the initial power asymmetry.

Chapter 5 zooms into the final stage of the acceleration process, when entrepreneurs have tested and refined their product and business model, defined a marketing strategy, created an impact thesis and indicators, and produced a compelling story around impact. Picking up on the investment committees, I examine how impact investors capture and evaluate the credibility of entrepreneurs' impact promises. By zooming into their evaluation practices, I show how investors move beyond self-reported intention, social mission, and visible characteristics, to examine entrepreneurs' impact promise in a way that is both analytical and subjective. Their evaluation centers on four interrelated aspects of entrepreneur's behavior: entrepreneurs' proven awareness and use of impact indicators and methodologies, selected biographical aspects that connect to their social goals, entrepreneurs' management of their venture and social impact, and their views about the future of the latter. In doing so, investors strive to detect opportunistic entrepreneurs while creating beliefs about the credibility of entrepreneurs' promises that embolden investment decisions.

Chapter 6 concludes by summarizing the argument presented in the book, before taking up the idea that impact emerges iteratively from a process of social engagement and negotiation. As the title makes clear, this book is about impact entrepreneurship. However, many books could be written about this topic, each with specific audiences in mind. I did not write this book just for entrepreneurship scholars. I like to think that *Impact Work* might interest social scientists in general. I also hope that the book might interest a broader audience of impact aficionados interested in discovering the dynamics underlying the production of impact work by examining the backstage of this production world. This book is not about prescriptive practical recommendations or general theory. Instead, it is about the lived experience of impact work by a group of passionate people.

## Bibliography


Adler, P., & Adler, P. (1987). *Membership Roles in Field Research.* Sage.

Aldrich, H. E., & Ruef, M. (2018). Unicorns, Gazelles, and Other Distractions on the Way to Understanding Real Entrepreneurship in the United States. *Academy of Management Perspectives, 32*(4), 458–472.

Appadurai, A. (1986). Introduction: Commodities and the Politics of Value. In *The Social Life of Things* (pp. 3–63). Cambridge University Press.

Austin, J., Stevenson, H., & Wei-Skillern, J. (2006). Social and Commercial Entrepreneurship: Same, Different, or Both? *Entrepreneurship Theory and Practice, 30*(1), 1–22.

Bacq, S., & Alt, E. (2018). Feeling Capable and Valued: A Prosocial Perspective on the Link Between Empathy and Social Entrepreneurial Intentions. *Journal of Business Venturing, 33*(3), 333–350. https://doi.org/10.1016/j.jbusvent.2018.01.004

Bacq, S., & Janssen, F. (2011). The Multiple Faces of Social Entrepreneurship: A Review of Definitional Issues Based on Geographical and Thematic Criteria. *Entrepreneurship & Regional Development, 23*, 373–403.

Bandinelli, C., & Arvidsson, A. (2013). Brand Yourself a Changemaker! *Journal of Macromarketing, 33*(1), 67–71.

Barman, E. (2016). *Caring Capitalism: The Meaning and Measure of Social Value.* Cambridge University Press.

Becker, H. S., & Geer, B. (1957). Participant Observation and Interviewing: A comparison. *Human Organization, 16*, 28–32.

Beckert, J. (2016). *Imagined Futures.* Harvard University Press.

Block, F. (2012). Relational Work in Market Economies: Introduction. *Politics & Society, 40*(2), 135–144.

Chliova, M., Mair, J., & Vernis, A. (2020). Persistent Category Ambiguity: The case of social entrepreneurship. *Organization Studies, 41*(7), 1019–1042.

Clifford, J. (1986). Introduction: Partial Truths. In J. Clifford & G. Marcus (Eds.), *Writing Culture: The Poetics and Politics of Ethnography* (pp. 1–26). University of California Press.

Clough, D. R., Fang, T. P., Vissa, B., & Wu, A. (2019). Turning Lead into Gold: How Do Entrepreneurs Mobilize Resources to Exploit Opportunities? *Academy of Management Annals, 13*(1), 240–271.

Dacin, P., Dacin, T., & Matear, M. (2010). Social Entrepreneurship: Why We Don't Need a New Theory and How We Move Forward From Here. *Academy of Management Perspectives, 24*(3), 37–57.

Dees, J. G. (1998). *The Meaning of Social Entrepreneurship*. Comments and Suggestions Contributed from the Social Entrepreneurship Funders Working Group.

Delmar, F., & Scott, S. (2004). Legitimating First: Organizing Activities and the Survival of New Ventures. *Journal of Business Venturing, 19*, 385–410.

Dewey, J. (1939). *Theory of Valuation* (Vols. 2, 4). University of Chicago Press.

Dumont, G. (2018). *Grimpeur professionnel: Le travail créateur sur le marché du sponsoring*. Editions de l'Ecole des Hautes Etudes en Sciences Sociales.

Ebrahim, A., & Rangan, V. K. (2014). What Impact? A Framework for Measuring the Scale and Scope of Social Performance. *California Management Review, 56*(3), 118–141. https://doi.org/10.1525/cmr.2014.56.3.118

Emerson, J. (2003). The Blended Value Proposition: Integrating Social and Financial Returns. *California Management Review, 45*(4), 35–51. https://doi.org/10.2307/41166187

Emerson, R. M., Fretz, R. I., & Shaw, L. L. (2011). *Writing Ethnographic Fieldnotes*. University of Chicago Press.

Hockerts, K., Hehenberger, L., Schaltegger, S., & Farber, V. (2022). Defining and Conceptualizing Impact Investing: Attractive Nuisance or Catalyst? *Journal of Business Ethics, 179*(4), 937–950.

Huybrechts, B., & Nicholls, A. (2012). Social Entrepreneurship: Definitions, Drivers and Challenges. In *Social Entrepreneurship and Social Business* (pp. 31–48). Springer.

Lamont, M. (2012). Toward a Comparative Sociology of Valuation and Evaluation. *Annual Review of Sociology, 38*(1), 201–221.

Langley, A., & Klag, M. (2019). Being Where? Navigating the Involvement Paradox in Qualitative Research Accounts. *Organizational Research Methods, 22*(2), 515–538.

Mair, J., & Martí, I. (2006). Social Entrepreneurship Research: A Source of Explanation, Prediction, and Delight. *Journal of World Business, 41*(1), 36–44.

Malinowski, B. (1922). *Argonauts of the Western Pacific: An Account of Native Enterprise and Adventure in the Archipelagoes of Melanesian New Guinea*. Routledge.

Mears, A. (2011). *Pricing Beauty: The Making of a Fashion Model*. University of California Press.

Moeran, B. (2013). *The Business of Creativity. Toward an Anthropology of Worth*. Left Coast Press.

Montgomery, A., Dacin, P., & Dacin, T. (2012). Collective Social Entrepreneurship: Collaboratively Shaping Social Good. *Journal of Business Ethics, 111*, 375–388.

Muñoz, P., & Kimmitt, J. (2019). Social Mission as Competitive Advantage: A Configurational Analysis of the Strategic Conditions of Social Entrepreneurship. *Journal of Business Research, 101*, 854–861.

Nicholls, A. (2010). The Legitimacy of Social Entrepreneurship: Reflexive Isomorphism in a Pre–Paradigmatic Field. *Entrepreneurship Theory and Practice, 34*(4), 611–633.

Patriotta, G., Gond, J.-P., & Schultz, F. (2011). Maintaining Legitimacy: Controversies, Orders of Worth, and Public Justifications: Maintaining Legitimacy. *Journal of Management Studies, 48*(8), 1804–1836.

Rawhouser, H., Cummings, M., & Newbert, S. L. (2019). Social Impact Measurement: Current Approaches and Future Directions for Social Entrepreneurship Research. *Entrepreneurship Theory and Practice, 43*(1), 82–115.

Reinecke, J., Van Bommel, K., & Spicer, A. (2017). When Orders of Worth Clash: Negotiating Legitimacy in Situations of Moral Multiplexity. In C. Cloutier, J.-P. Gond, & B. Leca (Eds.), *Justification, Evaluation and Critique in the Study of Organizations, Research in the Sociology of Organizations, 52*, pp. 3–72. Emerald Group Publishing Limited.

Schumpeter, J. (1911). *The Theory of Economic Development.* Harvard University Press.

Stark, D. (2011). *The Sense of Dissonance: Accounts of Worth in Economic Life.* Princeton University Press.

Tucker, R., Croom, R. M., & Bacq, S. (2019). Feeling Your Pain, Pursuing My Gain: Assessing Status-Striving, Empathy, and Social Entrepreneurship Intent. *Journal of Business Venturing Insights, 12*(C). https://doi.org/10.1016/j.jbvi.2019.e00142

Vatin, F. (2013). Introduction. In F. Vatin (Ed.), Evaluer et valoriser: Une sociologie économique de la mesure(édition revue et augmentée, pp. 17–37). Presses Universitaires du Mirail.

Zahra, S. A., Gedajlovic, E., Neubaum, D. O., & Shulman, J. M. (2009). A Typology of Social Entrepreneurs: Motives, Search Processes and Ethical Challenges. *Journal of Business Venturing, 24*(5), 519–532.

Zelizer, V. A. (2005). *The Purchase of Intimacy.* Princeton University Press.

Zelizer, V. A. (2010). *Economic Lives: How Culture Shapes the Economy.* Princeton University Press.

CHAPTER 2

# Seal

As a social impact accelerator, Seal selected, trained, and certified nascent impact entrepreneurs. The organization was, by many standards, a successful story and, in its decade of existence, had become a recognized actor of impact entrepreneurship in Europe. Since its creation, the staff had accelerated more than 200 early-stage impact enterprises and established durable partnerships with large corporations, business schools, foundations, the public administration, and investors. Within a few years, Jorge, Sofia, and Lola also created an impact investing fund operating independently and gradually contributing to funding ventures now considered the gold standard in impact entrepreneurship.

As in any entrepreneurial journey, Seal's early days were more modest. Jorge, Sofia, and Lola often recalled their beginning days to staff members, when they were piled in a cramped single-room office and with very limited resources, constantly struggling to get support for growing the organization.

"It was just the three of us, and our five volunteers in the small apartment we rented," explained Sofia proudly.

"Volunteers?" I asked.

"Yes, they were not getting paid but worked with us almost as employees; they had their own schedule, and they were like employees but without pay. Then, three of them became our first 'real' employees, way before Jorge, Lola, and I had a salary."

"And the entrepreneurs?"



G. Dumont, *Impact Work*,
https://doi.org/10.1007/978-3-031-64661-4_2

"We started by accelerating five ventures for one year. From the start we set a limited time for the program because we didn't want to become an incubator."

"Why?"

"Because we needed a business model. The incubator is something you find at universities, where there isn't the same imperative for rentability. The incubator also focuses on very, very, early-stage ideas, and we hoped to help more advanced entrepreneurs. We wanted entrepreneurs at a stage when they needed a clear push, so: the accelerator."

At that time, what would become impact entrepreneurship was largely unknown. Certainly, the social economy had been steadily growing across the country, with the Mondragon Corporation[1] being one of its most notorious examples. However, the widely shared view that making profit from socially oriented initiatives was not morally acceptable posed a significant challenge. Pedro, who participated in the ideation of Seal and now sat on the board, articulated this challenge to me the day we discussed their early struggles and the longstanding divide between the social and the economic.

"People were worried about that."

"That what?" I asked.

"Making money from the social."

"You mean, they thought it's bad to make money out of social issues."

"Yes. These were two different incompatible spheres."

"I see."

"But what's more, they saw us coming, all with a business school degree. We were the posh guys from the business school, you know, those who're going to make money out of NGOs! You know what I mean?"

"Yes. Like you're stealing money from the poor while you pretend to help them, right."

"Totally."

Frankly, I embarked on this fieldwork with this stereotype in mind. After a few months in the field, I would change my view to naturalize the social goals of the organization as part of my own conversion to impact entrepreneurship. It's only when exiting the field and having this view challenged by colleagues that I would infuse more critical distance into this belief. But, when I pushed the door of Seal's office on my first day, I was not alone in having strong doubts about the true motives

[1] See Flecha and Ngai (2014).

underpinning the organization's mission. I repeatedly listened to skeptical comments from colleagues and friends. As one colleague summarized to me once, as he forcefully tried to convince me that Seal was a boutique to achieve commercial goals, impact entrepreneurship was "just another way to make money."

Paradoxically, that impact entrepreneurship was largely unknown resulted in an opportunity for Seal. Concerns about companies' responsibility for social and environmental issues had accelerated the rise of corporate social responsibility (CSR), and those leading these departments were desperately looking to fulfill the CSR promise by integrating social, environmental, and economic concerns into selected aspects of their business operations. It was also a golden time for technological, early-stage entrepreneurship. Many governments and the European Union had put start-ups on their agenda. Accelerators and incubators opened doors at every corner of cities' innovation districts where entrepreneurship events were organized daily. A minimal number of success stories greatly magnified by the media fueled the aspiration of becoming an entrepreneur. Public institutions largely embraced this wave of interest, portraying entrepreneurship as the solution to increasing unemployment rates and creating dedicated training programs and resources for people to create their enterprises.

However, Seal's explicit mission to support the creation and development of early-stage enterprises to achieve social and environmental goals alongside profitability distinguished the organization from the non-profit sector. Since its inception, Seal greatly benefitted from the intersection of these two trends. Further, the networks of Pedro and Jorge, but also of Lorenzo, proved vital to convincing collaborators about the importance and possibilities of bridging technological innovation with social impact. "Lorenzo literally opened his address book, grabbed his phone, and called people, all well-known local leaders. He asked them and convinced them to join him on the board of Seal at a time when no one believed in us," recalled Sofia.

Pedro further explained, "Jorge had an excellent network and already knew who could be on the board and which company could fund us. I had other names in mind, Lorenzo as well, and we started working from there."

As I would soon learn, Jorge's family operated a leading multinational corporation and enjoyed a prominent reputation. As any nascent enterprise, Seal crudely lacked a consistent track record and a viable business model to assess its legitimacy and eventually attract much-needed resources. So, Jorge's network became crucial.

"How did you start, then?" I asked Pedro.

"We started by creating a board."

"Why?"

"The board matters a lot at the very initial stage, when you create something, for the reputation. If we had created a business, we would have chosen investors, powerful investors. You approach them based on the funding they can provide but also for their knowledge and network, for the prestige they will bring to you. But we didn't create a business, so we chose people who could help testify to the social goals more."

"So, you chose specific people to build the legitimacy of Seal, is that what you mean?"

"Totally. We chose people with a good reputation, and we convinced them to join us. So, people would look at us and think 'If they are with them, what they do should be great.' That was the idea."

Seal's mission was initially vague, Pedro confessed. It gradually took shape through a focus on supporting the development of impact entrepreneurship through five main objectives.

"First and foremost, what we do is help impact entrepreneurs. They're starving," said Jorge, laughing to emphasize their vital need for resources. "They're our focus, we're here to help them, we literally work for them although they don't pay us."

"So who's paying you?" I asked. If the entrepreneurs couldn't pay the bill because they literally had no money, someone else had to.

"Companies. Our corporate partners! They fund the accelerator."

"Ok. So you help impact entrepreneurs supported by corporate partners that fund Seal, right."

"Right. But their role is not only to provide funding."

"Ah, no?"

"Look, Guillaume, if we want to achieve systemic change we need to work with corporations because they hold the reins of the economy."

"You want them to work with entrepreneurs?"

"Exactly, we help them to work together. Not only because it's interesting for both. Without corporations, we won't be able to change much. So, we need to have them on board."

In other words, in addition to helping impact entrepreneurship and familiarizing corporations to impact, Jorge, Sofia, and Lola's third objective was to create a market for impact entrepreneurship.

Seal also aimed to develop new tools and methodologies. This fourth objective became more prevalent by the middle of the fieldwork. At that time, the acceleration methodology was slowly becoming established, and Sofia and Lola began to turn their sights on developing social impact standards. On the one hand, as the next chapter shows, the lack of standards raised tensions because of the coexistence of multiple understandings of impact. On the other, there was growing pressure from corporate partners and investors for a clear and shared methodology to evaluate the social performance of the ventures.

Lastly, Seal explicitly aimed to create an impact ecosystem. By design, the accelerator gathered previously disconnected actors; it would be the foundation for socializing those gravitating in the ecosystem to impact entrepreneurship.

These objectives make of Seal what organizational theorists call an "intermediary organization." Intermediary organizations play a central role in the functioning of markets by bringing together previously disconnected people with specific expertise.[2] Seal first created and disseminated bits of the culture of impact entrepreneurship, helping to define the content and boundaries of this novel category. By selecting specific entrepreneurs and rejecting others who, they believed, wouldn't have been able to qualify as impact entrepreneurs, Seal directly contributed to defining who and what belongs to impact entrepreneurship. In other words, Seal acted as a gatekeeper to a social world in the making by selecting new entrants under specific conditions. Seal also provided a "space of interaction" for these new entrants to interact and supported their socialization to core cultural categories. Such space enabled communication, eventually developing a sense of belonging to the culture and a collective identity.

When I started fieldwork in April 2017, Seal had set up its headquarters in a space leased by the city council and employed about 20 people full time. The office was strategically located in the rebranded innovation district, at the heart of a newly constructed building promoted for its sustainability and efficiency. Conceived as an industrial warehouse of the digital era, the building had been envisioned to boost innovation. As such, it was hoped to proudly pave the way toward a new digital revolution based on

[2] Economic sociologists have examined market intermediation by taking individuals as the primary unit of analysis. Organizational theorists, by contrast, have been more interested in organizations playing this role. It is thus natural that I build upon their work here, and primarily use the definition advanced by Johanna Mair and colleagues (Mair et al., 2012).

technological start-ups. I spent most of my time there during fieldwork. Then, Seal moved again to a nearby but smaller office space, also home to technological start-ups. Finally, after a few years and the creation of the impact investing fund, Seal relocated to the northern part of the city and opened two more offices across the country.

This first empirical chapter presents an overview of the organization. I begin by describing its three main areas of operation and introduce you to the staff members who will appear recurrently in this book. Next, I unpack the design and implementation of the acceleration program through which Seal shaped the entrepreneurs' experiences, including their thoughts and feeling and the ways they developed their ventures. Third, I turn to the funding model and the role of corporate partners. Finally, I examine the definition of impact entrepreneurship informing this process and promoted by Seal to produce a particular perspective on impact shared within the vast network of collaborators.

## The Division of Labor

On morning, Marcela and I were alone in the office. She had been handling the administrative duties at Seal for about a year but was now seriously thinking about quitting. She was exhausted, she said, because the day-to-day running of Seal was chaotic and always rushed. She aspired to a more peaceful work routine.

In many respects, the main room of the office embodied this chaos. Its small size of the room had everyone cramped and the only table was right in the middle, with enough space to move around, making any movement challenging and disturbing others' work. Every staff member worked with a brand-new MacBook Air, but additional screens were thrown on the table, between piles of paper. Posters and drawings from previous activities—to-do lists or the inspiring sentence of the week—covered the wall without much established order.

That is, the office felt like a storage space than a laboratory where impact entrepreneurship was in the making. Each "sub-team" had been carefully allocated a dedicated space around the table. On the far left side sat the investment analysts. They always jokingly called themselves "the dark side" as a *clin d'oeil* to those viewing with hostility the economic dimension of impact entrepreneurship. The middle of the table hosted the program managers of the acceleration program, several interns, and the communication officer, Andrés. Marcela, finally, was at the far right, next to a small Nespresso coffee machine and a water fountain. I sat right in front of her, at the small table corner that had been assigned to me.

The day-to-day running of Seal embodied the perpetual rush often described as an intrinsic feature of early-stage entrepreneurship. "Here, we're always on the move," Lola liked to claim every time an unexpected change upended the course of work. In such a small space, everyone was within earshot and communication was very straightforward, creating a joyful but constant cacophony. Digital communication was also pervasive. As a result, a good deal of time was spent writing, sending, and answering emails. The freshly launched WhatsApp groups were constantly buzzing. The long and intense workdays were always too short to complete all the assigned tasks by late afternoon. However, the fast pace of work was partly naturalized. Seal had been created from scratch a few years earlier, and the founders worked hard to cultivate the "lean start-up" spirit.

Many staff members ended up at Seal by accident. However, they were all deeply committed to its mission. There was something contagious, almost magnetic, about pursuing impact. The friendly atmosphere and the average age greatly contributed. Most staff members were in their late 20s, recent graduates, and eager to invest time and effort in a job they found meaningful. The three co-founders strove to create a feeling that what was happening was unique and visionary. In painting Seal as a pioneer in an entrepreneurial world that would have to embrace social impact sooner or later, they fostered organizational belonging. They aspired to bring transparency, constantly sharing information about the performance of the organization as well as their doubts and dilemmas. Ultimately, they would lessen status distinctions with the ambition to offer an egalitarian gaze where everyone had a voice.

That the atmosphere was energizing and exciting did not mean that work was always easy and pleasurable. Witnessing the progress made by the entrepreneurs was highly rewarding, but the long working hours put undeniable pressure on staff members. Most were strained beyond capacity. The anarchic organization and the ever-changing design of many activities did not help either, nor did hiring new collaborators instead of promoting existing ones. This was particularly the case for several program managers who left after I completed fieldwork. While satisfied with their experience at Seal, they were also eager to progress and gain freedom in their work.

In this space, where expressions of exhaustion coexisted with exhilaration, work was organized under three main areas. Seal's mission was first to help impact entrepreneurs through the acceleration program. This program took the lion's share of everyone's focus and was supervised by Sofia and Lola. It started with a stage of "recruitment" that involved scouting, agreeing, and selecting to create a cohort of a dozen entrepreneurs. Next, each cohort undertook a three-to-six-month training combining internal and external mentoring with collective sessions. During this stage of "inculcation" the staff shared social knowledge and role expectations with the entrepreneurs of the cohort. Finally, the stage of enactment enabled investors and social impact managers to evaluate the entrepreneurs' learnings from this training.

Taken together, this three-stage socialization process helped transform entrepreneurs into impact entrepreneurs regardless of their initial social or commercial orientation, as I will discuss in Chap. 4. In other words—and this is a fundamental argument of this book—Seal literally manufactured impact entrepreneurs and their ventures during the acceleration program.

Entrepreneurs were grouped into industry clusters. The three program managers—Santiago, Pablo, and Nina—carried out the day-to-day activities with the entrepreneurs within each cluster. They were occasionally helped by interns. At the inception of fieldwork, there were no less than eight different clusters addressing issues related to health care, social issues, natural resources, work and employment, and people and education. By the end of 2018, Sofia and Lola reduced these clusters to three. Indeed, clusters such as education were short of projects, and it was a nightmare to find competent candidates for each edition of the cohort. Also, each cluster had its own selection committees and some cluster-specific activities. The multiplication of the tasks considerably impacted the workload. The clusters' focus changed regularly according to the interests of the corporate partners providing funding. Finally, as mentioned above, Sofia and Lola were often experimenting with new ideas, leading to substantial changes in design.

Jorge led the second major area, dedicated to impact investing. Although his initial interest stemmed from the field of philanthropy, he was most captivated by the creation of an impact investing fund. As we chatted about Seal's early days one morning, I asked him how they started the fund.

"Well, from the start many people have been interested in investing in Seal."

"What do you mean by investing in Seal?" I asked, raising a quizzical eyebrow, as I thought investors were more interested in investing in the ventures than in the accelerator.

"They were not particularly interested in the ventures, but they wanted to invest in Seal. They were looking for something different."

"So you created the fund for people to be able to invest money through Seal, but not to invest directly in Seal."

"Not only that. It's true that for us it was important to be a lead investor for some of the ventures we accelerate. Back then, no one acted as lead investor in the ventures we invested in. So, we launched the fund with 31 investors."

"How much capital did you manage back then?"

"We started with tickets of 15k. Then, we had one investor giving us 200k. And from there, we built a small fund of one million and a half. We have a network of 450 business angels, the fund, and the support of the EIF."

"The EIF?"

"The European Investment Fund. It provided financial support. They give us three euros for each euro we invest in start-ups, so we will soon have about 4 million to invest in ten ventures, you understand."

"I do."

"It's great because it also signals to others that the work we do at Seal is good. Like 'These guys got money from the EIF!'"

Like the creation of the board described by Pedro, this aspect was particularly important to gain legitimacy. The fund provided entrepreneurs with small, entry-level funding of 40,000 euros, with the potential for follow-ups for a total of 300,000–400,000 euros per venture.

"So, entrepreneurs get into the program, and they can apply to the fund," I asked to better understand their chronological progression at Seal.

"Yes, initially yes. Our idea was to help the entrepreneurs who had undertaken the acceleration training to access funding. The acceleration program provided a deal flow for the fund. So, we helped entrepreneurs to develop the social and commercial dimensions of their ventures prior to applying to the fund."

"I always thought the problem was that there were too many ventures and not enough money," I answered.

"Not really. That's what everyone likes to say. But the real problem is that there aren't enough ventures to invest in. I mean, of course, there are impact enterprises. This is particularly true now because it's so trendy. But most of them ... they aren't worth investing in, to be honest."

"I see. So you make sure that entrepreneurs create 'ok ventures,' kind of?"

"Yes, but not only that. Because we accelerate the ventures, we get to know the entrepreneurs well. This is very important for investors."

"Why?"

"Because they trust us. They trust us so they believe that if we accelerate a venture and ask entrepreneurs to apply to the investment committee, it's a good venture. They should be thinking, 'Look, this must be a good opportunity for me to invest.'"

"So, you're a broker?"

"Sort of, but we also train the entrepreneurs, so the information we provide to investors comes from working closely with entrepreneurs for three months. You know, many of these ventures fail, so investors want the most accurate information to decide if they invest or not. And we help them to do that."

Luc and Patrick, the two investment analysts, helped entrepreneurs move into investment readiness. They oversaw and evaluated post-investment and reported progress. Gray-haired Luc was a seasoned entrepreneur and investor in his late 60s who had mentored entrepreneurial projects for years. By contrast, Patrick graduated from the local business school a few years prior. He was always well-dressed, even during the heat of the summer, and had worked at an independent financial advisory firm focusing on wealth management prior to joining Seal, a few months before me.

After six months of fieldwork, Irina joined the team. She was a renowned chief operating officer at a famous venture capital fund. After a stellar career, she opted enthusiastically for a risky shift at Seal. She was expected to lead this area and help professionalize the investment process to attract more capital. This acceleration area led by Luc, Patrick, and Irina received administrative support and the help of interns. The three had experience in traditional finance, often viewed the world quantitatively, and had walked into a new adventure with impact investing. Their initial inclination toward traditional finance, as we will see in the following chapters, would shape how they selected and evaluated ventures.

More broadly, the investment area was initially aimed to create success stories that would ideally support Seal's ambition to develop impact investing. This was one of Jorge's chief goals.

"If we cannot demonstrate that impact entrepreneurship works, we won't be able to attract investors consistently. Think about how everyone is looking at us right now. Everyone is looking at our super small fund. They look at what we do. They have expectations about what we can achieve."

Jorge strived to demonstrate to traditional investors that social impact start-ups were legitimate investment opportunities. To seduce the traditional finance sector, he had invited investment analysts and venture capitalists to sit on the board of advisors and participate in the decision making. They also participated in the boot camps for mentoring entrepreneurs about the financial aspects of their ventures.

A third area of Seal focused specifically on promoting the emerging culture of impact entrepreneurship. Proudly named "the inspiration area," the ambition was to create a vast community of impact aficionados. Not surprisingly, given his charisma and extensive network with local impresarios and thought leaders, Jorge led this area. Eva, a project manager, and Andrés, the communication and branding officer, supported him in his task. Indeed, thrilled by the prospect of sharing his passion for impact, Jorge had an irresistible bubbling enthusiasm. In the spirit of an entrepreneur pitching his product to convince others, he loved to describe his mission as inspiring others by developing social impact start-ups. He also viewed his role as one of converting people, literally evangelizing them by sharing his passion and providing successful cases demonstrating the value and timely need for impact.

While Jorge was literally all over the place and the spokesperson of Seal, Eva's explicit goal was to improve and facilitate the organization of events, which had recently grown in number and magnitude. Their planning and design inevitably required more human labor from the staff already overloaded with the daily acceleration and investment work. Indeed, at that time, Seal was organizing workshops for corporate partners, talks by leading experts in social innovation for larger audiences, and a yearly event gathering more than 1000 participants. To become a field leader, the staff created content and disseminated what they viewed as good practices, eventually collaborating with researchers and academics in this task.

These activities were also meant to serve the entrepreneurs that they accelerated by creating a national market for impact entrepreneurship. However, if the entrepreneurs had the opportunity to pitch and showcase their venture during this major event, its core focus was clearly on ecosystem building. Additionally—but equally important for the work of community building—paying partners, impact investors, and board members had exclusive networking opportunities over lunch and dinner. These meetings purposively created a clear distinction from the rest of the attendees and, as Andrés explained to me once, “the goal is to make them feel unique by showing that we bring them a differential value.” As the event kept growing year after year, by November 2023 this area of Seal exclusively focused on its preparation.

Subsequently, as I experienced myself, these events strengthened the bonds between staff members. Everyone actively participated in the hundreds of tasks, from preparing the rooms at 7 a.m. to running workshops and acting as panelists or moderators. I remember well my first participation in the yearly event. That same week, I had been helping Irina and Patrick to prepare a funding application for the EIF. The two were exhausted, but the stakes were high. They had been working longer workdays, sometimes nights, to meet the fast-approaching deadline. It was not that the application was complex, but it required the design of a clear and coherent investment process. The difficulty lay in envisioning a formal and routinized procedure that would, hopefully, also be co-funded by the EIF. At Seal, the investment process was relatively straightforward but had yet to be written down. The morning of the event, in the small room dedicated to the staff, the three of us reviewed the final details of the proposal in between allocating the chairs in the main room and eventually chairing sessions for Irina and Patrick. I sent them my last comments on Saturday afternoon, and they finally finished the revision on Sunday morning.

## Funding Structure

The funding structure of Seal deserves a pause. Not because it is one of a kind—many business accelerators rely on corporations to run their activities[3]—rather, its importance lies in that it shapes the organization in many aspects and, resultingly, how impact work is performed. During my field-

[3] According to Cohen and colleagues (Cohen et al., 2019), accelerators are primarily funded by corporations, then by investors. In some instances, entrepreneurs must either pay a fee or provide the organization with equity. Overall, accelerators combine funding from different types of providers and balance their demands. I believe that Seal’s case is particularly interesting in that corporations provided almost 100% of the funding although the accelerator operates relatively independently from their guidance. This contrasts with corporate accelerators that are funded by a single corporation and, therefore, designed according to its specific needs. Seal’s program, indeed, remained largely general.

work, almost 20 corporations from industries related to Seal's areas of expertise provided most of the funding. These corporate partners were drawn from Jorge's network of high-level executives and CEOs. I asked Pedro once why they seemed almost unconditional in supporting him and, more broadly, Seal.

"They like what we do, they trust the team, and they wanna be part of it."

"Part of it? What do you mean?"

"Well, they like being with us, to know that they're participating in what we do. Let's say they like being around. It's cool to be around. We do great things, and these things are related to social impact. Many of our partners are friends."

"They give you money because of the friendship?" I asked, provocatively.

Pedro then paused, thinking more thoughtfully about the future of these partnerships.

"What do partners ask in return?" I insisted.

"One day, there will be another financial crisis. Maybe within three or four years, and our partners will stop giving us money. Not all of them, of course, but some will have to cut down the cost, like 'I need to cut 50k ... your 50k.' These 50k were our 50k!"

"Yes, so you can't really assume that they will help out forever, right?"

"No, we can't. We cannot assume that they will give us money, we need to make sure that they give us the money because of our results, not because 'I like Jorge,' or 'I like Lola,' or whatever."

"And how do you demonstrate your results?" I asked, squinting.

He exhaled loudly. "I don't think we're currently doing it," he replied.

In fact, Pedro, Sofia, Lola, and Jorge's enthusiasm about the partners' unwavering commitment was very often tainted by their concerns about the lack of tangible results to testify to concrete outcomes emerging from these partnerships. Of course, they knew this was important. On the day of our conversation, Pedro's apprehension about the fact that Seal had yet to demonstrate tangible results to partners was deadly apparent.

Following Sofia's recommendation, I spent time reaching out and meeting with most corporate partners during fieldwork. I always traveled to their office and, in this more intimate atmosphere, gathered their views about their ambitions, interactions with entrepreneurs, and their experience at Seal. These partners concurred with Pedro's point. The outcomes from their partnership with Seal were hard to identify and, consequently, to evaluate. This challenge was problematic as they had to report to the top management.

Later during fieldwork, I thought it would be an good idea to share with Pedro some of the insights I had gathered while interviewing partners. He seemed an ideal person because he was not directly involved in the day-to-day running of Seal and, I believed, was someone with whom I could talk more easily and more directly about these issues than Sofia and Lola. I waited for the next Seal board meeting to ask. By the end of the meeting, when many participants had left and we were having a last drink, I approached him and raised this issue cautiously.

"You remember what you told me last year about the partners? I have been at Seal for about one year, and I'm stunned that the staff invests so much effort into the acceleration program."

"So where would you invest the effort?" he asked, amused.

"Who is Seal's paying client?" I asked.

"Partners."

"And what do they want?" I added, implicitly outlining that they had different expectations than entrepreneurs.

"I know, we aren't there yet," he answered, laughing. "To me, we should first define a product and talk about a product we sell to clients, and the paying clients are the partners, not the entrepreneurs. We need the entrepreneurs, and we must focus on them. But those who ultimately pay are the partners."

The struggle to demonstrate concrete results that would sustain funding over time was connected to the lack of concreteness of Seal's products for partners. Pedro summarized this idea well.

"If you create an interesting product, people will buy it. If the product is shit, then people won't buy it. We need to make sure we have it clear to make solid propositions. I already told them [Sofia, Lola, and Jorge] in September, during the annual strategic meeting! We must have it crystal clear, and we need to be able to measure it."

"How would you measure the result of networking, then?"

"Our partners must be aware of the value of networking because you cannot measure it. We provide you access to specific people and the network of these people, but I believe that you can't measure the result of the networking."

We can identify two main concerns in Pedro's comments. First, the products sold by Seal to paying clients were unclear. It hadn't been a problem so far, but partners were increasingly expecting and requesting tangible results after a few years of providing funding, participating in the selection committees, mentoring the entrepreneurs, and therefore investing time, effort, and money in the organization. Seal also lacked performance indicators to measure and eventually demonstrate the results of these partnerships. Nevertheless, indicators existed. For instance, at each meeting with the advisory board or during the biannual meetings with partners, Jorge shared the results captured by quantitative indicators of the number of start-ups accelerated. He showed the number of hours of mentoring, the number of events organized, or the volume of the audience attending these events. However, these indicators measured the acceleration's activities and centered on entrepreneurs. That the founders had not fully engaged with their paying clients was apparent.

To Pedro's concerns, Lola would often carefully recall the embryonic nature of many partnerships. One morning, when we reviewed the list of the current partners, she insisted on the short duration of their collaboration.

"Many partners have been with us for a year, maybe two in some cases, which means that we still need more time to obtain concrete results."

"But do you need to renew funding every year?" I asked.

"Yes, that's the problem. Every year, we must spend four months fundraising; that's exhausting and very uncertain for us."

I was not on the payroll at Seal but could sense well the stress that fundraising entailed when the end of the year was approaching. Internal changes within these partners, such as funding restrictions and the promotion or resignation of the person managing the partnership, often triggered the decision to cancel the funding. Sofia, Lola, and Jorge could not do much about this. Sofia recalled the case of Matías.

"Matías was the CEO and he truly supported innovation. But the sector, the social sector, relies on public institutions mainly. For Matías, it was clear that they had to engage with technological innovation. But there was a change in the board. The new members are more traditional, or conventional. They do not support technological innovation at all. So, he left."

"And this is when they stopped providing funding?"

"Yes, when he left, they [the partner] were gone. They did not fund us anymore."

This constant ebb and flow rendered the organization and execution of the work complex and, at times, tumultuous.

## We Don't Do Charity Work!

On a rainy evening in November 2017, I walked down to the harbor to meet with the rest of the team. Seal's major annual event would start the next day, and Jorge had convened us to a dinner with a well-known figure in sustainability and entrepreneurship. I had not planned on coming. The invitation had come through a general email to all staff members, and I did not consider myself as such. So, when Sofia told me "I'll see you tonight" as I was leaving the office in the late afternoon, I feigned surprise and asked her why we should see each other later.

"Why?" she asked, puzzled. "You're coming to the dinner with John Elkington, right?"

It sounded like staying at home was not an option. I groaned and explained, confused, that I was not planning because I did not know I was invited.

"Hum … I'm not a staff member," I said. She laughed.

"We sent a collective invitation to the team, and, of course, you're part of the team, this applies to you as well. Come on, stop being stupid."

"Who's John Elkington?"

"What?! Are you serious?"

I was. I had never heard of Elkington. Given Jorge's excitement, I expected him to be a notorious figure in the field. That he had reserved a whole room on the first floor of a fancy seafood restaurant only confirmed my hunch. Once inside, we were on our own. The red carpeting on the walls created a muddled and intimate atmosphere with an exclusive flavor. This, and my ignorance about Elkington, made me feel slightly uneasy and intimidated. But Andrés's jokes quickly relaxed the atmosphere, as always.

We were all seated around a massive wooden square table. Everyone was happily chatting while slightly glancing at the *invité*, who had been strategically seated next to Jorge. The usual latecomers finally arrived, and Jorge looked around before standing solemnly, eyes sparkling. We quieted down instinctively. For a few seconds, he stared intensively at everyone, as if he wanted to warn us of the importance of this moment. Then, he introduced John Elkington in his broken English, praising his visit and the work he had been doing for the last few decades. He then concluded his poignant speech by acknowledging him for being such an inspirational figure for Seal.

Jorge, Sofia, and Lola had picked up the concept of the "triple bottom line" from Elkington. The concept emphasizes the social, economic, and environmental dimensions that organizations should combine to create a more sustainable economy. To put it differently, any organization should care about people, profit, and the planet. While the traditional social economy already tackled the people and planet goals, the importance of being profitable was obvious in how Seal was ideated. As already mentioned, this was surprising at that time, although the overreliance on Elkington's work helped explain this view. One day I asked Pedro why they insisted so much on profitability.

"When I hear the term 'philanthropy,' I become quite tense," he said.

"Why?"

"Philanthropy is a relic from the past. Pure capitalism is under attack, and there are more and more companies, investors, and many others who say we need an alternative."

"An alternative? You mean CSR?"

"CSR is bullshit."

"Why? Jorge seems to like it, right?!"

"I know. But to be honest it's a marketing tool no one trusts."

"What's the alternative then?

"We must align social and economic goals. I don't want to hear about philanthropy. If we speak about philanthropy we're speaking about CSR, so it's the same."

If Pedro did not view CSR as a coherent path for Seal, he recognized that not all interventions for tackling societal issues had to be profitable. In fact, the choice of the presence or absence of profit in the design of the solution, whether it be a social impact start-up or an association, depended on the specific dimension of the problem being tackled.

"Look, what's happening in the field of employment is a good example of this. We all agree that employment is a serious issue, specifically in this country, but if we focus on projects that only help integrate vulnerable workers, we're making a mistake."

"Why? Do you mean we shouldn't help projects that facilitate workers integration?"

"I'm saying that this is exactly where NGOs, public institutions, philanthropy, and the like must come into play, because it's a different area."

"Like employment-related projects are a different area that must be supported by nonprofit actors?"

"Some specific segments of it, like integrating vulnerable workers. But if we focus on workers' access to the labor market more generally, and their training, we could intervene here."

"Why is this so different?"

"Because it's a space for business opportunities more than a space for public intervention. We need to focus on a space with business opportunities because this is where the state fails to provide money."

"I see."

"If we focus too much on the social, we will miss our goal."

Sofia and Lola often shared this view with partners by comparing Nelson Mandela and Steve Jobs. One morning, in front of a room packed with digital care executives, Sofia started by praising Mandela's ambition to make this world better and his constant fight for democracy and freedom, before contrasting him with Jobs.

"Mandela wanted to generate change at the scale of a continent and not only locally. But if Mandela focused on the people and had visionary goals, only Steve Jobs focused on the job! In fact, Jobs developed technological innovation that disrupted and revolutionized many of the things that we do, and he did this in a way that would be profitable," she emphasized forcefully.

Apple being one of the most successful companies out there, she insisted on the idea that "Technological innovation must be scalable." After pausing for her audience to make sense of these examples, she added, "Both were transformational leaders. They had a contagious passion for what they did, whether it was helping people or innovating. And they were truly hard workers."

As we will see in the following chapter, Sofia, Lola, and Jorge constantly emphasized the dual demand and the need to balance these two poles carefully. In fact, Jorge's ceremonial talk to each new cohort during the first hour of boot camp already highlighted this aspect by blatantly saying "Here we don't do charity work. We want real entrepreneurs!"

What does it mean to be an impact entrepreneur then? Jorge forced an emphasis on "real" and "entrepreneur," highlighting that any cohort members must give profit and social goals similar importance. Profit must serve the production of positive impact, whether it be for social or environmental goals, or both. Hence, by "impact entrepreneurs" the co-founders were referring to individuals who combined an acute awareness of a given social or environmental problem with a strong desire to address these problems and the capability to do so in an economically profitable way. This way, they aimed to share a single view of the term "impact" as being inextricable from either a social/environmental or a commercial aspect. As a result, an impact enterprise had both a social/environmental and an economic impact.

While the meaning given to "impact entrepreneur" was clear, I would soon realize that there was a discrepancy among staff members about the social dimension of impact. I became attentive to this issue after an investment committee during which Patrick and Sofia entered a heated debate about whether the venture would qualify as a social impact venture or a traditional venture. For Patrick, the social impact of the venture was clear, so the entrepreneurs could apply for funding. For Sofia, however, the venture was a traditional for-profit project. The two spent five long and tense minutes discussing whether to include the venture, until Patrick gave up. In the end, Sofia was the co-director of the acceleration area and he had to follow her view.

This debate raised concerns among Sofia and Lola, who understood their need to routinize impact measurement procedures and establish a clear, shared, and workable definition of impact. With this goal in mind, Nina, the newly promoted social impact manager, and Jackie, her assistant, designed and ran a one-day workshop for all staff members in October 2018. Their explicit goal was to have us "collectively think about impact," explained Nina. With this goal in mind, they hoped to have us review the existing definition of social impact and gain awareness about the different measurement standards at stake.

The workshop took place on a Friday morning in a room in the new Seal building. Laptops and mobile phones were ceremoniously left in a box next to the door, to maximize our concentration and foster participation. The atmosphere was playful, and jokes were buzzing, with staff members playing the entrepreneurs. It seemed like we were attending the educational modules usually taught to the cohort during the program. This annoyed Nina. She was struggling to have all of us silent. In a collective effort to control our excitement, we finally stopped chatting and joking so she could start. "As you all know, many start-ups fail in their social impact evaluation by the end of the program," she said. Her tone was, I believed, deliberately grave to emphasize the importance of this issue. "And this is a problem," she then added. "This is why we are here."

Meanwhile, Jackie was sticking three posters on the wall at the back of the room. Each presented a different definition of social impact. Within a few minutes, she asked us to choose the one we believed to be correct. I laughed at Patrick and Luc's puzzled faces.

"What's going on?!" I asked.

"Look, the definitions are almost the same."

"No, Luc, they vary," responded Patrick, amused.

"How can I choose one if they only vary in very minor respects? You've got to be kidding me," said Luc, insistent.

Santiago, Gisele, and I happened to share a similar view of social impact as having direct positive implications for the people. As we stood in front of the wall commenting on the definition, Jackie asked us to move to the left corner of the room and to create a group based on the definition of impact we preferred. From there, we watched a second group emerging in the room. Among them was Pablo. He had very little experience about social impact and had just joined Seal a few months earlier. He seemed hesitant about whether to stick to this definition or join another group, but Andrés was trying to convince him that he had made the right choice.

"Look at Pablo, he's lost," Luc told me, amused.

"Why are you standing there?" I asked Pablo.

"It seems to be the way to frame it, right?"

"No! We know what social impact is better than you!" answered Luc, laughing. "Come with us, you will see."

"Your definition only refers to positive implications, but social impact is also negative I think."

"You're wrong! Social impact cannot be negative, I'm telling you! Listen, I'm the oldest," Luc told him.

"Social impact can have positive and/or negative implications, right? It's clear enough, no?" said Pablo, now looking at Jackie.

We failed to rally Pablo to our group. Like Andrés, he felt more comfortable with a definition of social impact acknowledging the possibility of negative externalities. A third group had formed, of those who believed that social impact had to result from a clearly intentional decision and reflect a moral purpose. They stayed in the middle of the room. Nina then asked each faction to present its view. After 15 minutes of heated debate while each group defended their favorite definition, Nina stopped us to summarize the main insight from this exercise.

"We wanted you to realize that there are many different definitions of social impact out there. Even among us. Some of you already knew this, but that's important. Overall, they share similarities. First, impact results from an activity and the change results from this activity. Second, impact not only has implications for the objective target but also for its environment. Third, impact has long-term consequences. Fourth, impact can be positive or negative, and can produce both expected and unexpected implications. And finally, talking about impact means talking about measuring impact. So, indicators are key because otherwise we cannot demonstrate that we actually have an impact."

Our diverging views appeared clearly this morning and, as Nina and Jackie had purposively anticipated, nicely illustrated the polysemic nature of the term "social impact." This was particularly important to overcome the assumption of a unified definition held by some of the staff members, but also to insist on the importance of impact as a measurable output of concrete entrepreneurial activities. In the vein of Patrick and Sofia's argument, the multiple meanings of the term and the lack of shared measurement standards raised significant ambiguity in decision-making at Seal. Patrick was particularly concerned by this aspect. Once the workshop was finished and we had met with part of the entrepreneurial team he mentored, we left the building together. Recalling his tense conversation with Sofia about whether a venture should qualify as social impact, which had taken place weeks before the workshop, I asked him if he now felt satisfied.

"Not really."

"It's crazy that no one in there is able to agree on what social impact is."

"I agree. But that's not that surprising, right?"

"What you mean?"

"Well, do you think these projects have a real impact?"

"They're supposed to, right? Which is why you spend so much time at committees talking about it, right?"

"Oh yes. But for me the worst is the lack of criteria."

"For what, identifying a venture as impact, or measuring the impact?"

"To know that this is actually a *social impact* [emphasis added] start-up."

"I see, like the other day, right?"

"Right. You know, I work hard with entrepreneurs to prepare for the investment committee, but then they're told at the committee that they don't have a social impact. You know what I mean."

"Yes. That this could be waste of time for you."

"Totally."

"But you don't work on the social impact, right?"

"No. They should make sure that these guys have a social impact first, and then send them to me."

"Why don't you use impact standards then? It would solve this problem if everyone agrees on these standards," I asked.

"Because, to me, the only one that makes sense is the SROI [Social Return on Investment], but we aren't using it. We talked about it this morning; it was in Nina's slides, remember?"

"Why do you prefer SROI?"

"It gives you a number; it's easy, no?"

For investors, indeed, the number provided a foundation to easily compare ventures that actual standards and the theory of change capturing better qualitative dimensions of the ventures and used at Seal, did not allow.

As we reached his car, he reiterated his point to make sure I understood his dissatisfaction: "Nina has her definition, Santiago as well, you have yours, but we all ignore what social impact is exactly. Why? Because there is no definition, and everyone here has their own definition."

## Conclusion

This chapter has recounted the early days of Seal, presented its three main areas of operation, and examined its funding structure and the role of the latter for shaping the day-to-day running of these areas. Finally, I have also discussed the founders' pathway to impact entrepreneurship. Albeit brief, this description of the organization provides us with the foundation for the analysis to come in the following chapters. So far, we can draw three concluding remarks before moving forward.

Sofia, Lola, and Jorge launched Seal with the primary aim of helping entrepreneurs turn their ideas into an impact enterprise. This was clear from the start. With this goal in mind, circa 2013, they viewed the organizational form of the accelerator as ideal to serve some of the most crucial needs of early-stage entrepreneurs. They believed the design of the acceleration training to be critical to bridge nascent impact enterprises with established corporations. Not only did the corporate partners provide the much-needed funding to maintain Seal afloat, they actively participated in some of its most vital activities, including selecting ventures and mentoring entrepreneurial projects. Accordingly, it was not only that corporate partners could access entrepreneurs and their ideas—the entrepreneurs themselves could greatly benefit from the partners' expertise. And Seal would be the primary nexus between the two.

But Sofia, Lola, and Jorge also launched Seal with the explicit goal to develop the culture of impact entrepreneurship. Specifically, they had the ambition to not only create new knowledge and tools supporting its development, but also, and just as necessary, create a market for the entrepreneurs trained during the acceleration program. Their effort was taking place at a time when impact entrepreneurship was relatively unknown and, perhaps more importantly, rarely seen as morally acceptable and potentially condemned as a misappropriation of social means toward profit making. In this context, Seal and its outcomes would become the proxy by which they could create and share new cultural referents, reaching far beyond entrepreneurs and corporate partners.

Their audience, however, was primarily a business one. The small- and medium-scale events they organized gathered industrial leaders, executives from partner and non-partner corporations, academics, entrepreneurs, and investors. They of course also invited policymakers and representatives from third-sector organizations. However, the belief that change could not happen without industry support informed their emphasis on propagating impact entrepreneurship in the business world. Back then, their insistence on building profitable social ventures disrupted the dominant social economy approach. In their quest for impact, the founders strived to define and construct impact entrepreneurship as entirely revolving around a social and commercial demand. What constituted social impact remained unclear, but what was clear was that such impact could only be produced by coherently and consistently articulating the social and the commercial. This is the belief that provided the main guiding principle for the performance of impact work.

## Bibliography

Cohen, S., Fehder, D. C., Hochberg, Y. V., & Murray, F. (2019). The Design of Startup Accelerators. *Research Policy, 48*(7), 1781–1797.

Flecha, R., & Ngai, P. (2014). The Challenge for Mondragon: Searching for the Cooperative Values in Times of Internationalization. *Organization, 21*(5), 666–682.

Mair, J., Marti, I., & Ventresca, M. (2012). Building Inclusive Markets in Rural Bangladesh: How Intermediaries Work Institutional Voids. *Academy of Management Journal, 55*, 819–850.

CHAPTER 3

# Valuable Start-ups

On a Tuesday morning, I was seated in the small and fairly cramped meeting room with a dozen executives from the corporations funding Seal, who were eager to select the entrepreneurs for the new edition of the acceleration program. A screen and a projector were set next to the large window for entrepreneurs to play their slides. Lola quickly broke the by launching a quick round of introductions. There were, indeed, new faces among the chief innovation officers and heads of communication seated around the table. Next, she gave us an overview of the 13 entrepreneurs who would pitch their projects before concluding by reminding us about our goals for the morning.

"Your role today is super important," she said. "We're here to select the best start-ups for the program. For the most part, the success of the acceleration program relies on you! So, think deeply about your decision. Keep in mind that the entrepreneurs who are selected will spend the next three months with us. And we can't select everyone, obviously. You may not like all the ventures, but we will do our best to accommodate your needs."

Selecting promising impact enterprises in their very early stage was not only essential for Seal's success, but also crucial for the corporate partners who hoped to collaborate with the entrepreneurs. They expected to be introduced to top-tier entrepreneurs from their respective industries. By participating in the program, they could select ventures and meet with the


G. Dumont, *Impact Work*,
https://doi.org/10.1007/978-3-031-64661-4_3

entrepreneurs by mentoring them. They also expected to benefit from being publicly associated with an organization promoting impact entrepreneurship, and could use this association for their CSR and communication strategies. And because Seal's founders believed that companies are in the driver's seat in fostering change, they strove to create partnerships by providing space for them entrepreneurs to meet, exchange, and work with entrepreneurs.

Having introduced the organizational context of the book in the previous chapter, I now turn to the selection of the entrepreneurs to the accelerator. This process revolved around various steps and took place only a few weeks before the start of each edition of the acceleration program. During the selection committees, the short-listed entrepreneurs pitched their projects to enter the program. As Sofia told me, it was a great way for me to become familiar with the selection process and to forge bonds with the partners who participated as external evaluators. Indeed, I learned a great deal about their experience working with impact entrepreneurs, and I further deepened this understanding through one-on-one interviews with them.

Examining how partners evaluate early-stage impact enterprises was critical for sensing how the understanding of impact entrepreneurship was deployed at the ground level. It was also important to capture the role played by the exponential number of stakeholders increasingly involved alongside impact entrepreneurs, including business accelerators, impact investors, mentors, foundations, and governmental agencies.[1] These stakeholders provide support of different kinds, notably by training entrepreneurs, advising them on their social impact, helping to build their networks, testing their MVP with their clients, or generating novel ideas and opportunities through mentoring. This chapter uncovers the multiple ways they do so.

"Having partners select ventures is delicate," Sofia told me once, after recommending that I attend these sessions. She couldn't have been more right. My repeated observations of the heated debates among partners revealed the different interests driving corporations in their attempts to collaborate with impact entrepreneurs. These interests shaped their

[1] Stakeholders' participation in traditional accelerators and social impact accelerators varies greatly according to their goals. These goals, in turn, influence the design of the program, its target, and expected outcomes. See Cohen et al. (2019), Miller and Wesley (2010), Wright and Drori (2018), Yan et al. (2019).

criteria for identifying and, specifically, for evaluating and selecting impact enterprises with which to collaborate. Unpacking their evaluative practices, therefore, can shed light on how these stakeholders make sense of impact entrepreneurship. This is important given that the question of evaluation has mostly been examined from the perspective of investors.[2]

This focus on investors is hardly surprising given the persistent view that finance is chief among the resources needed by impact entrepreneurs. Of course, accessing finance is pressing. But financial capital is far from being the only resource they need. In fact, at such an early stage, securing investment is maybe the most complex task as entrepreneurs have very little to offer. This focus has largely undermined another, perhaps more important, feature of impact entrepreneurship: its collective nature. Resultingly, we lack an in-depth understanding of how stakeholders other than investors evaluate impact enterprises and make sense of their participation in impact entrepreneurship.[3]

As Lola reiterated to the executives seated around the table, selecting the best start-ups was a priority. "At Seal, we only work with the best entrepreneurs, and we have the best social impact start-ups." I believe her insistence was an attempt to prove Seal's value for the mentors, corporate partners, entrepreneurs, investors, and policymakers gravitating around the organization. However, what she meant by "the best start-ups" as the gold standard was puzzling. Indeed, while the dominant understanding of value in entrepreneurship is economic value, very early-stage impact enterprises are not attractive economically because entrepreneurs are still developing their products, building a team, and accessing a market. Although they tried to provide us with financial forecasting, assessing their economic value was tremendously challenging.

To explore this issue, I attended 23 selection committees, met several times with the selection officer to discuss scouting, interviewed the co-founders and partners, and carefully reviewed the characteristics of the ventures selected for each program edition. Still, I couldn't explain what the best start-ups were. None of the partners could articulate it either.

Cristina, who worked for one of Seal's long-standing partners, nicely summarized a shared view among partners as we met one day in the intimacy of her office. She noted that, at Seal, her firm competed with other

[2] See, for instance, the work of Huang (2018), Huang and Pearce (2015), Maxwell and Lévesque (2014).

[3] Clough et al. (2019).

partners belonging to the same industry but with different expectations about the entrepreneurs and upcoming collaborations. Importantly, she also emphasized the partners' embryonic knowledge of early-stage entrepreneurship but blamed Sofia and Lola for the absence of clear criteria for selecting the entrepreneurs:

"I know which products we need in my industry, that's my job, but I don't know how the process works for entrepreneurs."

"The process? You mean how they develop their venture?"

"Yes, that too, but what I mean is that I know what a start-up is, but from there, to assess whether entrepreneurs will make it or not, I have no clue."

"The problem is to evaluate if it's a good venture or not, right?" I asked.

"Yes. It's hard to know. I think part of the problem is not only that we don't know what a good venture is, or if they will succeed, but also that we have little guidance about which criteria we should use."

In this chapter, I start with Cristina's concern and examine what makes an early-stage impact enterprise worth accelerating. I use the term "worth" purposively, as my aim is to move beyond the dominant focus on economic value. The reason, as I show in the following section, is that what makes impact enterprises valuable is eminently plural. While it may sound trivial to say that an impact enterprise is a catalyzer for different types of evaluation and, accordingly, values, these values are often overlooked. Hence, I adopt an anthropological focus attentive to the question of values, which builds upon Brian Moeran's "ensemblage of worth" theory.[4]

This theory recognizes the plurality of values at stake beyond economic value to provide a more comprehensive account of worth. Originally formulated in the context of the creative industries, an "ensemblage of worth" reflects the criteria used to assess the worth of creative goods. As highlighted in the introduction, I believe that impact enterprises share a central feature with creative goods: they are singular in nature. Because of their singularity, impact enterprises raise similar challenges for evaluators who assess their worth, including creating evaluative standards and identifying concrete dimensions of the ventures. Indeed, the ensemblage of worth theory revolves around the premise that value is not an inherent property of things nor a mere individual preference. Instead, values are constructed by actors and the market in a dialogical and iterative process.[5]

[4] Moeran (2013).

[5] See, for instance, Moeran (2005, 2007, 2013), Moeran and Christensen (2013).

Brian Moeran's research is particularly illustrative in this regard. Moeran shows how the judgments of multiple people about the different properties of creative goods contribute to assigning them different values. In other words, values are created during the evaluation, located, and produced in a specific context. For instance, a stoneware pot made by a Japanese craftsman is not beautiful in itself; it is beautiful because of the different values brought to bear in its aesthetic and commercial judgment. This stoneware might hold material, symbolic, technical, aesthetic, and use values. An important implication is that things have no intrinsic qualities beyond the materials they are made from, and creative goods are "multidimensional singularities."[6] Applied to impact entrepreneurship, this insight challenges the dominant focus on economic value and calls for developing a comprehensive understanding of the multiple dimensions that imbue impact enterprises with worth.

Values are socially constructed. They are the criteria by which people judge what is legitimate and worthwhile.[7] Accordingly, evaluative practices play a central role in determining which aspects matter and for whom. They enable evaluators to produce a socially constructed understanding of what counts.[8] This insight is not too much of a stretch from the recent research on entrepreneurial evaluation. In fact, this research implicitly acknowledges that values are socially constructed through the very act of evaluation.[9] However, the theory of the ensemblage of worth extends this understanding by moving beyond the dualism between value (economic) and values (e.g., cultural, symbolic, social, and technical).[10] Hence, this ensemblage of worth constitutes the relative merits of an impact enterprise in relation to the overall estimation of the values granted to its different dimensions.

To uncover the ensemblage of worth of an impact enterprise, we must account for the different ways Cristina and her peers evaluate specific dimensions of the ventures and entrepreneurs because of their diverse interests and experiences. Consequently, we must consider evaluation criteria and the values they convey to understand how people construct

[6] See Moeran (2013).

[7] See Moeran and Strandgaard (2011).

[8] Lamont (2012).

[9] See, for example, Khaire (2013), Stark (2011).

[10] An exception is the work of David Stark (2011) on technological start-ups in the new media industry and, more broadly, his approach to the question of value where he adopts a similar position.

worth. Examining the worth of an impact enterprise should not be interpreted as an attempt to negate the importance of the economic and social value. Instead, it's an attempt to recognize the role of actors other than investors and the importance of their evaluative practices in the development of impact enterprises.

The following argument stems from what I learned during the different stages of the selection process. To move beyond the dichotomy between social and economic value, I advance five criteria: problem-solving capability, maturity, technical innovation, social impact, and network capability. I argue that their interplay informs of the worth of an impact enterprise because they convey use, technical, social, and relational values, raising two important points. First, the definition of what is valuable in impact entrepreneurship depends on the evaluators' view, be they corporate partners, policymakers, impact investors, serial entrepreneurs, or mentors. Subsequently, the creation of social and economic value expected from impact enterprises is, at its core, contingent on evaluation practice and, thus, involves multiple producers. Resultingly, an impact enterprise is not valuable *per se* but only becomes valuable when categorized as such as the result of an evaluation process.

## Scouting and Screening

One of the things I quickly learned at Seal was that impact enterprises were challenging to find. I found this shortage of impact entrepreneurs and ventures surprising. At the outset, the hype about technological startups was high and everyone seemed to be profoundly interested in impact. Why was it so challenging to identify them then?

All staff members were aware of the challenge that identifying entrepreneurs raised for the outcome of the acceleration program and, consequently, the development of Seal. Leire was assigned to this delicate task. The 23-year-old recent undergraduate's mission was to scout impact entrepreneurs across the country, reach out to them, and convince them to apply to the call. This task could quickly become tiresome and very stressful. This was particularly the case when the list of applicants remained limited in quality and quantity in the last weeks or even days before the closing of the call.

Leire embodied the urgency of her mission. She spoke fast, talked fast, and acted quickly. It was only after several days of chasing her through

Seal's corridors that she agreed to meet between two meetings. I was eager to learn about how she detected ventures and convinced entrepreneurs to apply to the call. In that sense, I believed that looking at how this task was performed would help me to clarify what type of entrepreneur and venture Seal favored. Indeed, the operations of selection and exclusion tell much about how intermediary organizations define things as valuable in a specific cultural context and, therefore, contribute to constructing a new market for impact enterprises.

On this particular morning, we sat in a room away from the hustle and bustle of the main office. Leire was truly exhausted. She waited a moment before turning on her laptop, enjoying these few stolen seconds of calm.

"Look, Guillaume, this Excel sheet gathers all the contact information of the entrepreneurs. I have also added small descriptions of the projects that I found. In total, we have over 200 applicants this time."

"Where did you find them?"

"Some entrepreneurs applied from our website. They go online, enter the application page, and fill out the form with the information we request. Others come from the network, our partners, the founders, or the mentors who may know interesting projects and send them to me. And the rest comes from me."

"From you?"

"Yes, I spend a lot of time searching for projects on the internet. What I do is review start-up websites and reach out to entrepreneurs. I attend events as much as I can. You can find entrepreneurs there."

"Which types of entrepreneurs do you look for?"

"I look for entrepreneurs who develop technological and scalable innovations of products or services," she said, almost rhetorically. "Of course, these must fall within our different clusters of interest."

"There are eight clusters, right?"

"Yes. That's a lot but we can accelerate ventures in health care, social services, resource management, work, future, and education."

"What happens then if you find a venture that educates workers for example? It may fit in the two clusters?"

"Yes. That's another of my many problems," she answered, laughing. "In practice many of the ventures belong to more than one category, so it's complicated to know which fits best."

"So, what do you do? Do you have any specific criteria?"

"No, not really. Getting the projects right is puzzling because you feel that they fit with the program, and then Lola, Sofia, and the program managers review them and disagree."

"What happens next?"

"Nothing, they reject them right away and I must get back to work," she said, discouraged.

I scrolled down the list, impressed by the number of applicants. She was right: I could count almost 200 ventures.

"But don't think they will all enter the program. Only a dozen will make it to the upcoming cohort."

Leire started recounting stories from the previous week's event, until Lola interrupted her by showing up at the open door.

"Quality over quantity!" said Lola loudly, as she had listened to the last bits of our conversation.

This led to a complete change of expression on Leire's face. Coming into the room to glance at the list, Lola stopped one meter from the table and stared at us intensively.

"I had a look at the list yesterday. This is not very promising," she said solemnly. "The selection starts on Monday. You remember? I hope to see more projects by the end of the week."

I felt concerned about Leire. She looked down, embarrassed, and agreed with Lola. "Yes, we're short of interesting start-ups. In fact, we've got a bunch of crappy ones."

Once Lola left, Leire seemed desperate and anxious. "What do you mean by an interesting start-up? Everyone talks about interesting start-ups, but what do you mean?" I asked.

"The entrepreneur must develop a product that is socially innovative. It could be a service as well, but they must develop something new and useful. Also, it must entail a clear business opportunity."

"Some newness is the key, right?"

"No, not only. They must be at the right stage. But most ventures have the same problem: they are either very early-stage or very advanced. Either way, they are useless. You follow me."

"Yes, I do."

"And then if the timing is right, the venture still must fit within one cluster."

Santiago, Pablo, and Nina would evaluate Leire's list on Monday. The three program managers were assigned to specific clusters and worked closely with the entrepreneurs. They also interacted on a weekly basis with the corporate partners and mentors to coordinate the meeting and organize their schedule, and reported to Sofia and Lola. This provided them with a nuanced understanding of the needs of their respective clusters, and they knew precisely which ventures could be of interest. While screening the list, they decided who was worth interviewing to get more details about the information provided in the online form, as most applications were made through the website. Next, they scheduled meetings to ask specific questions to contrast the information provided by the entrepreneurs in their application materials and to inquire about their professional experience and commitment to the project.

I observed the meeting between program managers and entrepreneurs many times. I found these meetings insightful for understanding what was expected from entrepreneurs. For instance, I learned that some entrepreneurs' lack of trustworthiness challenged program managers. One day, Pablo invited me to attend these pre-selection interviews with him. He had joined the organization soon after the start of my fieldwork to primarily manage the cluster in digital health. At 8 a.m. when we met, the office was still empty, and he briefed me about the upcoming meeting with a team of entrepreneurs. He was excited.

"I like them, they have been trying to develop a new medical device that is promising. They have potential. I knew about them from a coworker at the hospital. And the team looks very solid."

"What's the device about?"

"It's a device that gauges the probability of having a heart attack weeks before the typical symptoms appear."

"How do they frame their social impact?"

"That's one thing. It's unclear, so it could be just another medical device."

"There was no indication about it?"

"No. So we must be careful with these guys; they have been at this other accelerator before. That accelerator has no relationship with social impact. What they do is purely commercial."

"So why did they apply if they have no relationship with social impact?"

"They may have changed their business model and decided to go for impact, no clue. But the guys at that accelerator they don't care about impact, so if they have revised their plan to aim for impact it's not because of them."

"Why should they have changed their plan and decided to go for impact from one day to the next?"

"I don't know. To be honest, I like them but the truth is that the entrepreneurs aren't convincing as impact entrepreneurs, I think. When you look at their CVs, these are engineers, except the IT guy and the doctor."

"You don't believe in their social impact, is that it?"

"Hmm ... no, not really, at least from the document they sent us. They use the word 'social impact,' but it doesn't materialize in the venture."

During the meeting, the entrepreneurs were eager about the prospect of joining the accelerator. I found them very business-oriented, to which Pablo agreed. This was partly because of their look, as they wore executive shirts and carried briefcases, and because of how they framed their pitch, as Pablo later mentioned.

"They described their idea in a very commercial way. They focused on the product—which is typical with those entrepreneurs in health—and the market gap. I think that's because the other team member is from finance. And they've also pitched the project to investors. This is what investors expect."

Thinking about the gap with another venture we had reviewed earlier, I added, "Yes. And this other entrepreneur we pitched this morning was a university student. It was a very different perspective, right?"

"Totally. I mean there's a clear gap between them. Also, have you seen the contrast? The university student was truly passionate about social impact but did not shower before the interview."

"Hum, I see, and the others were very nicely dressed."

"Yes. You will meet potential collaborators and you don't even shower. But the guy sounded much more convincing than those two about social impact, that's obvious."

However, during the meeting, Pablo hid his doubts. The entrepreneurs presented in length about market gaps, their product, and their go-to-market strategy. When Pablo found the information satisfying, he interrupted them and jumped on to the social dimension of the venture.

"You've been talking a lot about the product and the business, that's great. But why would you like to have an impact? It's not clear to me why."

"Of course. We would like to talk to investors, you know, we need money," said the tallest, deviating from the original question.

"I see. But the social impact?"

"We have been talking to some doctors at the hospital and think that it might be great to care more about the social impact. We have a doctor on the team. After all, we belong to the health industry, no?"

"Yes. So what?"

"So, it's clear that we help people with our product, and we want your help to improve it. We want to be able to help more and more people!"

added the other entrepreneur in what sounded like as a desperate attempt to demonstrate their commitment to impact.

Pablo nodded, slightly taken aback from such a big claim. In closing, I asked about how Seal could help them. The entrepreneur reiterated his point about funding, "What we need is capital, we want to access investors."

At nearly midday, the two entrepreneurs finally left the meeting room. Pablo stared at me:

"You see, I told you, they don't care about impact. Entrepreneurs like these come here because they care about money. All they want is to access investors."

"Yes, you were right, but why is this incompatible with Seal? Entrepreneurs are also expected to have a business model and to generate profit," I said.

"Well, we don't want entrepreneurs only looking for money, because they're too advanced. We want entrepreneurs who care about impact. We help them develop their ventures and grow their impact. Then, they can apply for funding, but not vice versa. These were way too advanced to be able to make changes on their venture during the program."

"…."

"Frankly, they didn't sound very open to change. Don't you think so?"

I nodded in silence.

"He almost got angry at me when I asked how they would adapt their business model to integrate impact!"

The two ventures we had reviewed that morning were at the ideation stage and had minimal concrete features, such as an MVP, financial forecasting, a team. This was particularly the case for the university student.

"This is why I spend most of my time asking them questions about themselves. And we will be working together. So, I care about whether they work or not, if they have a source of income, what is their previous experience, how they would like to develop the venture, etc."

"Makes sense," I added.

"What I also look for is their capability to develop the venture in one way or another. What we do here is to help them to grow…thus their project is much more likely to change, and a lot. I want to see if they're willing and capable to undertake the work."

After Leire's list had been examined by program managers, and selected entrepreneurs invited for a pre-interview, only a handful of entrepreneurs convincingly combined social and commercial goals. Their scarcity roughly contrasted with the persistent view of the impact entrepreneur as someone who adequately, almost naturally, handles social and commercial demands. In fact, some staff members were even very skeptical about this possibility.

"There might be a sort of incompatibility between these goals—when you start looking deeper into the candidates, there's no one left," explained Santiago once at the end of a long morning filled with pre-selection interviews. An executive from a corporate partner named Lídia nicely conveyed this issue to me during an interview. I asked if she found the entrepreneurs convincing regarding their social goals. She thoughtfully looked out her office's large window for a few seconds, then turned back to me.

"You have two types [of entrepreneurs] here … the one who wants to make money but who pretends to be interested in social goals…and the one who wants to save the world but doesn't care about how they're going to make money. In both cases, we have a problem!"

Denis, an entrepreneur who applied to the program and who we interviewed with Santiago and Nina during the summer 2017, greatly exemplified Lídia's first type of entrepreneur. He looked like a "businessman" because of his tie, suit, and language. Freshly graduated with an MBA from a prestigious business school, Denis had one decade of experience in health and two decades as an entrepreneur. He showed strong business skills and quickly convinced us of his capability to develop his project.

This type of profile almost invariably raised suspicions among the two about the social goals. When Denis left the room, it was Nina who raised this point by saying, pessimistically.

"He loves dropping big names. He knows people in the industry, he has great presentation skills, he has a great CV, but I haven't heard anything about his social impact. Nothing. Well, he did say something about it at the end. Still, I have no clue. Lots of telling, great promise, serious but pretentious guy, but no concrete information about the social impact."

"He did say that he wanted to have an impact," I added.

"It's a lot of lies, of course," added Nina teasingly, underlying my inexperience without batting an eyelid.

In contrast, Lídia's "Type 2 entrepreneurs" sounded genuinely passionate about the social mission, which they located at the heart of their project:

"But the problem is that these guys typically don't care about the economic viability of their project. You remember Roger?" Santiago asked me.

"Sure."

"Look, Guillaume, Roger is an 'impact' [emphasis added] entrepreneur," Santiago continued, in a convincing tone.

I had met Roger during my first boot camp. He was late because he missed his Monday flight. He looked like a lunatic dreamer, with long curly hair, an oversized white T-shirt, and distressed jeans. Everyone connected instantly with him because of his irresistible passion for his project. However, he was laborious when pitching. I felt sorry for him. He was super stressed and started sweating severely by the middle of the presentation when he presented his product. He had begun his journey by creating handmade products. He then spent quite a few years volunteering for several non-profits, and quite a few more working as a commercial salesman for a medical distributor before launching his venture.

At this stage, the importance of evaluating credibility when screening entrepreneurs deserves a pause. I recurrently observed that the staff was particularly attentive to questioning and assessing the self-reported intention to achieve social impact and the entrepreneur's experience. Given that entrepreneurs make intensive use of "impression management,"[11] namely the performative activity by which people strategically manage their self-presentation in a way that they appear favorably and can influence others, this was hardly surprising. Santiago made this aspect clear to me one day during lunch. We had interviewed a candidate that morning, and he used his example to tell me.

"There are start-ups and entrepreneurs we meet during the selection process who, after a few weeks, you realize the only thing you'll get from them is hot air. You don't even meet with them anymore because they do nothing. They are worth nothing. You know what I mean?"

"Yes. Sofia told me the same."

"With these meetings we avoid the cast of professional entrepreneurs who are specialized in pitching, getting awards, and securing funding only because they are good at making the show and designing presentations but who have no interest at all in having a social impact."

"So, how do you detect them?"

"There are several aspects that matter. I like if they share financial information for instance."

"Financial information?"

[11] Goffman's (1959) well-known theory suggested that people attempt to influence the perception of others in the interaction. Applied to the organizational context, an organization could be seen dramaturgically because of the impression management strategies deployed by employees.

"Yes. Many don't show you this, but it's a signal that you can trust them. They [the entrepreneurs] have invested in their own company. They commit. Remember this other team we met this morning. The entrepreneur showed us information about who has shares in the company."

"So what?" I asked, squinting.

"Well, this is not typical. They don't show you this information. That they do signals commitment. With this information, you can trust them."

## Selecting the Best Start-ups

Scouting and screening resulted in a shortlist of entrepreneurs. These were then invited to pitch their idea to the selection committees, the final step to creating the cohort. Sofia and Lola organized one selection committee per cluster that gathered corporate partners and, occasionally, serial entrepreneurs and impact investors.

"This way, our partners can select projects of interest within the dozen short-listed entrepreneurs. Only two or three per cluster make it to the boot camp. The committee helps us to make sure that our partners select the right projects and not only those they like!"

"What's wrong with that?" I asked naively. "Aren't partners funding you to work with projects they like?"

"Not all the partners understand what impact entrepreneurship is, not even entrepreneurship!"

"Ah no?" I asked, mentally recalling that Cristina already warned me about her heterogeneous understanding of new venture creation a few weeks earlier.

"No. In fact, very often, partners don't know what's a good project."

"What's a good project then?"

"It's a project with potential."

"What do you mean?"

"That the project has potential to be accelerated. That we will be able to develop it further."

"But how do you select them, do you have specific criteria?"

"You'll see."

I hoped this would be easier, but found out later that they were not using any strict set of selection criteria. Uncovering what "the best start-ups" were made of, therefore, required working inductively to identify these criteria across committees.

Among these criteria was, first, the product's problem-solving capability. This criterion was a salient dimension of the evaluation because Seal's partners struggled to foster internal innovation. Most corporations struggle to foster internal innovation. This may be because of strategic misalignment, leadership conflicts, organizational issues, and multiple other motives. Accelerators such as Seal offer one way to address this challenge by providing corporations with a deal flow of entrepreneurship projects with the potential to address some of their innovation needs.

One morning, I discussed this aspect with Felix, the CEO of Nano, a corporation that creates and distributes teaching materials, and Fernando, Nano's head of innovation. He explained.

"At Nano we have hundreds of employees and hundreds of processes to have them work together. That's one thing. Everything you do takes ages. And also, we work in education. Education isn't very technology friendly. It's very slow to develop new products and services."

"So, you struggle at the firm level but also because of your industry, right?"

"Yes. We struggle to generate innovation. We are good at innovating when it relates to our core business. Still, there are so many new initiatives and methodologies and emerging ways of learning and teaching that we can't be innovative in all of them. Although yes, in education innovation is rather rare in my view."

"So here you are at Seal, right?"

"Yes. We want to generate new ideas about learning strategies and to discover new products that improve teaching-related issues."

Improving internal innovation by capturing entrepreneurial ideas created tensions. At one committee, for instance, the product ideated by the entrepreneurs of an environmental start-up met the expectations of Alain and Ivan. The two worked for corporations managing the distribution of natural resources in the city and the development of environmental indicators, respectively. Both sounded excited as they could foresee possible applications of the product, an electricity consumption device, in ways that would help their teams. Alain, who had a background in engineering, particularly loved the fact that the two entrepreneurs were engineers. While Alain and Ivan had disliked the ventures presented earlier that morning, they were now congratulating Sofia. This, in itself, would be bound to please her.

Alain and Ivan were clapping their hands but, on the other side of the table, Ricardo—the head of the marketing department of a long-standing partner—was nervously playing with his pen. "If I take the product alone, how should I use it to solve my needs?" he then asked in a provocative tone.

Ricardo openly questioned the decision to include the start-up in the cohort by outlining that he did not find the product helpful. Alain and Ivan turned to him, annoyed by his question. Ricardo continued.

"It's a great product, yes, but it is not unique at all."

"What you mean?" asked Sofia.

"I mean that it already exists," answered Ricardo, confident.

"Not exactly," said Alain.

"I know that the product is interesting for you guys, but what am I supposed to do with it?" added Ricardo ironically, in a rather direct way.

Taken aback by such directness, Sofia's thrill at finally meeting Alain and Ivan's expectations evaporated, as did Alain and Ivan's smiles. They did not dare answer immediately, as if they were waiting for other participants to stand up for their case. Sofia looked lost and darkly pessimistic. She had to arrive at an agreement to include the project to please them. This was key because the two were considering stopping their funding to Seal given the shortage of projects meeting their needs, as they would explain to me a week later.

Sofia also knew that Ricardo cared about projects developing regenerative systems. He was virulent at committees, and she knew he wouldn't give up that easily. It seemed that all of us knew this, and the room remained silent for what seemed to be an eternity. Ricardo was reading his notes, impassible, until he looked up at Sofia for approbation. She nodded in silence, in a way I found not very convincing. That his interest was not seriously considered made Ricardo look irritated. He tried to pressure the other participants by adding forcefully,

"As committee members, we should strive to reach a consensus by pondering these divergences!"

It was not unusual for partners to dislike the ventures. They often struggled to identify a fit with their needs, which was not surprising given that impact entrepreneurs developed their ideas individually. A few days later, I would discuss this point with Pedro.

"The projects are what they are. They haven't been designed to serve the needs of a specific partner, so we need to explain to partners that they'll have access to a cohort of entrepreneurs with ideas."

"What do partners say?" I asked.

"The partner must be smart enough to know which ideas are the most interesting."

I nodded in silence while he stared at me for a few seconds, to make sure I got it right.

"But the project itself, no. For example, it's like how some entrepreneurs sell the product, they should be inspired by the idea, right? There is one entrepreneur building partnerships with city councils in a way that is super interesting, for instance. Well, talk to him and take the idea if it's useful for you, then apply it! But to find projects that would exactly fit your needs. It's impossible."

As I learned from interviewing Seal's partners, they all struggled to understand and integrate this aspect. The week of my conversation with Pedro I also interviewed Paul, a partner from the health industry about whom Sofia had warned me:

"He's getting upset with the program, I think he's seriously thinking about leaving and not funding us next year. He comes less and less often, so you should talk to him," she told me.

As we progressed through the interview, Paul's dissatisfaction rapidly became apparent, but his was unsure who to blame. He sounded frustrated:

"I provided Sofia with clear indications about what I was looking for, but…!"

"They didn't find any projects for you?" I asked.

"It's unclear whether they haven't done the work well or whether this is because of our industry. I know that in other industries, it's pretty challenging to find innovative stuff, like for those working in education, but in health…"

"In health? What do you mean?" I asked.

"Well, in health, it shouldn't be that hard; there are dozens of projects!"

A second important evaluation criterion was the ventures' degree of maturity. In their design, accelerators typically focus on the idea stage or invest-ready ventures. Partners, however, struggled to clearly identify if the current development stage aligned with the program's focus. As for partners' conflicting interests, the challenge of evaluating the development stage popped up recurrently during selection committees.

That day's committee was a first for David, a young head of innovation at a firm in the healthcare sector. He had little idea what it was that made their project at an ideal stage to be selected, and asked multiple times about the stage of development: "These guys are green, very green, aren't they?" This aspect was obvious. Another representative nodded in agreement and answered, "Yes, they are at the green stage. I like the idea, but they need to develop it further."

"A venture must be green enough for entrepreneurs to benefit from the training and pivot, but not too green to envision potential collaborations," explained Sofia. Entrepreneurial ideas must be developed enough for partners to foresee how it could help them, while at the same time they must be nascent enough to revisit them significantly during the training.

This was challenging, as Michel, the chief innovation officer of a firm producing digital health technologies, explained to me during a coffee break outside of the building, in between two pitches.

"We do see exciting projects, but why select a project when the product is not developed enough, at least not enough for us to envision potential roads for collaboration?"

"How can you sense this?" I asked.

"You remember this start-up in biotech we listened to this morning?"

"Sure."

"I can see the potential value of the product for my firm, but this product is not developed enough to envision establishing a partnership within the timeframe of the program."

Generally, partners aligned with the views of Sofia, Lola, and the program managers because they believed in their expertise. Nevertheless, in some instances, their respective views collided. That morning, for instance, Pablo devoted a lot of energy to persuading partners to include a start-up in the cohort. Truly believing in the potential of the entrepreneurs, he advocated for their willingness to implement changes to their venture.

"The business model isn't very well defined yet, but this is something they will work on during the three months of the training. And, to be fair, I believe that the entrepreneurs are well aware of this, they told me. They welcomed your comments during the pitch. We will spend time with them and have them work with mentors to make sure they develop a proper business model."

Later that afternoon, we chatted with Sofia about the partners' resistance to Pablo's argument for including the venture. They did not see a clear fit with their own interests. Sofia sounded worried and raised a more general issue typically facing selection committees.

"Partners do not seem to be very familiar with what we do during the acceleration process, even if they have been told about it again and again."

"Why is that? What is it that they don't understand?" I asked.

"It's very hard for them to acknowledge what we can potentially bring to these start-ups, how much they will change, how they will grow during the program."

"You mean that they can't foresee how much the idea will evolve?"

"Yes. It's like they just think about how it is now, but not how it will look tomorrow. And much of the work that we do is to develop this idea."

"Hum, too present-centered, right?"

"It's also hard, sometimes, for them to detect what is truly innovative."

"What you mean?"

"They like the idea, but not because it's new. Because it seems to fit with their needs. But that's not enough to make it work."

As Leire mentioned earlier, entrepreneurial projects were expected to thrive because of the technologically innovative nature of their product or service. Accordingly, a third evaluation criterion was the technological innovation of the product or service supported by a valid business model. While corporate partners expected entrepreneurs to be at the top of the industry's development, this was not always the case. Marcus, the head of an innovation unit, exemplified this point by commenting on a start-up as we debriefed and made the final decision about which three out of the 12 projects presented that morning would enter the program.

"Yes, it's an interesting idea, but it has already been done."

"What you mean?" asked Sofia.

"That there are a lot of competitors out there. So, although the theory behind the idea is fascinating, the service will be tough to implement, especially the app," clarified Marcus.

"Do you already know an app like this?"

"Yes, there are millions of apps like this. And with this business model, it will be hard to grow."

The strict focus of the entrepreneurs on their product also posed challenges. Many of my interlocutors at Seal, from corporate partners to impact investors and mentors, recurrently pointed to this aspect. Marcus, again, nicely summarized how this made him exasperated when we conversed about the entrepreneurs later that day.

"Entrepreneurs only think about their product. They can't see further than the product, which is great as most of these products are new. But you need much more than a great and innovative product for this to work."

Further, the technical innovation embedded in the product and service must be socially innovative. Hence, these aspects must be evaluated jointly.

I remember well the case of a project named Triangle. Most committee's members found the socially innovative dimension to be problematic. After the pitch and the traditional round of questions, they started discussing the innovative nature of the technology. A chief technological officer started.

"It's true that this prosthesis is unique in how it builds on printing technologies. The product is very light and easy to use."

"The price is much lower than competitors if we trust the entrepreneurs," added José. This head of innovation at an insurance firm further explained to the room:

"At my firm, for a specific product we have to work with amputees, and there's a real issue here because prostheses are extremely expensive."

José found the new prosthesis to be both technically and socially innovative because of the final price for patients. The discussion soon shifted to a more intense debate as Pablo stepped in, cutting José short in his argument.

"Yes, José, the prosthesis will be cheaper. We'll agree on that. But the originals cost about 19,000 euros, which means the new ones will be around 10,000 euros. Please tell me, who can afford to pay 10,000 euros for a prosthesis? I mean, many people need them, but not everyone can pay that much. Let's say almost no one. If the entrepreneurs don't lower the production cost and the final price, I don't buy the idea."

José turned his head to Sofia, looking desperately for support. But Sofia agreed. "Pablo's right. Our mission is to support innovation while making it affordable for everyone, so we do not support technological innovation for rich people. I like the idea too, and the team, but we must find a way to lower the cost of the product."

Sofia's remark nicely conveyed the importance of the possibility for the project to have a social or environmental impact, or both. This may seem trivial given Seal's focus, but some entrepreneurs struggled to convince on the social dimension of their venture.

Additionally, partners typically viewed social impact as the positive impact of the technical and social innovation associated with the product or service and claimed to have a genuine interest in social impact. They also explained that this interest partly motivated their funding of the program and their willingness to collaborate with impact entrepreneurs. Cristina described this aspect enthusiastically during one of our meetings in her office.

"We're interested in a start-up because we're interested in the product. Consider this one, for instance: these guys will provide our clients with a device to regulate their use of our product and make it more efficient. But we don't want to sell our clients this product; we don't want to make money off of it. Our focus here is not on the business. It's a bit more social: we want this product to benefit society."

A deeper investigation of the motivations and practices of corporate partners allows for contrasting this point. Corporate partners agreed on the importance of the social dimension but gave it varying importance. For instance, at the end of a long selection committee for the cluster in health, Junca raised serious concerns about the limited interest that other committee members expressed in the social impact of the ventures. Specifically, the marketing officer disagreed with selecting a start-up called Hotuk. Hotuk's founder worked as a researcher in a public university lab. He pitched an attractive early-stage heart attack detection device that could be integrated with the detection toolkit used in hospitals. He mainly explained the social impact of the product by saying that it would be sold directly to hospitals and its use would improve patient care. Junca, however, disagreed.

"This is one of those typical medical devices to be sold for profit."

Junca's straightforward manner quickly made everyone uneasy. Among the executives seated around the table, some looked dismayed. But it seemed that Junca had made up his mind already. In fact, he was extending his point to how the committee had operated that morning and questioned the true goals of the other participants.

"We should not forget that our aim [as committee members] is not to make money but to foster global transformations in the health sector. We aim to change our patients' lives. This is fundamental. We mustn't forget that."

Two week later, we would discuss this conversation in his office, where Junca further developed his view about other committee members and what he thought was a truly limited appetite for social impact.

"You remember what you said the other day at the committee about making money? It sounded like you disagree with how other partners understand their participation," I asked.

"Well, they just wanted the project in because of the problem-solving capability of the product, right?"

I nodded.

"Hotuk has no social impact," he added defiantly.

"What do you mean?" I asked, surprised by his statement.

"You should have noticed this, you've been to many committees, right?"

"Yes, but what do you mean exactly?"

"Look, Guillaume, we've been presented with many start-ups that seek to solve health issues using technologies, but the entrepreneurs don't want to have a social impact."

He came back to his seat and sat thoughtfully for a few seconds. Finally, breaking the ice, I asked him:

"So what do these entrepreneurs want from Seal?"

"These entrepreneurs only focus on growing their business."

"How do you know?" I asked.

"Because we tend to take for granted that they'll have a social impact. We didn't even define the criteria we should use to evaluate social impact, we didn't agree beforehand about what is relevant as social impact."

In fact, like Junca, many partners also funded Seal to learn about social impact. They viewed their participation as one way to become familiar with impact entrepreneurs and the existing impact measurement methods and standards. Yet, on this specific aspect, many shared with me that they were unsatisfied.

"To begin with, one major problem is that we have no definition of social impact," added Junca. He sounded offended by this omission. "And they are no specific criteria to evaluate the social mission of the venture. How should we know then? You remember what Kevin said the other day to the committee?"

I did. Kevin, indeed, had already raised this point. He was the director of the CSR department of a firm in the food industry who expressed his frustration about this aspect. A few weeks later, I visited his office for an interview, and I asked him specifically about this aspect. He explained:

"What are the impact criteria? I mean, the social impact is not analyzed in-depth at committees, and I hoped this would have been the opportunity for me to learn more about impact. At the end of the day, this is also why we signed. But it's like they say the word 'social impact' and automatically there is social impact, that's it! Well, shouldn't we investigate social impact further?!"

Like Kevin, many partners initially thought the term "social impact" was universal. Yet, they learned during the selection committees that the term was polysemic. Additionally, they discovered that not all the impact entrepreneurs gave social impact the same level of priority. As we have seen in the previous section and will discuss in more detail in the following chapter, some made the social demand at the core of their endeavor while others had yet to consider it.

What was clear, though, is that partners expected all impact entrepreneurs to care about the social impact of their venture. After all, as Paul said, dissatisfied and echoing Junca and Kevin:

"They call themselves impact entrepreneurs, the staff calls them impact entrepreneurs, and Seal is an accelerator for social impact start-ups, right?"

To a lesser extent, partners also foresaw the possibility for the venture to act as a proxy, to grow their network. The networking capability of the venture thus provided a fifth evaluation criterion."One of the reasons we fund Seal is that we want to forge new collaborations with public and private entities, other corporations, foundations, and the like," explained Fernando.

And they viewed their collaborations with impact entrepreneurs as one way to achieve this, by acting as bridges to access firms. One morning, we discussed this point in detail with Julia, an innovation manager in the environmental industry. Particularly satisfied about her participation in Seal, she recounted a successful story from the previous year's committees.

"Do you remember that start-up we selected last year? The entrepreneurs were working with Botek [name of the competing firm]. What they do at Botek is very interesting because they have a very different business model. We learned they were working together during the presentation when the entrepreneur explained the different alliances she had established and who she was working with. After a few months, I asked her about this, and she connected me with someone from Botek. We now meet every month for lunch".

These connections could also be problematic. Luciana, the head of the open innovation unit of a pharma firm, once reminded committee members that already established connections can jeopardize the selection of entrepreneurs. She explained, "I guess we all agree that the inclusion of Kubik [name of the start-up] in the program is fascinating, but we need to know the terms of their collaboration with Bellsaat [name of the competing firm] and, if their collaboration is still operative, whether we can change it or not."

This was the case when entrepreneurs already worked with competing corporations. One Wednesday morning, for instance, the committee members were about to make their final decision. Stephan, a business angel who usually participated as an external advisor, then told us that the entrepreneurs had signed a sales agreement with a competing firm during the clinical trial of the product. "I've learned this from a good friend of mine who has invested in the venture and who sits on the board."

Circumspect, committee members halted the evaluation process and requested that Santiago reach out to the entrepreneurs to obtain information before deciding, a few weeks later, not select the project.

## The Worth of an Impact Enterprise

Over the years, Sofia and Lola revised and revisited this process more than once. Seal's clusters evolved, as did the deal flow of impact entrepreneurs, the quality of their projects, and the corporate partners' impediments. Despite these iterations, we can learn several lessons about how corporations envision impact enterprises and, more broadly, about how the worth of these enterprises reaches far beyond social and economic values. Picking up on Moeran's discussion of the ensemblage of worth, I now connect the five evaluation criteria unearthed in this chapter with different values. Finally, I propose that the ensemblage of worth of an impact enterprise revolves around four types of value.

The problem-solving capability criterion reveals expectations for the products envisioned by impact entrepreneurs to solve internal innovation challenges. Impact enterprises, indeed, often deserve multiple beneficiaries beyond those directly targeted by their proposed product. Corporate partners, thus, may assess the potential of the impact enterprise to create *use value*—that is, the benefits gained from the quality of the product or service through its use. This is visible, for instance, in the importance given to the fit between the product and aspects of the project that partners judge valuable for their firms. This is also visible in the "maturity" criterion, reflecting whether ventures are advanced enough to serve their needs. Their diverging interests raise tensions that can be solved by combining their individual evaluations of the potential of a product and, this way, agreeing on a higher understanding of what is valuable.

Next, the juxtaposition of problem-solving capability and maturity has implications for creating use value. This is because use value must be defined per the creation of *technical value*—that is, the technically innovative nature of the products and services contributing to make them valuable by putting the entrepreneurs' skills and knowledge to work. At Seal, corporate partners considered technical innovation to be central for products' competitiveness. More often than not, they rejected ventures replicating existing products. Beyond the technical dimension of the product or service, technical value represents their contribution to firms' technical innovation when coupled with a sufficient level of maturity and technical innovation.

Partners also presented their participation as a social contribution. They expected projects to have a positive impact on society, making social innovation and impact central to evaluating *social value*. What impact entails, however, was not defined beforehand. This ambiguity raised multiple interpretations and varying levels of commitment among partners. This aspect was another source of negotiation with, on the one hand, partners' interest in the use and technical value potential of the ventures and, on the other hand, the socially innovative nature of a product and its related social value. De facto, corporate partners adjusted these criteria on two levels. First, they agreed on social value by combining their understandings of the latter. Second, they articulated this result with their respective estimation of use and technical values. Resultingly social value connected with use and technical value, and vice versa. This mean that the impact enterprise's creation of social value was embedded in its potential to create use and technical value.

Ultimately, partners granted ventures *relational value* because they could act as a bridge with out-of-reach collaborators. Although partners positively evaluated the technical, use, and social values of a project, entrepreneurs had to demonstrate the absence of conflicting social connections that could endanger the overall estimation of their worth. Impact enterprises, therefore, could also become a proxy by which previously disconnected actors of the impact economy (and beyond) connected and interacted. From the present analysis, relational value emerges as the fourth type of value constitutive of the ensemblage of worth. Like use, technical, and social value, relational value was assessed and articulated with the other values to agree on which ventures to select. Taken together, the articulation of these different values reveals that impact enterprises can contribute to the impact economy in multiple, sometimes unexpected, ways.

Of course, in this chapter, my analysis approaches evaluative practices and the construction of worth in impact entrepreneurship from a specific vantage point: corporations and the particular setting offered by an accelerator. However, it raises two general points informed by the theory of the ensemblage of worth. First, what is valuable in impact entrepreneurship depends on the evaluators' view, be they corporate partners, policymakers, impact investors, serial entrepreneurs, or mentors. Although these evaluators claim to be fundamentally interested in impact, they have different interests, goals, and understandings of it. These may collide as they attempt to collaborate.

One important consequence is that the very meaning of impact entrepreneurship is created and negotiated at the nexus of these attempts to work together, and is revealed by these tensions. This process defines what an impact enterprise is. Although the resulting understanding of impact entrepreneurship may or may not be meaningful in other contexts, it outlines the importance of uncovering how people locally define and collectively impact entrepreneurship.

Second, the creation of social and economic value expected from impact entrepreneurs is mainly contingent on evaluative practices and, thus, involves multiple evaluators. Resultingly, an impact enterprise is not valuable *per se*. It only becomes valuable when categorized as such as the result of an evaluation process. Accordingly, the position taken here is that impact enterprises have no intrinsic qualities. In line with the above, this point outlines the importance of the evaluative context for the specific directions taken by impact enterprises as they develop. It also outlines the importance of this context for understanding how these impact enterprises become valuable and calls for capturing the role of actors other than entrepreneurs in this process. Consequently, capturing the collective dimension of impact entrepreneurship instead of remaining focused on the individual analysis of impact entrepreneurs is key. This book is one step in this direction.

In closing, from this description of the struggles, tensions, and learnings experienced by Cristina, Junca, José, Paul, Felix, and fellow partners emerges a structural aspect of this book, to which I will return in Chap. 6: the question of the credibility of the claims made by those involved in impact entrepreneurship. Credibility is critical for entrepreneurship in general.[12] In the present case, it reveals that those involved in impact entrepreneurship do not take impact for granted. They arguably have good reasons to do so. The circumstances under which impact entrepreneurship evolves are changing, as are the resources available for entrepreneurs' growth.[13] Corporations may be primarily or even exclusively

[12] Trustworthiness, perhaps more than credibility, has been of steady interest among entrepreneurship scholars, primarily in the context of the relation between entrepreneur and investor. See Bammens and Collewaert (2014), Kuckertz et al. (2015), Maxwell and Lévesque (2014).

[13] The institutionalization and popularization of the field raised new opportunities for impact entrepreneurs, for example, alternative types of finance providers (e.g., Agrawal & Hockerts, 2021; Hockerts et al., 2022) Nowadays, the social mission can become a competitive advantage (Muñoz & Kimmitt, 2019), with social entrepreneurship being viewed as a legitimate endeavor (Bruder, 2021; Dey & Steyaert, 2012).

interested in the benefits of making public their association with impact initiatives, rather than in impact itself. Contrary to what the literature almost unanimously suggests, some impact entrepreneurs may not have a prosocial intention upfront;[14] rather, they may initially follow an economic goal in creating their impact enterprise. Only later, in their encounters and interactions with impact entrepreneurs and organizations, they may develop a motivation for achieving impact. The following chapter examines this point by unearthing two dominant archetypes of impact entrepreneurs who strive to simultaneously address social and economic demands.

## Bibliography

Agrawal, A., & Hockerts, K. (2021). Impact Investing: Review and Research Agenda. *Journal of Small Business & Entrepreneurship, 33*(2), 153–181.

Bammens, Y., & Collewaert, V. (2014). Trust Between Entrepreneurs and Angel Investors: Exploring Positive and Negative Implications for Venture Performance Assessments. *Journal of Management, 40*(7), 1980–2008.

Bruder, I. (2021). A Social Mission is Not Enough: Reflecting the Normative Foundations of Social Entrepreneurship. *Journal of Business Ethics, 174*(3), 487–505.

Clough, D. R., Fang, T. P., Vissa, B., & Wu, A. (2019). Turning Lead into Gold: How Do Entrepreneurs Mobilize Resources to Exploit Opportunities? *Academy of Management Annals, 13*(1), 240–271.

Cohen, S., Fehder, D. C., Hochberg, Y. V., & Murray, F. (2019). The Design of Startup Accelerators. *Research Policy, 48*(7), 1781–1797.

Dey, P., & Steyaert, C. (2012). Social Entrepreneurship: Critique and the Radical Enactment of the Social. *Social Enterprise Journal, 8*(2), 90–107.

Goffman, E. (1959). *The Presentation of Self in Everyday Life*. Doubleday.

Hockerts, K., Hehenberger, L., Schaltegger, S., & Farber, V. (2022). Defining and Conceptualizing Impact Investing: Attractive Nuisance or Catalyst? *Journal of Business Ethics, 179*(4), 937–950.

Huang, L. (2018). The Role of Investor Gut Feel in Managing Complexity and Extreme Risk. *Academy of Management Journal, 61*(5), 1821–1847.

Huang, L., & Pearce, J. L. (2015). Managing the Unknowable: The Effectiveness of Early-stage Investor Gut Feel in Entrepreneurial Investment Decisions. *Administrative Science Quarterly, 60*(4), 634–670.

Khaire, M. (2013). Fashioning an Industry: Socio-cognitive Processes in the Construction of Worth of a New Industry. *Organization Studies, 35*(1), 41–74.

[14] I develop this point in more detail with Alice Mascena Barbosa (Mascena Barbosa & Dumont, 2023).

Kuckertz, A., Kollmann, T., Röhm, P., & Middelberg, N. (2015). The Interplay of Track Record and Trustworthiness in Venture Capital Fundraising. *Journal of Business Venturing Insights, 4*, 6–13.

Lamont, M. (2012). Toward a Comparative Sociology of Valuation and Evaluation. *Annual Review of Sociology, 38*(1), 201–221.

Mascena Barbosa, A., & Dumont, G. (2023). A new Understanding of the Role of Self-oriented Motivations in the Creation of Social Enterprises. *Journal of Business Ethics, 191*, 1–19.

Maxwell, A. L., & Lévesque, M. (2014). Trustworthiness: A Critical Ingredient for Entrepreneurs Seeking Investors. *Entrepreneurship Theory and Practice, 38*(5), 1057–1080.

Miller, T. L., & Wesley, C. L. (2010). Assessing Mission and Resources for Social Change: An Organizational Identity Perspective on Social Venture Capitalists' Decision Criteria. *Entrepreneurship Theory and Practice, 34*(4), 705–733.

Moeran, B. (2005). *The Business of Ethnography*. Berg Publishers.

Moeran, B. (2007). *Ethnography at Work (New)*. Berg Publishers.

Moeran, B. (2013). *The Business of Creativity. Toward an Anthropology of Worth*. Left Coast Press.

Moeran, B., & Christensen, B. (Eds.). (2013). *Exploring Creativity: Evaluative Practices in Innovation, Design, and the Arts*. Cambridge University Press.

Moeran, B., & Strandgaard, J. (2011). *Negotiating Values in the Creative Industries: Fairs, Festivals and Competitive Events*. Cambridge University Press.

Muñoz, P., & Kimmitt, J. (2019). Social Mission as Competitive Advantage: A Configurational Analysis of the Strategic Conditions of Social Entrepreneurship. *Journal of Business Research, 101*, 854–861.

Stark, D. (2011). *The Sense of Dissonance: Accounts of Worth in Economic Life*. Princeton University Press.

Wright, M., & Drori, I. (Eds.). (2018). *Accelerators. Successful Venture Creation and Growth*. Edward Elgar Publishing.

Yan, S., Ferraro, F., & Almandoz, J. (2019). The Rise of Socially Responsible Investment Funds: The Paradoxical Role of the Financial Logic. *Administrative Science Quarterly, 64*(2), 466–501.

CHAPTER 4

# A New Occupational Role

"I'm proud of having passed the social impact evaluation and been granted the social impact certificate! It wasn't an easy journey. As entrepreneurs, we must be able to innovate while creating economic and social value. This is super challenging. We must also adapt our business model and create processes to maximize and measure our social impact, making this task even harder. However, why should we talk about innovation if innovation does not help improve quality of life for the largest number of people? Thanks for helping us to understand this and to transform AbcHealth into a social impact start-up! We strongly encourage innovative entrepreneurs to work on the social dimension of their venture. If you want to achieve excellence in innovation, this is the way to go!"

Three months prior to the publication of this LinkedIn post, Leo was passionately pitching his venture to the selection committee. With extensive experience in entrepreneurship, the 42-year-old provided a solid market gap motivation and shined in convincing us of the value of his product. He also gave a clear and consistent description of his business plan and consistent financial predictions. His pitch would have been perfect if Leo hadn't disregarded the presentation of the social impact. In fact, at that time, he had no regard for impact. The idea behind his project, however, seduced some of the corporate partners. They praised the commercial potential of the product, and convinced Sofia, Santiago, and Luc to select


G. Dumont, *Impact Work*,
https://doi.org/10.1007/978-3-031-64661-4_4

him for the upcoming cohort. Three months later, Leo had undertaken a radical transformation, turning his commercial project into an impact enterprise in its own right.

One of the obvious things about impact entrepreneurship is that entrepreneurs must address a twofold demand as they ideate and progress in developing their project.[1] On the one hand, they are expected to have an intrinsic prosocial motivation resulting from a unique personality trait powering their drive to achieve social or environmental impact.[2] On the other hand, their attempt to achieve social impact must be profitable and scalable to attract stakeholders and access to financial and human capital. This may read as trivial, as these demands are the hallmark of impact entrepreneurship. Nevertheless, these demands have very often been studied in isolation and consistently described as contradictory.[3] Their articulation raises tensions impeding the development of impact enterprises as much as it informs their moral underpinning.[4]

The management of contradictory demands is not exclusive to impact entrepreneurs. Different occupational groups including knowledge workers,[5] athletes,[6] nurses,[7] police officers,[8] and artists[9] must also articulate similar demands to perform their work and to achieve career prospects. How? So far, scholars have advanced that people typically handle the contradictory demands of a new role by adopting avoidance strategies

[1] See Dees (2012), Huybrechts and Nicholls (2012), Smith et al. (2012, 2013), Tracey and Phillips (2007).

[2] Prosocial motivation has been long defined as the hallmark of social entrepreneurship. It reflects the desire to have a positive impact on society and/or the environment through commercial means, which distinguishes impact entrepreneurs from typical entrepreneurs (e.g., Austin et al., 2006; Dacin et al., 2010; Dees, 2012; Mair & Martí, 2006; Zahra et al., 2009).

[3] The juxtaposition of market performance and social impact has long been seen as contradictory because of conflicts with stakeholders demands (Molecke & Pinkse, 2020; Ramus & Vaccaro, 2017), diverging values (Mitzinneck & Besharov, 2019) and heterogeneous practices and motivations (Smith et al., 2013).

[4] See Bacq et al. (2016), Brieger et al. (2021), Bruder (2021), Dey and Lehner (2017).

[5] See, for instance, Arvidsson et al. (2016), Duffy and Hund (2015), Gandini (2016), Hearn (2010).

[6] See my previous work my previous work with professional climbers (Dumont, 2017) but also Clifton Evers (2019) and Katharina Rahikainen (Rahikainen & Toffoletti, 2021).

[7] See DiBenigno (2022).

[8] See Van Maanen (1973, 1984).

[9] See Banks and Hesmondhalgh (2009); Hesmondhalgh and Baker (2008), Lingo and Tepper (2013), Menger (1999).

stemming from engagement with one demand over the other.[10] Yet, that most people presumably fail to handle both demands simultaneously is problematic. At Seal, for instance, aligning these two demands is critical to profitably achieving impact, raising a pivotal question for the development of impact entrepreneurship: how can impact entrepreneurs handle the contradictory demands inherent to their new role?

This chapter provides one answer to this question by bringing to the fore the entrepreneurs' voices. Shedding light on their experience may seem trivial in a book about impact entrepreneurship. Surprisingly, however, most of our knowledge about how impact entrepreneurs recognize and manage these demands comes from collecting data with university students who have a limited understanding of the day-to-day of impact entrepreneurs.[11] In pointing this out I do not want to diminish the contribution of these studies that say much about what non-entrepreneurs think about impact entrepreneurship. However, I believe that explaining how people, whether they be impact entrepreneurs, police officers, professional athletes, or nurses, align these two demands requires uncovering the experiences of those who are actually engaged in this endeavor.

I examine how prospective impact entrepreneurs address these demands by picking up on recent discussions of organizational socialization, the process by which organizational members endorse new roles by learning and integrating specific skills, beliefs, values, and orientations.[12] While

[10] John Van Maanen developed the notion (1973, 1984) by studying police sergeant socialization, an employment context in which socialization activities and actors are formally defined and which revealed contradictory role demands linked to the supervisor role associated with this rank. To avoid the inherent conflict of supervising colleagues with whom they had recently shared the same rank, the organization often allocated sergeants to divisions where they had no previous history. The sergeants themselves anticipated this issue, avoiding interactions with colleagues in case they might remain in the same division. In a context of weak on-the-job socialization, medical institutions tried to get nurses to adopt a role that diverged from the one they associated with care work, and in which they maintained an idealized view of their patients through infantilization (DiBenigno, 2022). As a result, nurses deliberately avoided those who denied their idealized vision of their role (which involved infantilizing patients), enabling them to maintain their original views about their work. These scholars explain how contradictory role demands are negotiated in practice by pointing to individual or organizational "avoidance strategies" (Van Maanen, 1984).

[11] See Bacq and Alt (2018), Hockerts (2017), Smith et al. (2012).

[12] Overlooked in entrepreneurship, the socialization activities and tactics designed and deployed by organizations to socialize new members to well-established, long-standing professions has gathered a steady interest among organizational theorists. See, for example, Ashforth et al. (2007), Feldman (1977), Van Maanen and Schein (1977).

socialization has been widely studied across professional groups, in entrepreneurship the role of individual traits is the primary explanation for entrepreneurial behavior. This view has been forcefully extended to impact entrepreneurship, resulting in an analytical focus on the individual. And yet, it is only through their socialization that people make sense of a social world in a way that is consistent with its cultural norms, conventions, and beliefs. Organizational socialization, therefore, allows people to behave adequately within an organizational culture.[13]

One of the main objectives of this book is to explain Seal's role as a socialization organization enabling entrepreneurs to learn the ropes of impact entrepreneurship through the socialization activities of the acceleration program. Remember, for instance, Marc and Roger from the previous chapter. Marc initially focused on the commercial demand but then learned about social impact, the theory of change, and the existence of impact indicators. By contrast, Roger initially focused on the social demand and then learned about business models and developed his first financial metrics. Regardless of their initial orientation, they acquired the norms and values of the culture of impact entrepreneurship because of their socialization at Seal. There, they were put through a common set of experiences with other entrepreneurs. They also deployed socialization tactics by asking questions and observing the interactions and practices of serial entrepreneurs, mentors, policymakers, investors, and partners.

Investigating how impact entrepreneurs handle the contradictory demands inherent to their role requires a couple of digressions from the dominant assumption structuring existing scholarship. First, as a core argument of this book, we must move away from viewing impact entrepreneurs as primarily and systematically guided by a prosocial intention. Such prosocial intention results from a personality trait and is often described as the desire to positively impact society and the environment through commercial means, distinguishing impact from traditional entrepreneurs.[14] Of course, my point here is not that prosocial intentions are thoroughly absent among impact entrepreneurs. Instead, I suggest that their motivations are plural and multilayered and cannot be limited to prosocial intention.[15]

[13] See, for example, Ashforth and Saks (1996), Van Maanen and Schein (1977).

[14] See Austin et al. (2006), Dacin et al. (2010), Dees (2012), Mair and Martí (2006), Zahra et al. (2009).

[15] See Germak and Robinson (2013), Mascena Barbosa and Dumont (2023).

Second, if the prosocial intention is sometimes absent in the initial step of creating an impact enterprise, this means that the goal of achieving social impact must develop afterward. As the following pages illustrate, this development unfolds through the lived experience of impact entrepreneurship as entrepreneurs interact with stakeholders of different kinds, and in ways that feed the development of their venture. Moving away from the naturalization of prosocial intention as the primary motivation supporting the creation of impact enterprises, I propose that the goal of achieving social impact can be socially constructed through practices and interactions. Consequently, I advance that fully understanding how people come to create an impact enterprise requires examining the socialization process undertaken by entrepreneurs who have already ideated their project.

In the sections that follow, I uncover how entrepreneurs gained awareness of the twofold demands and integrated these demands by developing the role of impact entrepreneurs while implementing changes to their venture. Following the two analytical archetypes constructed in the previous chapter, I begin my exploration with those entrepreneurs who, like Roger, are primarily inclined toward the social demand of impact entrepreneurship. Then, I turn to those who, like Leo and Marc, were initially commercially oriented. At Seal, I followed both types of entrepreneurs during their day-to-day routine as they undertook the acceleration's activities. Hence, after examining in the previous chapter how they were selected to join Seal, I now unearth their struggles to make sense of these demands and integrate them.

## Acknowledging and Integrating the Commercial Demand

Berta was among the first entrepreneurs I met during fieldwork. Thin and tall, she had an intriguing and mischievous look. Two years older than me, she worked at a co-working space as an adjunct director for programs. She had heard about Seal from Javier, a fellow co-worker who had enrolled in the accelerator the previous year. Following his recommendation, Berta applied to Seal in March to move forward with her educational project.

On the first day, she told me, "I want to help unemployed youth access technology-related education by providing them with funding from public institutions."

"Cool. Where did the idea come from?"

"It's something I had in mind for a long time, when I was working with youth who can't afford education before moving here. I was talking about this with the director of the co-working space a few months. He liked this idea. I mean, most of what we do here is technology-related and it's true that many people can't, they can't afford it. It was just a random conversation. But then we talked about it again and again, and here I am."

"So you work at the coworking space, but you also work on your project? Or is the project part of your work there?" I asked, intrigued by how she was able to manage both jobs simultaneously.

"When we started, I just worked a little bit for the project. Then more and more. And then when we applied to the call, I had to put in the hours. And now I'm at Seal for three months. So obviously as I'm doing this with the director, he knows, in fact we're co-founders. But now I spend 70% of my time on the project."

"You manage to do it all alone?"

"Well, no. At the beginning it was ok, but now it's just too much time. I can't be everywhere. I come to Seal, then I go there, then I might go somewhere for some meetings. All day long. I basically work like 12 hours a day."

"What are you going to do?"

"I'm thinking about leaving my job at the co-working space. We've been talking about this with my co-founder/director. I just can't. But that would mean being unemployed for a while cause the project is not paying me anything.

"What did Santiago say about this?"

"He told me that I should be working full-time on the project."

"Yes. That's what they ask from most entrepreneurs."

Berta belonged to this group of socially oriented entrepreneurs who jumped into impact entrepreneurship with limited or no consideration for the commercial viability of their ideas. She had been working in the creative industries and had walked into an entirely new experience with entrepreneurship. As did Lisa on the lab researcher we met in the opening chapter of this book, Berta did not hide this aspect, though, but shared her lack of entrepreneurial knowledge to the room packed with entrepreneurs when she first pitched her project. I found her eager to learn the ropes of business creation and, as the two of us watched through the terrace's open door an entrepreneur pitching his venture, she described her main goal as being "to learn how entrepreneurship works."

When interacting with mentors, Berta consciously balanced her fine knowledge of the social problem, gained through first-hand experience, with her novice status in entrepreneurship. Later that week, she articulated a common starting point for a good number of the entrepreneurs I met at Seal by emphasizing her novice status in entrepreneurship: "This 'thing' of creating a venture, it's kinda coming out of nowhere for me!"

At this stage, Berta wanted to operate independently from public funding because of its volatility. Yet, she had been struggling to achieve her goal. We used to converse about this topic during our cigarette and coffee breaks. She did not like to talk about money in front of the other cohort members, I believed.

"I started by launching a crowdfunding campaign. This was a few months ago, before I entered the program. I wanted to be able to fund a first cohort of students to see this how it worked."

"Did you collect enough money?"

"No. I barely collected 25%," she said half laughing.

"So you applied?"

"Yes, I mean partly. I know that the way to go is to have corporations sponsoring me. Sponsoring the project and, this way, funding the students we would have selected."

"Have you thought about other business models?"

"What?"

"Other ways to generate some revenue, not only sponsorship from companies."

"Companies must give us money."

"Why would they do so?"

"They could advertise our collaboration on their website for their CSR program. It's advertising for them, right?"

As I quickly learned, Berta relied on the interpretation that companies would be willing to fund the project for the sake of it. "Because it's a great project," as she loved to say.

She was not alone in this view. In my view, many socially inclined entrepreneurs conveyed a similar belief in the pristine value of their idea. More broadly, and perhaps more importantly, these entrepreneurs had very limited consideration for commercial viability. Like Berta, they were guided by the belief that companies, investors, public institutions, or even business angels, would pay for their idea without monetary compensation in a purely disinterested way.

Resultingly, few of the socially oriented entrepreneurs had considered a business model for their project or were planning to do so. In other words, they still had to recognize and integrate the commercial demand of impact entrepreneurship. Recognizing and integrating was vital as Sofia, Lola, and Jorge believed that only a coherent business model would make a project profitable while enabling social impact. Along these lines, they launched a new training module during the program's first weeks to facilitating business-related knowledge to these entrepreneurs.

Their initial exclusive focus on social goals made acknowledging and integrating the commercial demand in the development of their new role of impact entrepreneur a tumultuous path. For instance, it took weeks for Berta to recognize and engage with the commercial demand in her project. Central to this change were several mentoring sessions with the Human Resources Director of one of Seal's corporate partners, Matías.

Matías liked Berta and was impressed by her project. He could have been a potential client, and, for this reason, Santiago assigned him to Berta. He took her under his wing, dedicating much effort to help her understand that not a single corporation wouldn't fund her venture without any compensation. To raise awareness about this aspect, he tried to have Berta switch roles from entrepreneur to Human Resources director. Matías also worked with her to pick a coherent business model by investigating ventures providing similar services. Finally, he suggested that having recently graduated students commit to work for the company afterward would make her project more attractive to clients.

"There's no way I will do that," answered Berta.

"Why?" he asked. "It's like a win-win situation."

"No. It's like working for the devil instead of helping people," said Berta convincingly.

"I don't see your point here. If you don't find a business model, you won't be working with anyone anyway."

"I told you, it's like working for the devil instead of helping people. I wanna help people. I don't want to work for companies and help them to make more money," she forcefully added.

"But you won't be working *for* companies!" [emphasis added]

"I will."

"Don't you think that, before 'helping companies to make more money' as you say, you're first and foremost allowing people to access education?" asked Matías.

"Yes. I get this. But the students should be able to choose where to work once they graduate. Wouldn't you like to choose where you work? Did someone forced you to work where you are now?" answered Berta provocatively.

"Of course not, Berta. But no one paid for my study. And the students will know this, this will be clear upfront in the contract with you. And it will be easier for them to get a job, don't you think so?"

"And if they don't like the company? Or if they don't like their co-workers? Or if they want to do something different? Or work for someone else? Or whatever…by doing that, I don't think you're fully helping them."

I spent much of my time with her program manager, Santiago, to learn the ropes of managing entrepreneurs. Like Matías, he was struggling to have her land on a coherent business model for her venture and revise her views about corporate partnerships. On this particular morning, I joined him to attend to his weekly follow-up meeting with Berta. As the two of us walked to her co-working space located about 30 minutes from our office, Santiago shared his enthusiasm for the relationship he got to develop with entrepreneurs at work.

"I very much like going out and visiting them. I could meet them online, from my desk, you know. But this way you get a sense of what they do, who they're. They also see how you gonna work with them."

"Building strong relationships with your entrepreneurs matters for the mentoring, right?"

"Yes, of course, it helps. But I like it too. I learn new things. It's always different. But yes, it's key if you want them to care about what you tell them."

"It's not easy to have them follow your recommendations?"

"Not always. So, I think it's important for them to see that we [the staff] commit to their project, that we take them seriously."

"Why would it be different?"

"Sometimes I feel that they believe that the entire world is against them. You know Berta is very much like this. She's very stubborn. She thinks that sometimes people do things against her; I don't know why."

We finally turned around the corner and reached the co-working space. We waited at the cafeteria. The place was earthy and artsy, with hand-crafted wooden tables and the menu hanging at the wall. Silently we watched some workers sitting at the individual tables on their laptops, searching for a familiar face, when Berta came out the front door to join us.

"So, have you thought about leaving this job to work full-time on the project?" Santiago asked within the first minute of our conversation.

That Santiago was straightforward was unconventional, and Berta raised an eyebrow signaling a particular annoyance. "It's not that easy," she said with her head held high while looking at the coffee machine.

"That's fine, but now you must look at this seriously."

"I know. But I must make sure that I'm eligible for unemployment money. That's why it's taking me so long. If I'm not eligible, there's no way I quit."

Santiago did not insist; rather, he quickly asked about her progress on the business model, their main topic of conversation during the previous weeks.

"I'm on it, I don't know yet. What's clear is that this project is not for companies. I don't want companies to make money out of it."

"I know, Berta, I know," he said reassuringly. "That's why I have scheduled meetings with several HR executives next week. They will help you think about this. I would like you to seriously think about it."

"I will. But not like this."

"Like what?"

"Like working for companies."

"Right. I hear you. But you will have to come up with an alternative otherwise you will never have an impact. You want to have an impact, right?"

"Yes."

"So, you would you have an impact if the project isn't operating? I mean if you are unable to fund students, they won't be able to access education, so you don't really have an impact, right?"

"Right. But still."

At that time of the fieldwork, the question of how to make Berta's project profitable was becoming pressing. On our way back to Seal, Santiago told me that he hoped Berta would finally understand the importance of coherently addressing the commercial demand by listening to mentors other than Matías. He was also unsure that she would finally quit her job.

"Do you think she will finally quit her job and work full-time on the project?" he asked me.

"Well, she's scared because she needs revenue. This unemployment money, you're never sure how much they will give you, and when."

"I see. Hopefully she will change her mind about the business model very soon," he added as we crossed the street.

I couldn't help but tell him that, from what I've seen of her, she tended to change her mind from one day to another.

"She will reconsider the business model. She knows that making money is vital for her, no?"

My effort to reassure him was in vain, as he remained perplexed. Prior to and during our meeting with Berta, he had sounded enthusiastic. He was now looking apprehensive about Berta's reluctance about integrating the commercial demand.

"If she doesn't progress, I will have to reconsider how we work together. Her project won't make it through the next evaluation committee."

A negative evaluation at the committee would mean that all the hard work Santiago had put in would have been useless. Accordingly, Berta's upcoming week was packed with meetings with the mentors he had recruited with this goal in mind.

When I met two weeks later with Berta at the co-working space to chat about the work in progress, she naturally talked about these meetings and sounded very pleased.

"The mentors, they were all super friendly and receptive about the project, they believe it's a great idea."

"What did they say about partnering with companies?" I asked, curious.

"They see the value of the project for their company. And I was super motivated as well, I couldn't stop asking questions."

"Great. Have you decided how you would like to work with companies?"

"We must work with companies because they have the money. They told me that these companies are looking for new hires. They need to hire people anyway, so yes."

The shift surprised me. It seemed that her previous week's meetings had been fruitful for rethinking her business model. Specifically, Berta started to acknowledge the importance of addressing the commercial demand for her project. To an external observer like me, it was great to see her motivated again and moving forward with the project in a direction that aligned with the expectations of Seal staff. We were now around the middle of the acceleration program, and I could feel how much her views had changed radically since her early days, when she systematically rejected any corporate partnership.

Having companies as paid clients gradually became acceptable for Berta, who designed a new offer tailored to those she called "my new client." This new client was "corporations seeking educated hires in the technological field," she said, reflecting how much she had begun to reconsider her project more commercially.

"I'm thinking about what I can offer and how can I present them the potential benefit to pay for my product."

"To whom?"

"To companies, of course."

Additionally, she realized that working with companies would boost impact in the mid-term, with corporate partners being the vehicle by which students would access the labor market.

"In fact, I stopped short when designing the project."

"What do you mean?"

"I mean that's its very true that students need to find a job. Finding a job is not easy in this country. So, if I can help with this as well it would be great."

Only by being repeatedly challenged by mentors did Berta recognize that addressing the commercial demand can positively influence the social demand while triggering social impact.

Socially oriented entrepreneurs at Seal also had limited business-related skills. Jon, an entrepreneur whose contagious passion and dedication to social impact seduced everyone at Seal, belonged to Berta's cohort. He aimed to help people suffering from mobility issues access medical prostheses in rural areas.

"What I do is connect people. I connect medical providers with people who need prostheses but can't access them in stores because they are unavailable."

"Why?" I asked.

"I mean, in cities, it's easy; there are a lot of stores. But in rural areas, like where I'm from, it gets super complicated."

"Like, there are few stores and limited options?"

"Totally. You visit the store, and they may have one, or maybe two, different models. You can only buy one of the two models they have available in the store. But these models do not always meet your needs. In fact, most of the time they don't!"

"You learnt this when working as a sales agent?"

"Partly yes. At that time, I was driving all day, visiting all these stores in the countryside. They had very few products when what you needed most of the time was a very specific product. And they didn't have it."

"Is this how you started?"

"No. It took me a few years. A few years after I quit this job. I was unemployed."

"You started with the website?"

"I first started by creating a Facebook page to see if my idea was worth a try. I didn't know it was going to be that useful."

"Useful?"

"Yes. I collected information about what people needed. They sent me feedback on my idea, and what they would like to have. I now have about 300,000 followers; I've created an online community."

"Impressive. How did you do that?"

"I learned some tricks to increase your follower base," he said, smiling.

"Are you making money off of it? I asked.

"Not really, that's my main problem. I'm at a stage right now where I'm thinking about how to turn this into real money."

In contrast with Berta, who viewed companies paying for the training of interns as contradictory to her social goal, Jon was aware of the need to develop the commercial potential of his project. Yet, for now, out of 300,000 followers he only had 40 people who paid an annual fee but did not purchase anything through the platform. With no income for the last two years, his team members were pressuring him to generate revenue, and specifically Rafa.

"Did you start together?" I asked.

"No."

"He joined the team later? How so?"

"We met a few months ago when I was pitching the project at an event. He came to talk to me. He was interested in the project, he told me he was a business angel. I asked him what this meant and if he wanted to join."

Rafa praised the merit of his idea and promised to turn online attraction into revenue while helping him build a business model.

"He invested 10,000 euros."

"Great. Against what?"

"Equity. He asked for equity."

"How much?"

"Too much," answered Jon, grumbling.

"Why? It was only 10,000 euros, no?"

"Yes, but I didn't know what it meant to give away equity. I knew that I had 10,000 euros, and I knew what I could do with 10,000, like paying to get more followers, pay rent, live for a while, very practical things!"

Rafa urged him to create a call center, arguing that, this way, they would sign new paid clients quickly. Jon accepted. By then, Rafa had started as chief financial officer while Jorge focused the development of a platform.

Santiago and Sofia witnessed first-hand the changes to the project resulting from Rafa's advice. They were pessimistic about him. Chief among their concerns was, perhaps, his lack of fundamental interest for the social dimension of the project. This concern came up during a mid-term meeting with Santiago to discuss Jon's progress. As often, Luc was the first to express loudly to the room his discontentment about Rafa and how the project was developing.

"He's only here for the money," said Luc.

"I agree, that's also my feeling," added Santiago. "But let's see, it may work out well."

"I don't think so," grumbled Luc.

"Why are you so pessimistic again?" asked Sofia.

"Rafa's not giving good results. He still doesn't understand what impact is and doesn't care about it."

As I would soon learn, staff members believed that Rafa negatively influenced Jon and slowed his progress. But Seal's philosophy was to avoid intervening in the founder's decisions. Accordingly, Santiago centered his effort on helping Jon to gain business-related skills for him to understand the problematic nature of the situation and move on. With this goal in mind, he introduced Jon to a professor at a leading business school by scheduling a couple of mentoring meetings. The professor insisted greatly on leadership.

"Jon, look, you must take the reins of the venture. This is your venture. You must grow by surrounding yourself with those who will help you to achieve it."

Jon described this meeting as a turning point. He started to understand and embody his role in a very different way, gaining leadership over Rafa, and closed the call center to reduce costs. He also started meeting investors and partners interested in the project instead of delegating these meetings to Rafa, whom he had always viewed as more business-savvy.

His growing self-confidence resulted from Santiago's work, who not only introduced him to "the language of business," as Jon liked to say, but also helped him to gain operational business skills. Jon acknowledged that he could not live off his wife's salary for the sake of his project any longer, but had to develop his business model coherently with his impact goals, access funding, and turn his online attention into revenue.

One morning, as the two of us were having coffee in the stairway of the accelerator building during one of his visits, we chatted about his progress since the first day of the boot camp, two months earlier. On this particular day, he sounded happy about the project so far.

"It took me time to understand my own business."

"What do you mean, if it's your business!"

"I always thought my business was to obtain a lot of information from many different people. Now I don't know how to manage all this information. I never understood this before."

"You never thought about how you would turn this into revenue?"

"No! And no one told me before that my business model was wrong, so I didn't know this."

"Where did you learn this then? From mentoring?"

"Yes. Definitely. I think that I'm now much more aware that the business model is key to developing the company. Understanding this was not easy. I don't know why, but I was obsessed with the Facebook page."

Berta's and Jon's cases provide an excellent introduction to a third aspect shared by most socially oriented entrepreneurs: they often resisted implementing commercially related changes to their idea, even when they had acknowledged the commercial demand and the need to address it. Berta, for instance, viewed corporate partnerships as "selling out" her project. She was no exception. Many impact entrepreneurs believed that the commercial viability would inevitably carry negative implications for their social impact goals. In response, they resisted calls for developing or changing their business model.

Mentors found this issue puzzling. They struggled to understand why entrepreneurs claimed to achieve social impact and make money out of it but rejected commercialization and corporate partnerships. For entrepreneurs, overcoming this initial reluctance was truly a lengthy and painful process, as was moving from acknowledging to integrating the commercial demand in the development of their new role.

In contrast with Berta and Jon's limited entrepreneurial experience, Alfonso and Luis had already launched a venture prior to their participation to Seal. In fact, they were still busy running this venture when we first met in May 2017 as they enrolled into the program to develop a second venture inspired by the learnings of the current one. In particular, the two engineers wanted to take action against climate change by helping companies plant trees in their inner-city buildings as a CSR strategy to compensate for carbon emissions. They would achieve this goal by hiring vulnerable workers, primarily people struggling to access the traditional labor market given limited qualifications, immigrant status, or disability.

Alfonso and Luis had already designed and implemented similar initiatives to address deforestation across the country, but their primary client was the public administration, primarily city councils. With this second venture, they now had to deal with a very different client, corporations. Resultingly, they expected to create a coherent value proposition attractive to corporations. Additionally, they also looked for building impact indicators for assessing the future social and environmental impact of the venture, as well as test a pilot with one of Seal's long standing partners.

Lola and Santiago were overly enthusiastic about the social relevance of the idea. They also fell in love with Alfonso and Luis, specifically Alfonso. The tall and charismatic entrepreneur had an irresistible bubbling enthusiasm and a straightforward manner that quickly put everyone at ease. Every time they discussed the project, people also praised its potential because of Alfonso and Luis's experience and commitment.

When Santiago designed their work plan, his core focus was making the project commercially sound and attractive to prospective corporate clients. The reasons was that their commercial communication was devastating, as Lola and Santiago recognized.

"Have you looked at their website?"

"Worst website I've seen in a while," answered Santiago, grumbling.

"These two are engineers. They work in the bush," said Lola, laughing.

"Yes. But they know what they're talking about. They've been there," replied Santiago.

"It's very true. And Alfonso is an outstanding speaker and communicator. You can sense it. But they have no clear message to communicate, and their website is rubbish."

In particular, Santiago hoped that Alfonso and Luis would create a compelling business narrative for pitching their project to partners and would soon run a pilot with one of them. He had high expectations about one of their mentors, a notorious marketing expert, to help him in this task.

I remembered very well the first encounter, when the two entrepreneurs, the mentor, a marketing intern, and I were packed in a small four-person meeting room at Seal's main office. The air conditioner was running loudly, but the atmosphere was suffocating. Enthusiastically, as always, Alfonso described the idea behind the project, spending a lot of time introducing us to the different tree varieties and explaining how they should be best planted in city centers. As Lola said, he spoke eloquently, intensively sharing his passion for his work and captivating our attention by making us feel we belonged to his project.

Alfonso gave explicit leads to the mentor about the embryonic stage of the venture. He almost called himself an imposter and reiterated that they were constantly learning new things since the inception of the boot camp.

"We've learned the word 'pivot' this morning, and we're now pivoting," he said. He was proud but prudent in clarifying that they were experiencing change and that their project was far from perfect.

Contrasting with Alfonso's enthusiasm, the mentor interrupted him abruptly.

"Great. You pivot," he said ironically.

"Yes."

"Hum. I want more details about the product. I want more detail about the product and what you sell to people!" he added trenchantly.

"We told you, we sell a service to companies for them to have trees planted. What we do is plant the trees."

"Hmm. But how do you brand this?"

"How do we brand this?"

"I mean, imagine that you must sell your product to a company. What would you say?"

"What would we say to the company?"

"Yes."

"Well, just that."

"Let's frame this differently. If you must brand your company, what would you say?"

"To brand?"

"Yes. You know what a brand is, right?"

"Yes."

"So what?"

"Which brand?"

The mentor began rolling his eyes while Alfonso and Luis watched each other, hopeless. They looked perplexed by the direction the meeting had taken. Uneasy with the mentor's suggestions for developing the project, they found it "too commercial." The words "product," "brand," and "strategy" I heard from the mentor to qualify aspects of their project were not incidental. They reflected a wide gap between their respective views of the project. For the mentor, the terms captured areas where work was needed. For Alfonso and Luis, however, they sounded contradictory with the essence of their initial idea. This made them irritable, which is understandable in light of Alfonso's late-afternoon comment to me in confidence, once the meeting was over, "These companies and their 'branding strategies' destroy the planet. We all know this!"

But we were not there yet. In fact, the epiphany came when the mentor suggested that they should build a bridge between their project and the smart city movement that had been flourishing in the city for the last few years. "This will give you more visibility and it has been supported by the city council." This last comment made the two entrepreneurs very upset. For Luis, "smart city" was a synonym for impact washing, particularly in managing green urban spaces. He found the comment insulting, as he told the mentor. Not very surprised by Luis's reaction, the mentor then questioned the project's name, with ridicule.

"This name. I don't like it. And I don't like the logo either."

It was easy to see why the mentor raised this point, but given the tone of the previous comment, the tension escalated.

"The term is a Latin name that all engineers know. This is why we choose it. We won't change it, that's not an option!" Luis answered aggressively.

"We don't care where it comes from!" said the mentor. "The only aspect that matters is whether your name makes sense to other people. So, who will you sell your product to? You aren't selling your product to engineers, right?"

"Right, we will sell it to companies."

"So frankly, this Latin name doesn't make sense for anyone except you and two more engineers, as you say."

Luis felt insulted. The situation was becoming uncomfortable for myself and the marketing intern seated next to the mentor. The mentor started again.

"And, you know, the problem isn't that I don't like it, I'm not paying for your product, but you must invent something that sounds much more emotional to create your brand and attract people. And your name and the logo are not emotional at all. Believe me."

A few weeks later, I spoke on the phone with Alfonso, who would soon be traveling to the city to meet with a potential corporate partner. Given the heated nature of the interaction with the mentor, I expected that they would stop working together. I couldn't have been more wrong.

"We have a new marketing strategy!" Alfonso exclaimed excitedly, emphasizing the words "marketing" and "strategy."

"A new marketing strategy, you're the one saying that?" I asked, amused. "What about?"

"You remember this mentor?"

"The nasty one?"

"Yes. We've been working with him."

"What? The one who got mad at Luis?"

"Look, he was partly right. We haven't changed the name, but we agreed on a new logo and slogan. And now we're working with a guy from his team on a new website. I'll send you the link when it's ready!"

They were now developing a branding strategy with several "strategic goals," including a partnership with a leading grocery store chain. While they had acknowledged the importance of addressing the commercial demand because of their prior experience, only the socialization activities provided by Seal, specifically the mentoring, enabled Alfonso and Luis to move away from the belief that improving the commercial attractiveness of their project would negatively impact their social goal and integrity. Instead, they grew a new understanding that addressing the commercial demand, by developing a coherent and attractive branding strategy, was central for achieving social impact through signing partnerships with corporations.

Let's summarize the chapter so far. From the stories of Berta, Jon, Alfonso, and Luis, we have learned that the entrepreneurs inclined toward the social demand struggle to acknowledge the commercial demand. They lacked business-related skills and often resisted implementing concrete changes in their ventures to address this demand. Socialization activities resulted in moving away from the belief that acknowledging and integrating the commercial demand means "selling out" social impact. Santiago and Pablo's close follow-up and the external mentoring are critical pieces of Seal's offering to entrepreneurs. These activities also helped commercially oriented entrepreneurs to acknowledge and integrate the social demand, as I develop next.

## Acknowledging and Integrating the Social Demand

In the large sunlit meeting room of Seal, Tony stood by the window, attentively listening to Santiago giving suggestions about the acceleration program before he started pitching his project. In his late 40s, with his dark business suit and white shirt paired with jeans and sneakers, he conveyed a relaxed look with a touch of seriousness.

While our previous three candidates struggled to articulate their ideas, Tony nicely and coherently summarized the different facets of his project. An energetic and smiling man, I felt strongly that how he described his career choices established his credentials. This was not only because of his self-confidence; he also spent time sharing and reflecting on his strengths and weaknesses. For Santiago, self-criticism was an essential characteristic among impact entrepreneurs. It signaled a much-needed willingness to learn and progress.

Tony had just created a learning platform for professors to develop and certify their skills. After a couple of opening remarks, he turned to the business at hand.

"Most higher education institutions struggle with training their professors. Professors receive pedagogical training, but they are largely underskilled. We tend to think that professors learn how to teach, right? But we found that they lack tailored training to improve the way they deliver content to students. I'm sure everyone here remembers more "bad teachers" than "good teachers," right?"

After pausing for a few seconds for us to read his next slide, he then continued by emphasizing the issue at stake.

"As you can imagine, this situation is problematic. We learned by working for months alongside professors at different institutions. We designed our platform from there. Our platform offers training and monitoring to guarantee continuous improvement. It also creates an online community where teachers can interact, exchange good practices, and learn collectively."

"Who pays? Teachers?" asked Luc.

"I'm getting there! Our main clients are institutions. They can be universities, professional schools, and the like. First, they buy the product. Then, they pay a fee based on the volume of courses they want. We've segmented the prices based on the type of course. And the more courses they sign up for, the cheaper."

"And teachers?"

"Well, we also believe that teachers may want to follow some courses. So, we have other pricing options for them. It would be like attending an online course, but with an individual follow-up."

"So, they just follow the course?"

"Yes. Then at the end there is a test and we deliver a diploma."

"Is that an official diploma?"

"Great question. Last week, we've been exploring ways for this diploma to be certified by the Ministry of Education. This means that we must partner with a public institution. We are negotiating potential partnerships with three institutions."

Like most commercially oriented entrepreneurs, Tony conveyed a clear market gap. According to Santiago, he also offered a comprehensive competitor map, a coherent business model proposition, and financial metrics. During the pre-selection process, these aspects motivated him to call Tony for an interview, as he explained to me later that morning.

Perhaps as crucial for the selection of the venture was the deal flow concerns. Indeed, the limited number of start-ups addressing education-related issues had become problematic for Seal, with the staff struggling to fill all the seats for the cohort. Sofia, who oversaw this cluster, and Santiago who worked closely with the entrepreneurs, wrestled to provide partners with new projects. In response, they broadened the scope of their search, sometimes lowering quality criteria or inviting projects not directly related to educational issues.

Tony was less successful in his understanding of the social demand. As for most commercially oriented entrepreneurs, one reason was his lack of consideration of this aspect in the presentation of his motivation and the mission of the venture. In fact, by the end of the pitch, Tony hadn't mentioned anything about social impact yet. We were all waiting for him to expand his speech and talk about social impact, but he remained silent. Sofia broke the ice.

"Tony, are you aware that Seal focuses on social impact ventures?"

Many commercially oriented entrepreneurs applied to Seal to access funding. Their obsession with funding was unsurprising, as nascent entrepreneurs struggle to contact and convince early-stage investors given their limited network and lack of concrete evidence.[16] They viewed Seal as one way to bridge this gap.

[16] Early-stage entrepreneurs, be they commercially oriented or impact, typically struggle to access funding because of the high uncertainty of their endeavor. See, for example, Drover et al. (2017), Huybrechts and Nicholls (2012). At this stage, entrepreneurs are still developing their products, building a team, and accessing a market. See, for example, Hsu et al. (2013), Huang (2018), Mason et al. (2017), White and Dumay (2017). They lack evidence and strive to demonstrate that their ideas have the potential to fulfill meaningful market needs, as well as their aptitude to develop these ideas (Macmillan et al., 1987; Shepherd et al., 2021).

This became particularly clear when Luc, the investment analyst, inquired further into the project's roots. Tony explained that the project belonged to a private institute employing him. While they granted him some time to develop the project at work, the institute had minimal funding to pay for the creation and development of the platform. For this reason, Tony thought that applying to Seal would help him connect with investors and corporate partners.

"In fact, this project is not new. We already had funding. We did an investment round last year. But we've spent all the money, and we need an additional 300k to hire a bigger team. We need to develop the website and launch an app. All this is expensive. Because the accelerator also specializes in education, we thought it would be a good idea to apply. And here we are!"

Rodrigo, an entrepreneur belonging to Tony's cohort, applied to Seal with a similar goal. Trained in applied economics, he worked as a sales representative for multiple start-ups, some of which he had co-founded. At that time, digital health was on the rise, and he firmly believed in the commercial potential of his platform connecting doctors and patients. He claimed repetitively that the platform differed from existing ones, and we were all eager to learn how.

"Our platform focuses specifically on creating bonds between the doctor and the patient to identify the proper treatment. So we connect them and enable communication in a more efficient way, without having the patient come to the hospital.

"My dad already uses an app like this. What's new here?" asked Pablo.

"You're right. Some apps try to do this as well, but we bridge the two by providing a hybrid follow-up of the patient's needs."

"Yes. But how exactly?" asked Sofia.

"Because of the unique interface we created," he said, vaguely.

"I get it, but what's unique about it?"

"We spent time working closely with doctors on that. And you, know, two team members are medical doctors. So, they know."

"They know what?"

"They know what's needed. And they also know that it would be easy to commercialize it. Many hospitals are interested in using such platforms. They're saturated, it's obvious. The platforms have them saving space, time, and money!"

"Is that what your doctors said?" asked Luc, perplexed.

"Yes. They're key for us in that they provide the much-needed medical expertise for the project. They played a pivotal role in identifying the need."

As for Tony, Sofia asked the conventional social impact question. This led to an expression of surprise on Rodrigo's face. As he answered, Rodrigo did not connect social impact to a personal motivation or the project's mission this time.

"We work in health. All we do is help patients and doctors forge better relationships and improve care. That we have a social impact is obvious, no?"

Both Luc and Sofia raised eyebrows but remained silent. Luc sighed and then turned to Pablo. His face contorted with annoyed disbelief as Rodrigo waited for them to approve his view. But such approval never came. Not particularly interested in the social demand, Rodrigo believed that belonging to the digital health sector testified to his impact goals. Later that day, as we chatted outside of the meeting room, he asked me about the implicit connection between the industry and social impact. "That's normally how it works, right?"

As they progressed in the accelerator training, entrepreneurs gradually acknowledged that industry belonging did not automatically qualify their project as *for* impact. In other terms, it's not because the project belongs to the social sector or is related to health or the management of natural resources, that it has a social or environmental impact.

A few weeks later, I met Fanny, one of the doctors who cofounded the venture with Rodrigo. She worked at a private hospital and detailed at length their struggles with impact investors' expectations. She explained that they were trying to secure a funding round of 250,000 euros. In this process, they found surprising that investors cared about their project's social impact and requested concrete information about impact indicators.

"We have a fundamental problem. Investors ask about our social impact; they ask about how we will measure this impact."

"Did you think about this before?"

"Well, no! And we still have no idea about how to do so [laughs]."

"Didn't they tell you that impact investors aim for impact?"

"Yes. But I don't know, I didn't expect them be so precise about it."

For Tony and Rodrigo, developing the venture's social impact became a key priority as they wished to access impact investors and, ideally, secure funding. They needed funding to move forward, specifically to hire computer scientists and to develop their respective platforms alongside a communication strategy. Interestingly, however, they managed the social demand in very different ways.

Rodrigo used an avoidance strategy. He outsourced the work needed to frame, develop, and measure the social dimension of the venture by hiring an external social impact consultant. The consultant would then create a theory of change, artificially locating social impact at the core of their mission. He also created impact indicators. As Rodrigo explained to me, he did not have the necessary knowledge and skills, and told me confidently, "Why not hire someone more competent than me?"

Pablo and Sofia approached his decision from a very different angle. In particular, they strongly disagreed with his decision not to undertake this work himself or, at least, internally. During the mid-term evaluation when the staff assessed the progression of health-related projects, Sofia told Pablo that not undertaking the necessary work to develop the venture's social impact was not what was expected from an impact entrepreneur.

"If we ask them to follow the social impact training, why does he ask someone else to do it for him? This is precisely what I call doubtful social impact."

For Sofia, Rodrigo's decision testified to his obvious dearth of interest in social impact, not his willingness to address the social demand seriously.

"It doesn't look like he cares about becoming an impact entrepreneur. Don't you think so?" she asked Pablo.

As it turned out, a few days later, Pablo explained during his next one-on-one meeting to Rodrigo why the social demand had been negatively evaluated.

"The main problem is with social impact. We like the idea, we like the platform, and the business model makes sense. But the social impact is underdeveloped."

"Yes, that's true, that's why I hired someone," answered Rodrigo.

"Well, that's another problem."

"Why? You don't like how he managed social impact?"

"It's a bit more complex than that," said Pablo, annoyed.

"I mean we do care about social impact, that's rather clear, no? We've invested money into this guy because you asked us to work on our impact, right?"

"Look, Rodrigo, how could you care about your social impact if you're not even taking care of it yourself?" said Pablo trenchantly.

While Rodrigo disregarded social impact, Tony fully embraced the training on impact measurement to further develop his platform for professors. In particular, he developed a theory of change for his project and, from there, created a portfolio of impact indicators. During the mid-term evaluation, Santiago praised his motivation and progress in addressing the social demand. At the end of the three-month training, I sat with Tony to conduct a final interview about his experience at Seal. He spoke about this aspect enthusiastically.

"What happened is that I never thought about the project through an impact lens. Of course, it's great if you have a social impact, but that has never been my goal."

"What was your initial goal?" I asked.

"My goal was to provide new tools to institutions for assessing the quality of their teachers and training them if needed."

"How did you come to social impact then?"

"I learned that the social impact dimension added value to the venture. It also becomes mandatory for accessing investors, at least the ones that we met here at Seal."

The fact that some entrepreneurs were not initially interested in their venture's social impact should give anyone pause. Even those entrepreneurs claiming to have social goals often showed a limited understanding of the meaning and practicalities of social impact. The view that social impact was industry-related was commonplace.

Hélias, for instance, belonged to the third cohort of entrepreneurs I observed. In his 40s, he worked as a senior researcher at a university. He had spent the last two years developing a medical device before applying to Seal. His goal was to access funding to commercialize the device.

"Last year, I had funding from the university, and I applied for additional grants. It has worked well for us, but developing the prototype is very costly."

"I see. You need a lab, right?" I asked.

"The lab isn't the problem, we can use the university's lab. But I need to buy new equipment and the lab cannot pay for it. So I'm looking for a partnership with hospitals to finalize the device. And then I will commercialize it."

Mentioning my own research, for me to understand the abyssal gap between our respective fields, he added.

"Perhaps in your field, it's easier because doing research is much cheaper, right? But in my case, it's not cheap. With no money, I had to stop working on the project."

"So, you applied?"

"Yes, that's why I applied. I saw they had an acceleration program for health-related projects like mine."

Recognizing that many of the selected entrepreneurs had a limited understanding of social impact, for the following boot camp, Sofia and Lola added a speech from the social impact manager, Nina. Her speech was eye-opening for Hélias to acknowledge the social demand inherent to the role of an impact entrepreneur.

"Right after I started the program, on the first day of the boot camp, there was this speech from Nina. I realized that I was wrong. I knew there was something related to social impact at the accelerator, but, you know, I believed that producing the device would be enough."

"Enough?" I asked.

"Yes. That it would be enough to be an impact enterprise. With the device, we will have a positive impact anyway. After all, we work for hospitals, we help people suffering from disease."

"So, what happened?"

"I had to change my mind! This happened on the first day of the program. When they explained social impact to us, it was like a revelation moment."

"What did you do next?"

"I tried to follow what they told us, but developing the social impact was much more complicated than expected," he said laughing.

"Why? You struggled to create indicators?"

"Not really, the indicators were actually the easiest part once you got all the theory of change framework."

"Ah ok, this framework is challenging, right?"

"Hell yes. I struggled with almost everything in the framework. Like the social mission—what is a social mission? We had no social mission. So, we had to create one. And this mission would become *the* [emphasis added] mission."

"What you mean?"

"I mean that our mission was developing and commercializing a product. Of course, if we have a social impact while doing that, that's great. But that was not our main goal, having a social impact I mean. So, we had to reorganize many things around this new mission, our client, those who would benefit from using the product, the outputs. All these things."

"You sound like it was harder than developing the device at the lab," I added, amused.

"Well, almost. I mean, what's complicated is that you must see your project in a very different way than how you originally thought about it. You need to understand what social impact is, then you must revise the mission, etc."

"You can't only say to people 'I have a social impact' and that's it, right?"

"No, Nina would kill me!" he said laughing.

During the training, Hélias moved from discovering the social demand to gradually integrating this demand into his role and project by identifying and overcoming some of its inner contradictions. For instance, he recognized that one way to broaden the scope of his social impact was to select partner hospitals from the public sector.

"I don't know why, but I have initially thought about private hospitals because they work better, more efficiently, but at the end of the day, they're right in saying that I should work with public hospitals."

"Do you think that because they're public it means that you have an impact?"

"No, not really. You also impact people at the private hospital, right? But it's true that not everyone has access to a private hospital because not everyone has medical insurance as we do.

"So, it was not accessible to anyone, right?"

"Right. So, the point was that people who may really need my device won't be able to access it if we only focus on private hospitals."

I remember well his final pitch on the demo day at the end of the training. The narrative of his deep motivation to address the social problem revolved around the story of a relative who suffered and eventually died because of not being able to access healthcare. This narrative was everywhere; it was the recurring element underpinning the whole pitch. Hélias worked for weeks with Marta who trained entrepreneurs to build convincing and compelling impact-related stories. Resultingly, he made the social demand a natural occurrence by developing a narrative establishing his motivation to use his expertise to help patients.

A quick look beyond the curtain of these narratives is therefore essential. For instance, his journey at Seal revealed that achieving social impact had not been an influential aspect in his career as a medical researcher, nor had addressing the social demand through venture development been a straightforward process. The moment when his struggles appeared, perhaps, more clearly, was when I shared with him my surprise about this new narrative.

"Hélias, the first day of the program you told us a very different story, you remember. There was no social impact back then!" I said.

"You're right, I agree. It's something I learned here, for sure. And with Marta we integrated this in the pitch."

"Yes. Many of those who are here do that. Did you like the process?"

"I first struggled to understand what social impact means. I struggled to make sense of it."

"Why? They provided you with a definition, right?"

"Yes, they did. But it's like everyone you talk to understands it differently, so it's confusing when you don't come from this field!"

But his appropriation of the social demand was not only a discursive move. Hélias spent time filling and refining his theory of change. He also reflected these changes into the venture and, later, created indicators of his project's resources, products, outputs, and outcomes supported by the social impact officer and his program manager.

"They gave us two tables, one with the theory of change where I had to write down some aspects of the project, and another with some indicators. It was complicated."

"But you had understood what social impact means, right?"

"I did. But it was complicated because the project is still at a prototype stage, you must project yourself quite a lot to think about how it will affect people in the future. But it makes sense to me."

"What?"

"Thinking about how many people I will touch, what would be the tangible and intangible benefits for these people. How I could measure them and collect data to do so."

In other words, in daring to imagine a future for the venture's social impact, which means nothing more than clarifying the beneficiaries and the extent to which they would benefit from using his product, Hélias had to frame concrete plans about how he would achieve this future. It was these plans that would then guide his work for the following months as he went on to finalize the design of his product and start early commercialization.

If the social impact training provided by Seal aimed to have entrepreneurs embracing one single definition of social impact, how they handled the social demand inevitably varied. For some, it remained subordinate to the commercial demand. Virginia, for instance, navigated the training by imbuing impact indicators with economic meaning. She belonged to the team of a venture developing an application fostering virtual interactions between diabetes patients and medical staff. These interactions would increase patient autonomy in treatment by limiting their travel to the hospital.

Sofia and Pablo had already raised doubts about Virginia's social impact goals when she entered the program. As usual, Luc was, by far, the most expressive in his assessment. One day, the two of us were listening to Virginia's pitch from the back of the main room of the accelerator's building. He said to me, half covering his mouth and with his customary directness,

"I don't like her, I don't like the project, I don't think it will ever have an impact."

"Uh, no?" I said, looking inquiringly at him.

"Look, I think she just doesn't care about impact at all."

After three months in the program, Virginia pitched her project to the social impact committee. As we waited for Virginia, the comments from some participants revealed skepticism. Like Hélias and Tony, Virginia created a theory of change and impact indicators for her project. She explained to us that the social impact of her venture was twofold. First, the device enabled budgetary savings by anticipating treatments and, second, it saved patients time. "Time is money because they don't travel to the hospital that often," she added while sharing with us a complex Excel table. To our surprise, she had quantified several facets of social impact (e.g., the number of hours saved) and converted those numbers into economic profit (e.g., how those saved hours could be dedicated to paying additional workers).

In other terms, while the socialization process aimed to produce a homogenous approach to social impact among impact entrepreneurs, it resulted in different approaches as they learned and made sense of the knowledge shared with them. In the case of Virginia, Luc found her approach choking. For him, the direction chosen by Virginia reflected her original focus on the commercial demand. At the end of her pitch, he asked ironically, "How can you try to make money out of your social impact?"

## Becoming an Impact Entrepreneur

What we learn in this chapter is that the process of becoming an impact entrepreneur is gradually constructed as reality through patterns of interactions taking place over time among actors, forming an enduring group of people striving to endorse this new occupational role. Hence, the experience of the entrepreneurs at Seal can be, first and foremost, theorized as one of organizational socialization. Berta, Alfonso, Luis, Jon, Tony, Rodrigo, Hélias, Virginia, and their fellow cohort members had to learn a new role and develop their venture in a way that reflected the central convention of impact entrepreneurship, and that placed the juxtaposition of the social and commercial demand front and center.

Handling contradictory role demands is essential for integrating this new role. The internal and external mentoring, as well as the cohort training, provided entrepreneurs with shared social knowledge and raised a refined understanding of behavioral expectations. These learnings resulted in salient adjustments in their role and in new skills, allowing them to turn their idea into an impact enterprise. As they moved from being either a socially oriented or a commercially oriented entrepreneur to combine both and became an impact entrepreneur, the outcome of their socialization to impact entrepreneurship was assessed and certified.

As we also learn in this chapter, this process of socialization is, of course, not straightforward. In fact, it may be better described as an intense and tumultuous learning-by-doing process. Additionally, the socialization activities helped entrepreneurs acknowledge and make sense of these demands, although not all were willing to integrate them. Each demand carried specific beliefs that might negatively impact the implementation of these changes, outlining the importance of developing a new mindset when engaging in impact entrepreneurship.

The social and commercial demands are culturally defined, as shown in Chap. 2, and socially constructed, as shown in this chapter. They are not intrinsic to the entrepreneurs. Addressing these demands therefore requires developing new skills and expert knowledge, calling for approaching impact entrepreneurs as a new occupational group and for moving beyond the persistent focus on the individual characteristics of the entrepreneurs. This is particularly important in a context where we know relatively little about the skills and tasks required for the ideation, creation, and development of an impact enterprise. In other words, the entrepreneurial work involved in producing impact ventures and dilemmas and anxieties underpinning this transformative process.

This approach also allows for tracing some similarities with other occupational groups facing contradictory role demands. This is particularly the case when the content of the role is vaguely defined, the institutionalization of socialization processes is limited, and individuals must generate their own income. These three circumstances are clearly visible in impact entrepreneurship and shape how workers address contradictory role demands in other contexts. For instance, knowledge workers experience tensions between their personal and professional aspects as they build a reputation to secure work. Athletes must handle the demand for peak athletic performance and self-branding despite the fact that gaining expert skills in either field undermines the other. Artists strive to be authentic to their original audience while simultaneously addressing the commercial demand of their occupation to generate revenue.

Failure to align contradictory demands jeopardizes career prospects and avoidance strategies may not work when the two demands are inherent to the culturally accepted definition of the role. In fact, I believe that the internalization and management of contradictory role demands require three enabling conditions. First, these demands are at the heart of this new role, such that individuals cannot otherwise become part of this occupational group. Second, the socializing organization relies on interactions with both internal and external actors to inculcate this role, such that new members are accountable for handling contradictory role demands beyond organizational boundaries. Third, newly socialized members aspire to retain this role in the future despite no longer participating in the socializing organization. In contrast, members of occupational groups who experience contradictory demands not inherent to a new role will adopt avoidance strategies and focus on one demand over the other.

So far, we have a picture of impact entrepreneurs as individuals striving to learn the values and conventions of a new occupation that is, for the most part, still in the making. They are driven by different motivations and these motivations cannot be reduced to prosocial intention. Their work experience and knowledge are heterogeneous, and they have embarked on a journey that is eminently collective and during which they must learn new skills. As we have seen in this chapter, mentors are central to any progress in the journey to becoming impact entrepreneurs. Finally, mentors are deeply engaged in the socialization orchestrated by Seal and shape this process of becoming. The following chapter, thus, specifically focuses on the interactions between mentors and impact entrepreneurs.

## Bibliography

Arvidsson, A., Gandini, A., & Bandinelli, C. (2016). Self-Branding among Freelance Knowledge Workers. In M. Crain (Ed.), *Invisible Labor: Hidden Work in the Contemporary World* (pp. 1–27). University of California Press.

Ashforth, B. E., & Saks, A. M. (1996). Socialization Tactics: Longitudinal Effects on Newcomer Adjustment. *The Academy of Management Journal, 39*(1), 149–178.

Ashforth, B. E., Sluss, D. M., & Harrison, S. H. (2007). Socialization in Organizational Contexts. In *International Review of Industrial and Organizational Psychology* (Vol. 22, pp. 1–70). Wiley.

Austin, J., Stevenson, H., & Wei-Skillern, J. (2006). Social and Commercial Entrepreneurship: Same, Different, or Both? *Entrepreneurship Theory and Practice, 30*(1), 1–22.

Bacq, S., & Alt, E. (2018). Feeling Capable and Valued: A Prosocial Perspective on the Link between Empathy and Social Entrepreneurial Intentions. *Journal of Business Venturing, 33*(3), 333–350.

Bacq, S., Hartog, C., & Hoogendoorn, B. (2016). Beyond the Moral Portrayal of Social Entrepreneurs: An Empirical Approach to Who They Are and What Drives Them. *Journal of Business Ethics, 133*(4), 703–718.

Banks, M., & Hesmondhalgh, D. (2009). Looking for Work in Creative Industries Policy. *International Journal of Cultural Policy, 15*(4), 415–430.

Brieger, S. A., De Clercq, D., & Meynhardt, T. (2021). Doing Good, Feeling Good? Entrepreneurs' Social Value Creation Beliefs and Work-Related Well-Being. *Journal of Business Ethics, 172*(4), 707–725.

Bruder, I. (2021). A Social Mission is Not Enough: Reflecting the Normative Foundations of Social Entrepreneurship. *Journal of Business Ethics, 174*(3), 487–505.

Dacin, P., Dacin, T., & Matear, M. (2010). Social Entrepreneurship: Why We Don't Need a New Theory and How We Move Forward From Here. *Academy of Management Perspectives, 24*(3), 37–57.

Dees, J. G. (2012). A Tale of Two Cultures: Charity, Problem Solving, and the Future of Social Entrepreneurship. *Journal of Business Ethics, 111*(3), 321–334.

Dey, P., & Lehner, O. (2017). Registering Ideology in the Creation of Social Entrepreneurs: Intermediary Organizations, 'Ideal Subject' and the Promise of Enjoyment. *Journal of Business Ethics, 142*(4), 753–767.

DiBenigno, J. (2022). How Idealized Professional Identities Can Persist through Client Interactions. *Administrative Science Quarterly, 67*(3), 865–912.

Drover, W., Busenitz, L., Matusik, S., Townsend, D., Anglin, A., & Dushnitsky, G. (2017). A Review and Road Map of Entrepreneurial Equity Financing Research: Venture Capital, Corporate Venture Capital, Angel Investment, Crowdfunding, and Accelerators. *Journal of Management, 43*(6), 1820–1853.

Duffy, B., & Hund, E. (2015). "Having it All" on Social Media: Entrepreneurial Femininity and Self-Branding Among Fashion Bloggers. *Social Media + Society, 1*(2), 1–11.

Dumont, G. (2017). The Beautiful and the Damned: The Work of New Media Production in Professional Rock Climbing. *Journal of Sport and Social Issues, 41*(2), 99–117.

Evers, C. W. (2019). The Gendered Emotional Labor of Male Professional 'free-surfers' Digital Media Work. *Sport in Society, 22*(10), 1691–1706.
Feldman, D. C. (1977). The Role of Initiation Activities in Socialization. *Human Relations, 30*(11), 977–990.
Gandini, A. (2016). *The Reputation Economy: Understanding Knowledge Work in Digital Society*. Palgrave Macmillan.
Germak, A., & Robinson, J. A. (2013). Exploring the Motivation of Nascent Social Entrepreneurs. *Journal of Social Entrepreneurship, 5*, 5–21.
Hearn, A. (2010). Structuring feeling: Web 2.0, Online Ranking and Rating, and the Digital 'Reputation' Economy. *Ephemera. Theory & Politics in Organization, 10*(3/4), 421–438.
Hesmondhalgh, D., & Baker, S. (2008). Creative Work and Emotional Labour in the Television Industry. *Theory, Culture and Society, 25*(7–8), 97–118.
Hockerts, K. (2017). Determinants of Social Entrepreneurial Intentions. *Entrepreneurship Theory and Practice, 41*(1), 105–130.
Hsu, D., Haynie, M., Simmons, S., & McKelvie, A. (2013). What Matters, Matters Differently: A Conjoint Analysis of the Decision Policies of Angel and Venture Capital Investors: Venture Capital. *Venture Capital, 16*(1), 1–25.
Huang, L. (2018). The Role of Investor Gut Feel in Managing Complexity and Extreme Risk. *Academy of Management Journal, 61*(5), 1821–1847.
Huybrechts, B., & Nicholls, A. (2012). Social Entrepreneurship: Definitions, Drivers and Challenges. In *Social Entrepreneurship and Social Business* (pp. 31–48). Springer.
Lingo, E. L., & Tepper, S. J. (2013). Looking Back, Looking Forward: Arts-Based Careers and Creative Work. *Work and Occupations, 40*(4), 337–363.
Macmillan, I. C., Zemann, L., & Subbanarasimha, P. N. (1987). Criteria Distinguishing Successful from Unsuccessful Ventures in the Venture Screening Process. *Journal of Business Venturing, 2*(2), 123–137.
Mair, J., & Martí, I. (2006). Social Entrepreneurship Research: A Source of Explanation, Prediction, and Delight. *Journal of World Business, 41*(1), 36–44.
Mascena Barbosa, A., & Dumont, G. (2023). A new Understanding of the Role of Self-oriented Motivations in the Creation of Social Enterprises. *Journal of Business Ethics, 191*, 1–19.
Mason, C., Botelho, T., & Zygmunt, J. (2017). Why Business Angels Reject Investment Opportunities: Is it Personal? *International Small Business Journal, 35*(5), 519–534.
Menger, P.-M. (1999). Artistic labor markets and careers. *Annual Review of Sociology, 25*, 541–574.
Mitzinneck, B. C., & Besharov, M. L. (2019). Managing Value Tensions in Collective Social Entrepreneurship: The Role of Temporal, Structural, and Collaborative Compromise. *Journal of Business Ethics, 159*(2), 381–400.

Molecke, G., & Pinkse, J. (2020). Justifying Social Impact as a Form of Impression Management: Legitimacy Judgements of Social Enterprises' Impact Accounts. *British Journal of Management, 31*(2), 387–402.

Rahikainen, K., & Toffoletti, K. (2021). "I Just Don't Wanna Deal With the Headache of People Fighting Over the Internet": A Study of Sponsored Female Climbers' Digital Labor. *Sociology of Sport Journal, 39*(3), 251–260.

Ramus, T., & Vaccaro, A. (2017). Stakeholders Matter: How Social Enterprises Address Mission Drift. *Journal of Business Ethics, 143*(2), 307–322.

Shepherd, D. A., Souitaris, V., & Gruber, M. (2021). Creating New Ventures: A Review and Research Agenda. *Journal of Management, 47*(1), 11–42.

Smith, W. K., Besharov, M. L., Wessels, A. K., & Chertok, M. (2012). A Paradoxical Leadership Model for Social Entrepreneurs: Challenges, Leadership Skills, and Pedagogical Tools for Managing Social and Commercial Demands. *Academy of Management Learning & Education, 11*(3), 463–478.

Smith, W. K., Gonin, M., & Besharov, M. L. (2013). Managing Social-Business Tensions: A Review and Research Agenda for Social Enterprise. *Business Ethics Quarterly, 23*(3), 407–442.

Tracey, P., & Phillips, N. (2007). The Distinctive Challenge of Educating Social Entrepreneurs: A Postscript and Rejoinder to the Special Issue on Entrepreneurship Education. *Academy of Management Learning & Education, 6*(2), 264–271.

Van Maanen, J. (1973). Observations on the Making of Policemen. *Human Organization, 32*(4), 407–418.

Van Maanen, J. (1984). Making Rank: Becoming an American Police Sergeant. *Journal of Contemporary Ethnography, 13*(2), 155–176.

Van Maanen, J., & Schein, E. (1977). Toward a Theory of Organizational Socialization. *Research in Organizational Behavior, 1*, 84–89.

White, B. A., & Dumay, J. (2017). Business Angels: A Research Review and New Agenda. *Venture Capital, 19*(3), 183–216.

Zahra, S. A., Gedajlovic, E., Neubaum, D. O., & Shulman, J. M. (2009). A Typology of Social Entrepreneurs: Motives, Search Processes and Ethical Challenges. *Journal of Business Venturing, 24*(5), 519–532.

CHAPTER 5

# Good Match

By 3 p.m., the kitchen was empty, with most staff members back at the office. Located in the east corner of the main floor, this bright room was decorated with motivational slogans. Its single communal table often hosted our lunches when it was too cold to use the terrace. There, Sofia was listening to voice messages and scribbling on her phone, probably dealing with late emails. I thought it was the ideal moment to ask her to discuss fieldwork, and I stopped by on my way out to invite her for coffee. We moved to a café nearby and sat outside, glancing at the imposing metallic skeleton of Seal's office building.

"You know, it's like they don't speak the same language," she said.

"What do you mean?" I asked.

"You remember what I told you on your first day?"

"What?"

"That they have the same goal. Entrepreneurs need resources, and mentors want to work with them. But it's not always working as we would like, it's like they don't speak the same language."

I found her comment puzzling. Indeed, why would they struggle so much to work together if they shared the same goal? I kept a mental note. As the two of us walked back to the building, Lola came out of a meeting with Cristina, the head of innovation for one of Seal's long-standing partners, who had been involved as mentor. She looked irritated.

"What's going on?" Sofia asked her, surprised.

"Cristina."


G. Dumont, *Impact Work*,
https://doi.org/10.1007/978-3-031-64661-4_5

"Why?"

"She has been complaining about a team of entrepreneurs, saying that 'they don't really care about my comments, and I feel I'm just wasting my time,' you know."

"What did you say?"

"Nothing yet. She said that the project was interesting but asked to be assigned to another team."

It's not that Lola was particularly surprised by Cristina's complaint. Cristina was not the one greasing the wheels. That time, she touched on a recurrent and pressing matter. Some entrepreneurs showed very little consideration for external advice. This issue exasperated Lola and Sofia, in addition of carrying important implications for Seal's success in developing impact enterprises for two reasons.

First, as in any accelerator, mentors at Seal were a central piece of the acceleration training because they offered guidance in their area of expertise. This is partly why Lola, Sofia, and Jorge strove to cultivate an extensive network of mentors with whom they developed trustable bonds. They liked to describe this network as "our community." It included serial entrepreneurs, business angels and investment analysts, policymakers, lawyers, business school professors, and top executives. These mentors shared bits of their experience without monetary compensation. They invested considerable time in traveling to Seal, meeting with the entrepreneurs, and commenting on their documents.

Second, the attractiveness of an accelerator tends to be thought of as based on mentors' reputation. If social connections help entrepreneurs to access resources, it is not surprising that accelerators are primarily designed to help entrepreneurs build such networks.[1] Seal provided both a physical space and an orientation for fostering network building in a unique way, and Lola and Sofia strongly believed that their mentors were a driving force in attracting the best entrepreneurs to the program. Certainly, there is a link between mentors' reputations and the prestige of the accelerator. Surprisingly, however, the entrepreneurs I interviewed had yet to articulate the importance of this aspect when they considered applying. In fact, as I soon learned by attending dozens of their meetings with mentors, most entrepreneurs were unaware of who the mentors were, except for corporate partners with whom they hoped to establish bridges.

[1] See, for instance, Cohen et al. (2019) and Krishnan et al. (2021).

That early-stage entrepreneurs benefit extensively from the network built during the initial steps of venture development has been widely documented.[2] Most literature has examined the structure of the network enabling or constraining action among those constituting the network. This focus has been very valuable in showing who within a network can provide entrepreneurs with specific resources and when. However, how the social relations constitutive of this network shape resource exchange remains unclear. In other terms, network analysis tends to foreclose a rigorous examination of the content of the social relation. However, resource exchange depends not only on the strength of the tie but also, and perhaps more importantly, on the quality of the relationship between those involved.[3] Because we cannot speak of relations without emotions, without explaining how to turn ties into pipes we can hardly explain the bigger puzzle of how one relationship develops to enable resource exchange during the interactions.

This chapter develops an approach to resource exchange in impact entrepreneurship grounded in its emotional and meaningful dimensions. While I previously examined how impact entrepreneurs acknowledge and integrate the dual demands of their role through mentoring, I now zoom in-depth into the micro-interactions that constitute mentoring and use Zelizer's relational work framework.[4] Picking up on her discussion of relational work as the efforts involved in matching relations with appropriate transactions and media of exchange for them to become meaningful and turned into a good match,[5] I emphasize the role of meanings, emotions, power asymmetry, and broader organizational forces in enabling the transfer of resources between impact entrepreneurs and mentors.

In other words, my goal in this chapter—and indirectly in the whole book—is to bring people back into the analysis and engage with aspects other than efficient outcomes, risk, and performance. Relational work, indeed, refers to the "creative effort people make establishing, negotiating, transforming, and terminating interpersonal relations."[6] Because any economic activity involves a set of relationships, and because some of these

[2] See, for instance, Arenius and Laitinen (2011), Busch and Barkema (2022), Hoang and Antoncic (2003), Jack (2005), Klyver and Arenius (2022), Newbert et al. (2013).

[3] Marc Granovetter (1973) and Brian Uzzi (1996, 1999) showed well the importance of uncovering the quality of the relation to explain the exchange.

[4] Zelizer (2005, 2012). See Nina Bandelj (2012) for a review of the concept.

[5] See Block (2012).

[6] Zelizer (2012).

relationships are more meaningful than others, relational work concentrates on the negotiated meanings, enabling actors to set boundaries between relationships by marking them as specific.[7] Relationships are effective when meaningful, and the type of transaction and medium of exchange must be aligned to create good matches.[8]

Accordingly, good matches must be worked out during social interactions marked by a specific set of transactions.[9] Yet, most relationships between entrepreneurs and resource holders are non-contractual, and the exchange must be framed to overcome the absence of the monetary transaction. Many additional, yet no less important, resources—such as social connections, reputation, information, and expertise—are exchanged in a non-contractual and emotion-driven way.[10] The approach of relational work incorporates this aspect and allows for analyzing the efforts involved in generating matches between social relations, economic transactions, and resources.[11]

Building on these insights, I argue that relational work is a central aspect of impact work. In. particular, I propose that the emergence of a good match requires the creation of a shared understanding of the situation and the media of exchange. This understanding enables them to overcome the initial framing of the interaction by the accelerator and to redefine initial roles. I develop this argument by uncovering the relational infrastructure created by Seal and cemented by expertise, reputation, and behaviors of "giving back." This infrastructure frames mentors as resource holders and redefines entrepreneurial needs according to their subjective experience. Entrepreneurs, by contrast, are assigned the role of resource seekers. Then, I show how entrepreneurs negotiate these roles by framing their endeavors as distinct from resource seekers, by presenting themselves and acting as resource holders. This reveals that for the exchange to unfold, both impact entrepreneurs and mentors interpret and accommodate roles to match the relationship, transaction, and media and to negotiate the power asymmetry originally constructed by Seal.

[7] Zelizer (2005).
[8] Zelizer (2010).
[9] Bandelj (2016).
[10] See, for example, Huang and Knight (2017).
[11] See Bandelj (2016).

## Pairing Impact Entrepreneurs with Mentors

"We've got brilliant people in the house, and our entrepreneurs care about this a lot!" Sofia claimed proudly as she listed the names of Seal's mentors to me. I could recognize well-known leaders, serial entrepreneurs, top executives, business angels, and fund managers. Sofia knew most of them personally. She worked out these relationships by taking the time to talk to them individually, publicly showing her gratitude to have them "in the house." She also introduced them to each other, guided by her intuitive sense of "who would like to meet whom."

At the end of Seal's annual event dedicated exclusively to mentors, I asked her about the rationale for such practices. She explained, "Mentors are not only here for the entrepreneurs, they want to build their network. They want to develop new connections by meeting with people, be part of the community. And we help them to do just that!" However, sustaining their commitment to the program also required not contacting too often nor assigning to too many entrepreneurs. Finding the right balance was vital for their motivation all year long. "We must take care of them," she concluded.

Jorge had a slightly different view on the situation. Indeed, if Sofia and Lola strove to help mentors grow their network, he strongly believed that "belonging to Seal" was chief for their motivation to dedicate their time freely to the organization. "They wanna be with us. They wanna be around us," he used to say pompously during our team meetings, when he encouraged staff members to take great care of the mentors. "They must feel that they belong to Seal!" which required sustained communication and the organization of this "mentor-only" event.

Mentors were incredibly busy. Their full-time positions at companies made them reputable and attractive for Seal, but also partly explained their struggle to find time to fit entrepreneurs into their schedule. Additionally, many of the mentors described to me how the often-chaotic organization and the entrepreneurs' variable commitment rendered their participation even more challenging. Occasionally, mentors had traveled to Seal on the wrong day because of misleading information, or had to leave earlier because the entrepreneur did not show up on time. "How can you work in these conditions?" a mentor once asked me rhetorically, exasperated about waiting for a team of entrepreneurs.

Mentoring occurred through meetings between mentors and entrepreneurs and aimed to enable resource exchange. I use the term "exchange" on purpose. On the one hand, mentors offered entrepreneurs feedback, guidance, industry expertise, and potentially networking opportunities. They did so at a time when entrepreneurs' access these resources were limited or, for most, nonexistent. On the other hand, most of the mentors I talked to explained cultivating the hopes that they might identify investment opportunities, meet new collaborators, or eventually integrate the project in one way or another for those mentors who worked freelance.

Yet, continuity over time in the relationships between entrepreneurs and mentors was rather exceptional. Although I witnessed some mentors formally joining the team of a venture or investing in the latter, these situations remained rare. In fact, mentors invested their time with no other compensation than the joy of advising entrepreneurs, sharing their experience, and "giving back to the community," as a serial entrepreneur once said.

Further, the interactions between mentors and impact entrepreneurs did not systematically lead to resource exchange. Sofia already raised this issue in the opening of this chapter by saying metaphorically that mentors and entrepreneurs did not speak the same language. For her, what was particularly enigmatic was that both parties shared similar goals and, therefore, should organically "find a way to work out the relation, no?" she asked me as we were discussing at the café. I nodded in silence, and she added to reiterate her point, "Entrepreneurs need resources, and the others want to work with them."

This relational mishmash jeopardized Seal's goals. Sofia, Lola, Jorge, and the program managers had to enable exchange by creating good matches. This task was necessary to satisfy their collaborators—be they impact entrepreneurs, devoted mentors, or corporate partners—and to sustain their participation. Lola described good matches as momentum when "our entrepreneurs and collaborators connect. They understand each other and can engage in a conversation leading to a collaboration." Although she tended to frame this momentum as a natural occurrence, it did not unfold alone but required an understanding to emerge between both parties. In fact, Sofia and Lola dedicated much time to supporting its emergence by strategically constructing it as part of a broader relational infrastructure orchestrated by Seal.

A first step in this process was to provide a context for the interaction through discursive framing assigning specific roles to impact entrepreneurs and mentors. Because part of the thrill of joining Seal lay in accessing an exclusive network of mentors, Sofia and Lola constantly built mentors' attractiveness by over-promoting them as well-known experts wishing to share their resources. Of the three, Jorge was the most eager about emphasizing their high status.

"Ahead is an exciting week during which you will meet many people. They're coming exclusively *for you* [emphasis added]. All of them are experts in their respective areas. We've got top executives from leading corporations in your sector, policymakers, business angels and investment analysts at major VC funds, professors from top business schools, and successful entrepreneurs. I'm sure you all know well who they are. Meeting them is, in itself, a fantastic opportunity, cause they're very busy people, but they kindly agreed to dedicate their time to *your* [emphasis added] project. Make the best of these opportunities!"

When interacting, Jorge carefully weighed each word while staring intensively at his interlocutor, to the extent that I found some of our one-to-one meetings slightly discomforting. To the entrepreneurs seated in the meeting room this morning, his insistence on "top" and "leading" emphasized the high symbolic capital of mentors as he shared the week's schedule with entrepreneurs. "Look, entrepreneurs must feel privileged to be here and grateful to the mentors for devoting their time to them," he explained to me once. In fact, most seemed captivated by him, their eyes sparkling. And while entrepreneurs were already assigned to the position of learner when they entered the program, Jorge also enforced their subordination to mentors.

Having set up the context for the interaction, the staff proceeded to strategic pairing. Nina managed the network of mentors and jointly evaluated with Pablo and Santiago the needs of each entrepreneur and the resources each mentor could provide them. At this stage, their focus was primarily on what they viewed as the "objective needs" of entrepreneurs.

"How do you know upfront what they need?" I asked.

"We interviewed them, you don't remember?"

"I do, I've been to dozens of interviews already."

"So, we start from there. Of course, we revise their needs during the bootcamp, then after. We always know them better as they progress through the program. The idea is that they develop their venture, right? So, depending on the progress, we may assign them other mentors."

"But how do you choose them?" I asked again.

"We choose mentors that will teach entrepreneurs something. So hopefully, they will soon improve their business model, their product, their communication strategy, whatever they need."

While Nina remained vague about this process, strategic pairing helped entrepreneurs understand and integrate the culture of impact entrepreneurship as they saw it. Lola and Sofia used mentors to familiarize entrepreneurs with the conventions ruling interactions, as they (Lola and Sofia) would like them to behave. Among these conventions was being passionate about one's venture, Jorge explained eloquently.

"Someone who's not passionate is not an entrepreneur, he doesn't have credibility. You must share it with passion. You must be able to share the passion that drives you. Those entrepreneurs who are just passing through impact entrepreneurship don't convince anyone. If you're here because you don't have anything else to do, well, people see this quickly, it's obvious, and your credibility is low. You may have an impressive CV, work experience, etc., but at this stage, you have minimal credibility and must find ways to compensate with good *logos* and *pathos*. You may have the best career out there, you must have demonstrated your value, but it doesn't give you the necessary legitimacy…at least for now."

For Sofia, maybe chief among the characteristics of a great impact entrepreneur was being humble.

"They must come down from the clouds, you know what I mean?"

"Not really," I answered.

"Being humble is not precisely a defining characteristic of entrepreneurs!" said Nina while winking complicitly at Sofia.

"Yes. Of course, not all our entrepreneurs are overly confident about their venture. Not everyone thinks they're the best!" added Sofia.

"That's true. Some are very shy. Look at Manu, for example. He's super shy, he always doubts his project. He has very little self-confidence, don't you think?" asked Nina.

"Yes. Santiago is working with him precisely on that aspect. Much of his work focuses on having Manu believe that he can make it," clarified Sofia.

"This French guy, Clement, really doesn't need this type of help," added Nina ironically.

"Who's he? I haven't met him yet," I asked.

"If you see someone telling everyone he's the best, and his project is dope, that's him. You will find him easily," Sofia told me, laughing.

"He can't stop praising himself. That's so annoying. The kid is just so ego-driven. It's like he thinks he has created the new Facebook and everything else is bullshit!"

"So who would you assign him?" I asked.

"Good question," said Sofia. She sat thoughtfully for a few seconds, intensively looking at the list of mentors, before turning back to Nina and me.

"Nina. Why don't you assign him to Rob? Have you met him, Guillaume?"

I met Rob during my first boot camp. In his late 40s, he worked as an investment analyst at a major venture capital fund. In a dark suit, hair combed to the side, he always looked very sober. I saw him smile only once, when talking to Lola. Harsh and direct, he was among the first people I asked for an interview at the inception of my fieldwork. He rejected my request immediately.

"Yes. I asked him for an interview."

"Ah, great, you interviewed him," said Sofia.

"Well, no. He didn't agree. He told me, 'I have no time,' that's it," I explained, dismayed about my first and only interaction with Rob.

"That doesn't surprise me," said Sofia, laughing. "I have known him for a long time, so I'm used to him. He's a bit rude, that's clear, but this is also exactly what we need to shake entrepreneurs sometimes."

"Like to shake Clement?" I asked.

"Exactly."

"No doubt he will beat Clement in less than five minutes," added Nina, excited. "I totally forgot about him. Yeah! Let's do this, that's so great! This Clement comes straight from university. He's a 'Uni kid,' who thinks that because he won some prizes already, he's hot shit…No doubt Rob will turn him down!"

The kind of work performed by Sofia and Nina, and that goes into the production of strategic pairing, enforced the role of resource seeker assigned to entrepreneurs while increasing the power of mentors. It started when staff members engaged in relational work for entrepreneurs to lower their expectations about their venture. With the explicit goal "to bring entrepreneurs back to the ground," Sofia, Santiago, Nina, Pablo, and others constantly recalled overly enthusiastic entrepreneurs in the very early stages of their ideas.

Mentoring was also aimed at tempering entrepreneurs' aspirations to secure funding because they saw their venture as "investment ready." During pre-selection interviews, for instance, I was more than once shocked by entrepreneurs' insistence on accessing impact investors, although they had yet not developed and tested their product and, more often than not, provided inconsistent financial metrics. One day after another pre-selection interview, I shared these thoughts with Santiago, who did not find this surprising.

"Most of these guys enter the program believing they are in the investment readiness stage. You ask them for metrics, and they always claim, 'Yes, of course we have metrics,' you see my point?"

"So what, that's great, right?" I asked.

"Well, in theory, yes. But then you check the numbers, and they all have over-valuation. Most of it is just hot air."

We laughed.

"What do you do then?" I asked.

"Our work starts with having them recognize where they stand. You want them to question those numbers. So when they meet with our collaborators, they don't overdo it…or at least less!"

"I see."

"What I mean is that they can't do whatever they want! They must behave themselves and treat mentors well."

"What should they do differently?"

"You will see yourself soon."

The response to my question came later that week when working with Pablo. He had arranged a couple of meetings between a team of three entrepreneurs and the head of innovation of a leading corporation in the food industry. That morning, the two of us visited the entrepreneurs' office for the weekly work-in-progress meeting. On our way to their office, Pablo shared with me his expectations for the meeting.

"I wanna make sure that everything goes smoothly."

"What would go wrong?"

"Entrepreneurs don't like to be questioned."

"Questioned on what?"

"On their idea, on what they have decided, and what they should do."

"Why?

"They believe they are the new Facebook, and everyone must love them and applaud their idea!"

During the meeting, Pablo spent the first five minutes inquiring about the work completed thus far and the result from the recent trial of their product. Then, he got straight to the point in a solemn tone.

"These guys [the mentors] are at the top of their game. You might hear things that you don't like, or that you don't find relevant, or they might even critique your ideas, but don't get mad about it. Take these comments as an opportunity to learn by asking them why they don't like it!"

Foreseeing the potential irascibility of the entrepreneurs about having their idea questioned, Pablo recommended they consciously induce their own behavior.

"Make the best out of the situation," he reiterated as we left.

In other words, part of the relational work involved in building a good match required entrepreneurs to produce "emotional labor."[12] That is, they had to manage their emotional state and expressions, for the mentor to have a suitable experience. Persistently engaging with mentors and constantly revisiting one's idea was seen as much-desired behavior. Jorge always highlighted this aspect of the cohort by linking this personality trait with what defines a "good impact entrepreneur," as he liked to say. "A good impact entrepreneur asks for things all the time. He solicits people, asks, asks, and asks again all the time. Good impact entrepreneurs always return for more and don't take things for granted!" That is, "A good impact entrepreneur is a pain in the ass."

## Making Pre-established Roles Meaningful

Zoé stepped into Seal's building on the fourth day of the boot camp with a clear plan in mind. Wearing a black suit, heels, and a Dior handbag, her elegant style contrasted with the laidback attitude of other members of the cohort. She explained her elegance by her concern not to be taken seriously by mentors, "I do my best to look professional and to behave professionally."

Zoé had also reviewed the list of mentors available on Seal's website. She noted some of the names of the mentors she had met the day before and had collected information about those that she would meet today. "I spent two hours last night looking at their LinkedIn profiles. I want to know who they are, what they know, and how they can help me." When available, she also watched videos of their talks on YouTube "to get a sense of who they are," she explained.

Zoé's careful investigation of the mentors was atypical. "I do this all the time," she proudly cleared up for me. On that particular morning, we coincidently met in front of the building and walked through the main hall toward the lift together.

[12] Hochschild (1986) developed the notion based on a study of flight attendants to emphasize the labor performed by women to self-induce particular emotions to behave adequately in a commercial relationship.

"I want to know who I'm talking to and make the best out of each meeting; you know what I mean? I searched you as well," she added, laughing.

"Me?" I said, surprised.

"Of course. There are two people in your network who I would like to talk to."

She gave me their names and asked about our relationship, wondering if we knew each other well enough. "A lot of people know a lot of people on LinkedIn, but I want people who actually know each other because I need them to help me out," she added carefully.

Zoé applied to the program with the primary goal of growing her network. At least, this was how she articulated her motives to me. What she did not tell me, however, was that she also knew precisely which aspects of her venture needed great care. She was developing a food-related application and needed to find a chain of grocery stores where she could test the app. She also needed to work on her branding strategy.

She embodied proactivity and persistence to the extent that, a few weeks into the program, Santiago confessed to me his vain effort to slow her down. Her self-determination was palpable. She liked to describe it as a personality trait and explained her proactive attitude by using the following rhetoric. "Well, I've quit my job, moved, and invested everything in this project, so there's no way I would do it differently." I nodded silently, and she added, "I have to kick ass … otherwise all these efforts aren't worth it."

We jumped in the elevator and went up to the second floor. As the door closed, I asked how she felt about the program. She took her time answering, "I feel a bit like I'm going back to school." After 15 years of a career in the marketing department of a multinational corporation, the 40-year-old had shifted paths the year before. She switched from managing teams to being managed by Pablo, who was only 25. "It's not always easy!" she confessed, half smiling. Building upon her savings from her last job, she had relocated in town and enrolled in an MBA. She was now striving to turn her final year project into an impact enterprise.

"And I finished school two months ago," she says, laughing. She foresaw this project as the next step in her career, "I mean, I like it. I have many things to learn, of course, and this is how it is, I guess; so far it has been great. I like the people there, and we're a good group, but, you know, I'm not like those 25-year-old kids. I need to make this happen because I need to make a living out of it soon."

A few weeks later, I would meet again with Zoé to follow up on the work in progress. She had chosen a café close to her office, apologizing for her decision by explaining that she was "too busy for meeting too far from here!" I found her to be slightly uneasy about Seal but didn't know why. I couldn't have been more wrong, as I soon realized when she started telling me about her most recent meeting with a mentor operating a chain of supermarkets in town. I could feel the excitement in her tone.

"That would be so great if we could collaborate, you see. It would be a great way for me to test the app with 'real clients.' That's exactly what I need now."

"Did you meet him because of your network from the business school?"

"No. No way could I have met him alone. I could have asked some of the people in my network, but I'm not sure I would have been able to talk to him."

"So, you met him here?"

"Yes. He's a good friend of Jorge. You know his family works in that sector, right?"

"Yes. What do you need to know exactly about the app?"

"I spent the last three weeks developing several new features. I need to make sure they're functional and easy for people to use."

A few weeks later came the approval from the mentor. When we met, she was about to test the app with a sample of customers and in a supermarket from another group focused on high-end products. We discussed her recent success.

"You see, that's why I spend so much time networking with people and working out the connections."

"Congrats, I'm so happy for you! Have you asked anyone else?"

"What do you mean?"

"Well, other supermarkets, I would like to try the app at different places."

"I do contact potential partners in the sector, I go meet with them, I invite them to our events, I interview them for my blog and the newsletter, and I also invite them to give a workshop here to gain visibility. And all the time and effort I invest has mid-term benefits. I take care of them!"

In terms of a set of practices and beliefs, Zoé was not the only entrepreneur believing that she brought value to companies. Very often, this belief guided entrepreneurs' efforts as they came to negotiate the initial framing of their role as resource seekers within the relational infrastructure offered by Seal. This resulted in power asymmetry. Nevertheless, most entrepreneurs did not take their role of resource seekers for granted. Instead, they worked toward positioning themselves as resource providers, making sense of the relationship by demonstrating the value they could provide to mentors and partners.

"It's like they see us always asking for things. But it's not always true," Zoé added.

"What, you mean they also ask things of you?" I asked, slightly provocatively.

"For the partners I'm meeting these days, what I offer is great because I help them save money, I help them do things better."

"You help them do things better? Which things?" I asked, recalling Berta. Indeed, the entrepreneur who developed a venture to help unemployed youth access technology-related education also largely took for granted the benefits partners gained by collaborating with her.

"These partners, they're mainly small distributors and supermarkets, that's true. But if they work with me, they can promote our collaboration for their communication and CSR strategies."

"Why?"

"It's always nice to say you work with a social impact enterprise, no? Otherwise, why would they sit down with me?"

The process of role negotiation in which engaged Zoé appeared even more readily in how Gabriel and Benjamin envisioned their meetings with mentors and corporate partners. The two entrepreneurs had almost two decades of experience in work integration. Quite ordinary looking (jeans and sneakers), they created a spinoff from their previous company that connected job seekers, employers, and educators. On a sunny afternoon of June 2017, I visited their office in the city's suburbs. After being introduced to the team, we moved into the intimacy of Benjamin's office. They had a mentoring meeting the day before with an executive from Seal's network. Gabriel, the team's spokesperson, described the meeting with sudden emotion.

"A priori, it looks like we don't bring anything to companies, like we're only asking for help." Pausing for a few seconds, he described Seal's framing of their role as frustrating too, then adding forcefully, "These companies are interested in our product. ICO [name of the company], for instance. They launched a similar product five years ago. It failed because they're not experts in the sector."

"You guys bring in the expertise, right?" I asked.

"Sure, they don't have the expertise we have with educators and job seekers. We all have many things to learn, which is also partly because we do this program and spend our time meeting with so many people. But we also have a lot to offer!"

Zoé, Gabriel, and Benjamin were not alone in negotiating their role. Mentors also strove to negotiate their roles for their participation to be meaningful. As we have seen, Jorge, Sofia, and Lola insistently promoted mentors as leading experts wishing to share their skills, sectorial expertise, networks, and material resources. They also insisted that their participation was voluntary and non-financially compensated, and that they made invaluable efforts to free some time in their schedule.

This was partly true. Anna, a 45-year-old marketing director, had been mentoring projects at Seal for about two years. We met in a cozy café on a Wednesday morning. Her phone was buzzing constantly. I feigned annoyance to implicitly suggest that the noise was interrupting our conversation. To my relief, she turned off the volume. She placed the phone in her bag, hanging from the chair next to me.

"You see, when I tell you I'm always super busy, is that I'm always super busy," she said to me, winking and pointing to her bag. "That's why I like to come here. I had a meeting earlier in a building nearby, and the next one will come here at 11 a.m."

"How do you find time for mentoring, then?" I asked.

"I do it because I like it. I like to listen to new projects and ideas and be in touch with entrepreneurs. These guys don't pay me, but it's a passion. Now, of course, I don't like to waste my time."

"When do you waste your time?"

"What I do now is that, if I am with a team that is not advanced enough, or that I feel [is] not prepared enough for our meeting and that we're not on the same line, I say no!"

Mentors systematically described to me, albeit in different ways, the existence of what Anna named, smiling, "a sort of passion for entrepreneurs."

"I like their enthusiasm. They're always super excited to tell you about their idea. They're doing new things."

I could only agree, as my interactions with entrepreneurs resulted in a very similar feeling—their enthusiasm was often contagious.

"I think it's great because they're people who have been making an important decision, starting a business. That this business has a social impact makes it even more special to me."

"Have you been an entrepreneur yourself?" I asked.

"No, not at all. But each of us plays a role in that; some people helped me back then, and I think we must give back knowledge and expertise for free and voluntarily."

Likewise, David, a successful entrepreneur who advised and invested in start-ups, conveyed well this sort of "giving back" behavior. This was particularly clear when he explained to me his involvement in three local business accelerators, including Seal. We were sharing a coffee in the brand-new office of his company, in the heart of the city's technological district. The district had recently been remodeled to host technological start-ups and foreign entrepreneurs like him. Showing me around, he provided me with a glamorous view of his life as a successful entrepreneur who had sold two of his companies and was about to start the third.

I inquired about what mentoring meant for him. He breathed deeply, sitting back on his black leather executive chair while passing his phone from hand to hand.

"It's much like trying to contribute to the ecosystem. I believe that if I help ten people, they will help another ten once they succeed, so we can create a solid ecosystem of people helping each other."

"And do you believed it has worked so far?"

"Of course, Guillaume! All my tips won't work. I can't solve everything, but since we often come through the same process, we face similar challenges and often need similar solutions."

Mentors' motivations were more complex than that. Involved with Seal for the last two years, Silvia was the head of procurement for the international markets of a biotech firm. For our first meeting, she suggested the bar of a well-known luxury hotel near the city center.

I had never been to this hotel before, and it was only by glancing at the façade and its doorman that I realized I should have worn my suit instead of a white T-shirt. Inside, Silvia sat in the rear of the large reception room beside the bar. Dimmed lights and the dark green velvet curtain covering the large windows created an intimate atmosphere with an exclusive flavor.

"You should have warned me about the place," I said, half smiling and pointing out my T-shirt to explain my relaxed outfit.

"I like it here. I like to have most of my business meetings here. I'm a member, in fact. It's nice and quiet."

Indeed, we were alone. I added, "I wanted to meet because Lola told me you're thinking about leaving Seal, right?"

"Yes. For now, I've asked her not to assign me too many projects. But yes, I may not resign next year."

"The mentoring isn't going well?"

"No, it's not for that reason. I just can't deal with them all, and I'm unable to provide good advice when rushed. There's not much that you can do during a 15-minute mentoring meeting. It's just not enough."

"You never meet the entrepreneurs longer?"

"No, I don't have time. I meet them at Seal when I go there. And the meetings there are only 15 minutes. Sometimes a little bit longer. But not long enough, I think."

But time was not her primary concern. She continued.

"The quality of the projects is lower this year, I think, at least to me, so it is not that interesting, to be honest."

"What do you mean by quality?"

She looked to the bar thoughtfully before turning back to me, "Most of the projects are underdeveloped, you know."

"Most of the corporate partners I talked to mention this aspect as well. But that's also the goal of Seal, right? To help develop new projects," I said.

"Sure. But because they aren't developed enough it's not easy to envision potential collaborations."

I nodded in silence, waiting for her to complete the sentence, and thinking that partners also struggled with this aspect.

"Well, you know, the truth is that they don't bring much newness. Maybe it's because I attend so many industry events that I'm aware of what's going on, but still, it shouldn't be like this."

"Okay. I thought that you also learned from the entrepreneurs because they were developing revolutionary stuff, aren't they?"

"Yes, in general yes. I mean, most of the time, I feel that I learn from them. I meet with so many start-ups every year, entrepreneurs with different backgrounds, ideas, sectors, everyone with a specific way of doing things. You always learn things in unexpected ways."

"But it was not as much the case this year, right?"

"No. It was not. But, you know, last year I learned a lot about alternative go-to-market strategies. You remember Jack?"

I did. Jack was a character, the entrepreneur from October's cohort who always made jokes and asked funny questions during the seminars.

"In January, I invited the entrepreneurs to my company. We discussed their products with my team for an entire morning. This was very insightful for us."

By contrast with Silvia's experience, Saïd, a highly committed 36-year-old digital marketing freelancer, was more reserved about the learning opportunities offered by meeting with the entrepreneur for mentoring.

"It's not because you mentor a team of entrepreneurs that you learn something. Sometimes it can be super annoying. They don't tell you anything new or only speak about themselves."

As an alternative, during the boot camps and the events organized for mentors, he always chatted amiably with everyone to build his network. "It's definitely a great place to make new contacts with people I won't meet elsewhere." He also hoped to meet new clients among the entrepreneurs, "You know that many of the entrepreneurs you talk to, well, most of them, nothing happens!"

"What you mean by 'nothing happens'?"

"They talk about stuff that they have no idea about."

"So, why drives you here?"

"Let me put it to you this way, Guillaume. Some might become my clients, or you can have a contractual involvement in the company."

"Cool. So, you're working with some of the entrepreneurs of the cohort?"

"Not yet, not yet!" he clarified, laughing.

Despite his efforts to build working relationships with entrepreneurs by being proactive, sending them additional materials, and spending extra time on their projects, Saïd was not very successful. This disappointed him, but he signed up for another year as a mentor. For now, he was satisfied enough with having his picture on the accelerator's website for him to gain visibility and be associated with a social impact initiative. This new line on his CV mattered, as he explained later, "It's great that Seal does social impact, it's different from the other accelerators and programs I already participate in."

My point here is that mentors think of their involvement in multiple ways. These include gaining new learning, networking, and selling paid services, depending on the mentor. In contrast to how they were depicted and promoted at Seal, mentors were not disinterested collaborators. They firmly expected to "get something back from the relationship" and their involvement. Impact entrepreneurs and mentors alike thus negotiated their respective roles in interactions, which was necessary to arrive at a transactional understanding of the exchange.

## Building a Transactional Understanding of the Exchange

So far, we have seen that Seal provides a physical infrastructure gathering impact entrepreneurs and mentors. This infrastructure becomes relational as soon as the staff strives to pair them in ways that would support the development of their venture and enable them to learn the values and conventions of impact entrepreneurship. This relational infrastructure creates a situation of power asymmetry. Impact entrepreneurs hold the role of resource seekers. Mentors are depicted as resource holders. Resource seekers are presented as low-status while, by contrast, resource holders are granted high power. Resultingly, entrepreneurs are in a subordinate position while mentors enjoy high symbolic status and resources.

While the previous section showed that impact entrepreneurs and mentors negotiated these roles, I now examine how roles are enacted during social interactions, leading to a shared transactional understanding enabling exchange and indicating the construction of a good match. Indeed, relational work involves an intentional effort to achieve a goal, explicitly here enabling resource exchange. This effort consists of adapting to the other parties' expectations and beliefs as the interaction between impact entrepreneurs and mentors unfolds.

At Seal, the staff ceaselessly advised entrepreneurs to welcome comments from mentors and to adopt humble behavior. Such behavior belongs to the constellation of expectations raised around impact entrepreneurs. In fact, the "best entrepreneurs" were often portrayed as open to new ideas, humble, and welcoming feedback. This behavior was required for the success of mentoring because of the belief that it would greatly facilitate mentors' enthusiasm to commit to the relationship. This, in turn, would support the development of a transactional understanding of the exchange, namely a shared perspective about the relationship built during the social interaction.

Mentors, however, described their interactions with entrepreneurs in slightly different ways. Among them was learning about the limited willingness of entrepreneurs to listen and take their advice seriously. In her late 50s, Maya described this aspect at length when sharing with me the ups and downs of her experience as a mentor of digital health start-ups. In particular, I asked what she had learned from interacting with entrepreneurs during the mentoring meetings. She explained, pensively,

"One thing I've learned by working with entrepreneurs is that they don't like having you say that they're doing it wrong. Which is fine, they must learn...but then they think they already know everything. This is common; now I'm aware of this, I try to frame things differently."

"What do you mean by framing things differently?"

"I may want to spend a lot of time congratulating them for the quality of their project. I ask them many questions to show them that I'm interested in what they do, I tell them that they're doing a great job, these kinds of things."

"It helps?"

"I think so. I do my best to make them feel confident, and once I feel they are I start commenting on the project."

If building confidence with entrepreneurs was necessary, in some instances, these emotions were not always actually felt but faked, because they were believed to be essential for creating new relationships. Mentors, indeed, also performed emotional labor. And even though mentoring at Seal was not financially remunerated, their emotional labor had an exchange value because it helped frame the interactions in ways that could potentially enable the exchange. Of course, not all mentors worked out the interaction this way. For example, Rob, the antipathic mentor Sofia and Nina assigned to Clement, did not work it out at all.

Half of the mentors believed their expertise was not truly appreciated and that entrepreneurs did not acknowledge their status of expert. "It's very much like they believe that they know more than me...in my industry, while I've been around for 25 years," Marcos, a retired CEO of a national educational business, told me, slightly irritated. Another mentor, Georges, was the most explicit on this aspect. In his late 30s, he successfully launched an online consumer health and wellness product marketplace in 2011. A long-time friend of Jorge, he had been mentoring projects for a few years and occasionally participated in the selection committees as an external advisor with entrepreneurial experience. He also often gave a motivational talk during the boot camp to recount his story by discussing the critical success factors of his career and, at the same time, validating himself as a successful entrepreneur.

The day before, he sent me the location of a busy Starbucks located on the other side of the city, in a wealthy neighborhood. There, Georges made sense of his participation in Seal by recalling his early entrepreneurial debut. Remembering his experience emotionally, he told me with a mix of reflexivity and frustration.

"Most of the time, entrepreneurs don't care. I see that all the time. On the one hand, it's okay because I'm not always 100% correct, and I'm not involved in every day of the company. But I'm also where I am because of my track record. I've created quite a few successful companies now. I've been through the same path and succeeded more than once. They should all know this quite well… I have a lot of experience on quite a few things, although I could be wrong as well, of course. But too often it's like they don't care."

Georges then paused for a few seconds to look through the window. He stared at me again.

"Look, Guillaume, many times when I advise them, they don't trust me, like they don't take it seriously. Do you know what it means for me not to be taken seriously?"

"Not exactly."

"This is just a waste of time, for me, them, for all of us."

"Why?"

"Because it's worse than no meeting at all."

Entrepreneurs, indeed, sent him informational signals that negatively impacted the opportunity for resource exchange to unfold. I observed that mentors tended to lower their commitment to the program when doubts about the credibility of their view emerged. But I also believe that what vexed Georges the most was that he knew entrepreneurs crudely needed his help to progress.

"I've been there. I've been sitting on that chair, struggling day after day, with very few people to help me. So trust me, this is when you need help. This is when you need people like me to spend time on your project. Otherwise, you go nowhere," Georges explained to me.

Arriving at a transactional understanding of the exchange, indeed, requires impact entrepreneurs to show "coachability." Coachability refers to the willingness to seek, consider, and integrate feedback.[13] As illustrated by Georges and Marcos, it also required that impact entrepreneurs show gratitude for mentors' time and effort. Without paid remuneration, the mentoring interaction and, eventually, the resulting relationship had to be emotionally rewarding. In some cases, it may also require mentors to adopt the same humble attitude as the entrepreneurs. All the mentors I met during fieldwork were grateful for their interactions with entrepreneurs when their feedback was heard, and their status acknowledged.

[13] See Ciuchta et al. (2018).

Likewise, entrepreneurs questioned the behavior of mentors. Chief among their complaints was their hostility toward the project. Entrepreneurs often experienced such hostility as a personal offense. Ernesto, for instance, was a 41-year-old entrepreneur who teamed up with Rita, a lab scientist to develop the business model of her venture and a coherent branding strategy. Two weeks after the start of the program, the three of us met the investment analyst assigned to them. The intimidating attitude of the mentor became acute when he incessantly questioned the financial forecasting Ernesto had prepared with a colleague experienced in finance. His rude comments generated animosity among the entrepreneurs, who gradually stopped answering his questions, only providing him with bits of answers. Their attitude bothered the mentor, and the apotheosis came suddenly.

"Look, Ernesto, if you don't care, I can just go."

"Yes," said Ernesto. I looked up at him, surprised by such uncharacteristically refreshing directness. We will contact you once we have revised our numbers."

This last sentence led to a complete change on the mentor's part, and he left the room almost immediately. We then looked at each other silently, shocked by the interaction but relieved that it had finally ended.

Later that week, Ernesto and I discussed this event over a coffee. He remembered the event emotionally, expressing mixed feelings about the investment analyst and mentors. Sensing himself to be less affected than he would like, he said.

"That's great, for sure, all these people know a lot, and I would love to work with them; no doubt my business would make a tremendous step forward. But some look at you as if you don't know shit, like 'I'm gonna tell you how life is out here.'"

"I see. You found him pretentious, right?"

"Yes. No way could I work with people like them, and you feel this very quickly. Like this guy, for instance. I can be wrong on my numbers, but don't look at me like that."

"Yes. He was not very friendly, you're right."

"Totally. I was shocked. It's not easy for us. He might be right, he knows his shit, and he's helping us, but at the same time, we can't say yes, all the time. We must fight for our ideas until we find a consensus, right?"

The following week, I met the investment analyst at a demo day. I wanted to know his opinion and walked straight up to him to ask how he felt about that meeting. He stared at me, not very surprised by my question.

"Well, he didn't like me!"

"Ernesto?"

"Yes, Ernesto. But also, there was no real spark. You know this feeling when you meet someone?"

"Like you feel sort of a connection?"

"Yes. Kind of. I can't explain what it is."

"Is that the first time this has happened to you?"

"Oh no, it often happens when you meet people, or entrepreneurs. But with Ernesto the fact that he wasn't receptive to my comments didn't help!"

This "real spark" was often connected with shared attitude and value, two critical aspects for arriving at a transactional understanding. This point was well-illustrated by the case of Roberto, an entrepreneur from Ernesto's cohort mentored by Alex. Rodrigo explained, "Alex is helping us on the legal side. We found an agreement to formalize our relationship and to 'pay' him, as we have no cash. Now, I help him develop one of his projects, but we did sort this out because we are on the same page. I mean, there is good personal chemistry, and he likes our ideas."

For Ernesto, the chemistry never emerged and he never sent any of the documents to the analyst. He also failed to attend the following meetings. "Not the best way to start a relationship with someone, huh!" Pablo told me ironically. He had not yet, I believed, fully understood that Ernesto found the mentor's behavior inappropriate and, accordingly, had decided not to pursue the relationship. More broadly, Ernesto's behavior is illustrative of a complaint shared among mentors highlighting the entrepreneurs' scant communication.

For instance, Cristina—one of the Seal's long-standing partners we met in Chap. 2—had met twice with an entrepreneurial team until she stopped receiving emails from them. She explained.

"Look, we met twice, I liked the project, and we had a good feeling. I asked for more information. I invited them to come to my office. The idea was to have them meet our team and discuss how we could use our network of clients to test their pilot."

"Sounds like a promising start, no? What happened next?" I asked.

"What happened next? Well, what happened is that I sent them a few emails, but they never replied. They did not even come to the meeting. I'm waiting for Lola to tell me what's wrong with them.

Lola assigned Cristina to another team. As Ernesto described and acted regarding mentors, Lola designated the entrepreneurs' behavior as inappropriate. Indeed, arriving at a shared understanding of the transaction also required sustaining communication among parties. Nevertheless, although all entrepreneurs reiterated their wish to meet mentors, and vice versa, sustaining communication was often an issue. In many situations, either the mentor or the entrepreneur complained about this issue, typically blaming the other party to explain failure in the mentoring relationship.

## What Makes a Good Match?

Once we understand that a good match between impact entrepreneurs and collaborators is not only the result of common interest or a sense of chemistry alone, it is much easier to understand the challenges underpinning their social interactions and how these jeopardize resource exchange. This is important because, at the earliest stages of an impact enterprise, mentors are the most precious resource for entrepreneurs. Without them, entrepreneurs couldn't access the knowledge necessary to learn and make sense of the social and commercial demands. They would struggle to revisit their prototype, integrate social impact in their communications, develop impact indicators, or pick up a business model.

The relational work perspective helps bring back agency into the analysis of impact entrepreneurship and reveals that arriving at a good match requires the performance of relational work, although several aspects constrain this performance. Chief among them is the framing of the role of impact entrepreneur and mentor. The relational infrastructure allows physical gathering and interactions between impact entrepreneurs and mentors, but fosters power asymmetry. This power asymmetry calls for a process of role negotiation in which both parties make sense of their role, acknowledge the bilateral nature of the exchange, and eventually arrive at a transitional understanding. This transactional understanding provides the foundation upon which impact entrepreneurs and mentors exchange things of different natures, primarily information.

Accordingly, the crux of my argument is that resource exchange is constructed through, and enabled by, relational work. Indeed, good matches emerge because relational work makes the relationship meaningful by creating an alignment between relations, transactions, and media of exchange. For the exchange to unfold, it must be meaningful for both parties.

Meanings are not given, nor should they be taken for granted. Instead, they are socially constructed in interactions as people continuously challenge and rework them.

Further, if role negotiation has been theorized as a "soft power strategy"[14] deployed by the entrepreneurs, this negotiation process is fundamentally a practice of imbuing the emerging social relation with meaning. When the exchange is not formalized nor monetarized, the emotional benefits derived from the interaction may overcome its material and informational value. In other words, good matches are the outputs of a relational process involving pairing actors who mutually acknowledge their roles and expectations. This results in the construction of a transactional understanding of the exchange adapted to the features of the relational infrastructure.

This insight is vital for understanding how the exchange of resources unfolds among those involved in impact entrepreneurship. It means that, in order to explain how relational work generates good matches, we need to closely study the micro-interactional processes and the broader infrastructure hosting them. Doing so requires moving beyond depicting structures of relations, or ties, between actors to, instead, zoom into the content of the ties. Accordingly, by building upon the relational work approach, this chapter challenges a critical piece of conventional wisdom, namely, the dominant market logic and instrumental view governing most of our current understanding of resource transfer and, to some extent, the interpersonal relations governing it.

## Bibliography

Arenius, P., & Laitinen, K. (2011). Entrepreneurial Teams and the Evolution of Networks: A Longitudinal Study. *The International Journal of Entrepreneurship and Innovation, 12*(4), 239–247.

Bandelj, N. (2012). Relational Work and Economic Sociology. *Politics & Society, 40*(2), 175–201.

Bandelj, N. (2016). Thinking about Social Relations in Economy as Relational Work. In I. P. Aspers & N. Dodd (Eds.), *Re-Imagining Economic Sociology* (pp. 227–251). Oxford University Press.

Block, F. (2012). Relational Work in Market Economies: Introduction. *Politics & Society, 40*(2), 135–144.

[14] See Santos and Eisenhardt (2009).

Busch, C., & Barkema, H. (2022). Planned Gerardk: How Incubators Can Facilitate Serendipity for Nascent Entrepreneurs Through Fostering Network Embeddedness. *Entrepreneurship Theory and Practice, 46*(4), 884–919.

Ciuchta, M. P., Letwin, C., Stevenson, R., McMahon, S., & Huvaj, M. N. (2018). Betting on the Coachable Entrepreneur: Signaling and Social Exchange in Entrepreneurial Pitches. *Entrepreneurship Theory and Practice, 42*(6), 860–885.

Cohen, S., Fehder, D. C., Hochberg, Y. V., & Murray, F. (2019). The Design of Startup Accelerators. *Research Policy, 48*(7), 1781–1797.

Granovetter, M. (1973). The Strength of Weak Ties. *American Journal of Sociology, 78*(6), 1360–1380.

Hoang, H., & Antoncic, B. (2003). Network-based Research in Entrepreneurship: A Critical Review. *Journal of Business Venturing, 18*(2), 165–187.

Hochschild, A. (1986). *The Managed Heart. Commercialization of Human Feeling*. University of California Press.

Huang, L., & Knight, A. P. (2017). Resources and Relationships in Entrepreneurship: An Exchange Theory of the Development and Effects of the Entrepreneur-Investor Relationship. *Academy of Management Review, 42*(1), 80–102.

Jack, S. (2005). The Role, Use and Activation of Strong and Weak Network Ties: A Qualitative Analysis*. *Journal of Management Studies, 42*(6), 1233–1259.

Klyver, K., & Arenius, P. (2022). Networking, Social Skills and Launching a New Business: A 3-Year Study of Nascent Entrepreneurs. *Entrepreneurship Theory and Practice, 46*(5), 1256–1283.

Krishnan, R., Cook, K. S., Kozhikode, R. K., & Schilke, O. (2021). An Interaction Ritual Theory of Social Resource Exchange: Evidence from a Silicon Valley Accelerator. *Administrative Science Quarterly, 66*(3), 659–710.

Newbert, S. L., Tornikoski, E. T., & Quigley, N. R. (2013). Exploring the Evolution of Supporter Networks in the Creation of New Organizations. *Journal of Business Venturing, 28*(2), 281–298.

Santos, F. M., & Eisenhardt, K. M. (2009). Constructing Markets and Shaping Boundaries: Entrepreneurial Power in Nascent Fields. *Academy of Management Journal, 52*(4), 643–671.

Uzzi, B. (1996). The Sources and Consequences of Embeddedness for the Economic Performance of Organizations: The Network Effect. *American Sociological Review, 61*(4), 674–698.

Uzzi, B. (1999). Embeddedness in the Making of Financial Capital: How Social Relations and Networks Benefit Firms Seeking Financing. *American Sociological Review; Albany, N.Y., 64*(4), 481–505.

Zelizer, V. A. (2005). *The Purchase of Intimacy*. Princeton University Press.

Zelizer, V. A. (2010). *Economic Lives: How Culture Shapes the Economy*. Princeton University Press.

Zelizer, V. A. (2012). How I Became a Relational Economic Sociologist and What Does That Mean? *Politics & Society, 40*(2), 145–174.

CHAPTER 6

# Impact Promises

Gerard had just left the room after pitching his project. Seated on the other side of the large white table, Sofia seemed very pleased with his pitch. She looked around, confident that the investors attending the meeting would fund Gerard's venture. This was especially important because a favorable funding decision would help position Seal as a leader in the national impact entrepreneurship ecosystem. The fund was starting to develop a consistent portfolio of funded ventures that attracted attention across the country.

The investors, however, remained silent. They were still conscientiously reviewing their notes, making up their minds about the final decision. Marc, an external investment analyst invited to this investment committee, finally broke the icy silence to say solemnly, "Financial forecasts are excellent … but we must take a leap of faith to believe that Gerard has the intention to launch a social enterprise." His sentence raised several eyebrows around the table. After clearing his throat loudly, Marc continued, "We must take a leap of faith in believing him because, right now, we don't have any solid evidence showing that he actually cares about having a social impact."

Marc expressed aloud what many of us had kept to ourselves. We had little concrete information to evaluate the credibility of Gerard's self-reported prosocial intention and social mission. We knew that he had recently quit his well-paid job at KPMG Paris with the ambition of



G. Dumont, *Impact Work*,
https://doi.org/10.1007/978-3-031-64661-4_6

creating an impact enterprise training care workers, certifying their skills, and connecting them with employers through a platform. Such a life-changing decision, he confessed emotively during his pitch, was motivated by a recent personal crisis that had raised a burning desire to "have a social impact." Gerard also emphasized his personal relationship with care work, using the example of a relative to claim a deep knowledge of the social problem.

While investors applauded his financial metrics that convincingly showed the economic viability of his project, his promise to achieve social impact "seemed too great to be true," asserted another investor. As Marc summarized, a pressing question remained: "Does Gerard *really* [emphasis added] care about social impact?"

One thing that has emerged in earlier chapters of this book is that those engaged alongside impact entrepreneurs, be they executives, mentors, policymakers, or staff members, did not always take entrepreneurs' promises to achieve impact at face value. Rather, they scrutinized their claims by juxtaposing them with entrepreneurs' past behavior and actual action. The previous chapters also showed that some of these actors, including the impact entrepreneurs themselves, did not engage in impact entrepreneurship with the explicit aim of achieving social impact, or of helping others to do so. Rather, they developed the motivation to achieve social impact once they were already involved in this process.

A central argument of this book is that entrepreneurs can be socialized to impact entrepreneurship *after* they have created a venture. Resultingly, they may decide to turn their project into an impact enterprise later, for instance, in this case because of the socialization at Seal. Further, Seal also acts as a socialization organization to impact entrepreneurship for actors other than entrepreneurs. Many of the actors of the impact entrepreneurship ecosystem introduced in the previous chapters, including corporate partners, mentors, and investors, walked into a new experience at Seal. Initially attracted by the prospect of participating in socially related projects, their understanding of these projects was very heterogeneous. Their time at Seal signed their conversion to impact entrepreneurship.

As I have also discussed in the previous chapters, regardless of the nature of the original motivation to engage in impact entrepreneurship, impact entrepreneurs are conventionally expected to articulate a prosocial intention to achieve social impact. We have seen that this prosocial intention may be socially constructed during the training at Seal, or it may be at the heart of entrepreneurs' behavior, as described in Chap. 4. In either case, it must be expressed coherently and convincingly to signal the distinctive organizational identity of the venture.[1] In the impact economy, self-reported prosocial intention is a shared moral standard. There are, thus, solid expectations for entrepreneurs to display a prosocial intention, as Gerard expressively did.

Accordingly, impact investors looked for prosocial intention and a clear social mission, two aspects they believed were critical to achieve impact. However, as the debate taking place at this morning's investment committee illustrates, doubts may arise on the credibility of these aspects. The main reason is that, as Marc also carefully noted, the eloquence of the impact entrepreneurs about their noble goals to make this world a better place is profoundly embedded in their pervasive discursive strategies to convince others. While at Seal they explicitly learn to create a compelling impact narrative, all impact entrepreneurs engage in discursive practices to frame their prosocial mission and social mission in a way that align with field conventions. This situation raises a fundamental question that must be solved to make an investment decision: how to evaluate the credibility of such a promise.

This chapter addresses this question by looking more specifically at how impact investors carry out this evaluation beyond observable characteristics and self-reported prosocial intention and social mission. Impact investors' primary goal is to fund innovative market-based solutions addressing societal problems,[2] and central to it is "the intention to generate positive social and environmental impact."[3] Their decision-making process, therefore, is twofold. On the one hand, they evaluate the economic promises made by the entrepreneurs by using tools from traditional finance. On the other hand, they scrutinize the social impact accounts to evaluate the credibility of the social impact promises.

Previous scholarship on this process brings to the fore the observable characteristics of the entrepreneurs and proposes that impact investors

[1] See, for example, Miller and Wesley (2010), Nicholls (2010).

[2] Although they tend to accept lower return rates, impact investors expect financial returns from their investments and use conventional financial metrics and impact indicators. See, for example, Agrawal and Hockerts (2019), Casasnovas and Ferraro (2022), Thirion et al. (2022).

[3] See the definition of the principles for impact investing by the Global Impact Investing Network. https://thegiin.org/impact-investing/need-to-know/#what-is-impact-investing

would view gender or skin color[4] as a proxy reflecting attributes such as care, compassion, empathy, and altruism. This chapter challenges this claim and seeks to explain more comprehensively how to assess something as volatile as a promise by building on previous understandings of the evaluation process of traditional ventures. Traditional investors, indeed, avoid over-relying on entrepreneurs' promises and surface level characteristics. Rather, they scrutinize their actual behaviors and assess their aptitude for successfully achieving their goals.[5] They also evaluate the credibility of such promises by weighing entrepreneurs' skills, professional experience, industry experience, storytelling skills, and track record. They try to gauge their personal qualities and commitment to make up their mind and decide.[6]

These evaluative practices enable investors to construct a belief in the investment, which is critical because it emboldens investment decisions. Brought to impact entrepreneurship, this insight means that impact investors should capture the credibility of entrepreneurs' promises to achieve social *and* economic goals. This is particularly important at the earliest stages because entrepreneurs have little concrete evidence to offer and many obstacles to face. Indeed, existing impact metrics only capture aspects of operating ventures, including the activities that are assumed have an impact (e.g., creating a school or developing a work-training program) and the outcomes of these activities.[7] That is, these indicators measure the social mission at advanced development stages, not when they are still ideating, testing, and finalizing their products.

Under these circumstances, I argue that investors view the credibility of the impact promise as central for overcoming the challenges jeopardizing

[4]We know little about the criteria used by impact investors and, more broadly, social finance providers, although they face new challenges in measuring the social mission and aptitude of entrepreneurs. See, for instance, Anglin et al. (2022), Barman (2016), Lee and Huang (2018), Miller and Wesley (2010), Nicholls (2009), Rawhouser et al. (2019).

[5]Investors build their assessment based on three interrelated aspects: the venture, the entrepreneurs, and the perception of their capability to execute the plan (e.g., Cardon et al., 2009; Huang & Knight, 2017; Huang & Pearce, 2015; Lee & Huang, 2018).

[6]They judge entrepreneurs' personal qualities and commitment to goals during their interactions. See, for instance, Feeney et al. (1999), Hsu et al. (2013), Mason et al. (2017), Maxwell et al. (2011), Mitteness et al. (2012). Consequently, a more subjective assessment relies on investors' "gut" but is key to decision-making (Huang, 2018; Huang & Pearce, 2015; Maxwell et al., 2011).

[7]See, for instance, Agrawal and Hockerts (2021), Hehenberger and Harling (2018), Rawhouser et al. (2019), Reisman et al. (2018).

entrepreneurs' social goals and that may threaten investors' investment thesis.[8] I develop this argument by documenting how investors evaluate the impact promise analytically and subjectively. With this goal in mind, I describe and analyze four aspects of the entrepreneurial behavior under scrutiny: entrepreneurs' proven awareness and use of impact metrics, biographical aspects informing their social goals, how they manage their venture, and how they envision its future. I then articulate these aspects to show that the evaluation results in a collectively constructed belief in the credibility of the promise made by entrepreneurs to achieve their social goals, which reflects the alignment between self-reported prosocial intention, social mission, and actual behavior.

## Impact Metrics

"They could have searched for better indicators of impact, and for more indicators," Luc told the room, with his casual mix of exasperation. Taking a deep breath, he then continued with a wry smile:

"There is a lot of work ahead for them to create reliable indicators. They didn't think about social impact!"

"Well, they said they want to have an impact, right?" said Sofia.

"Yes, they told us something about the impact [during the pitch], but just something... not even a slide. Their indicators are useless," continued Luc.

"What do you mean by useless, Luc?" asked Sofia.

"These indicators are useless, useless! They don't measure anything. The entrepreneurs didn't take care about it, no doubt."

Luc couldn't stop questioning the information provided by the two entrepreneurs. His frustration, I believe, came from the fact that the entrepreneurs had been successful on the economic dimension of their venture but failed to clearly articulate a clear impact thesis. Also, they did not provide tangible indicators. This omission, Luc knew, strongly jeopardized their chances of receiving funding.

A few days before this conversation, Luc had shared solid expectations about the entrepreneurial team. As the two of us were reviewing the document the entrepreneurs had shared with him to receive feedback prior to the pitch, I asked his predictions about the investment committee's upcoming decision:

[8] See Grimes (2010), Miller and Wesley (2010), Smith et al. (2013).

"I don't know, I hope. I mean, they have done a very good job. They almost tick all the boxes."

"You've been working with them, right?"

"Yes. I was the financial advisor. Great product, coherent business model. A true innovation. They have already signed a couple of partnerships. That's good, investors like this."

"Why?"

"It shows that they're able to promote their idea and get people on board. They also have a couple of business angels supporting them and received two grants for product development."

"Does this matter as well?"

"Yes. I helped them on the financial forecasting. This forecasting is solid for that reason. That was great, I like them. And, you know, it's great to invest your time in entrepreneurs who actually care about what you say."

Entrepreneurs' willingness to listen and integrate external feedback was central for Luc, who dedicated a lot of his free time to Seal. But this morning at the committee, it was with a mix of frustration and despair that he talked about the entrepreneurs. "It's like they have forgotten the social impact," he concluded sarcastically.

That impact metrics are a prevalent aspect coming into play while evaluating impact promises is not surprising. Indeed, impact measurement standards are the only formalized way impact investors can attempt to capture social impact. Quantitative in nature, impact indicators are believed to provide objective information upon which impartial decisions can be made. This was particularly clear in the early days of impact indicators, with the development of the social return on investment (SROI) that, as Virginia did in the previous chapter, attempted to monetarize impact. This attempt to quantify qualitative aspects of the impact enterprise to assess their performance has been a powerful force shaping the development of impact investing as many investors come from the world of traditional finance. Yet, numbers are also enablers of qualitative discussions. They help provide a common ground for impact investors, as do financial metrics that provide a shared language and understanding of what is valuable and what is not.[9]

[9] Vandebroek and colleagues (Vandebroek et al., 2020) showed that numbers are not supposed to be the determinant of a decision but to provide a common ground for impact investors, as financial metrics do. In other words, quantitative tools can also encourage dialogue.

An issue I observed recurrently among entrepreneurs is that they typically forgot about the prospective nature of impact indicators. At this stage, it was obvious to everyone on the investment committee that they still had to further develop, test, and commercialize their product before being able to measure its social impact. Hence, impact indicators could only provide indicative information about prospective impact. Earlier that day at the committee, David summarized this point nicely to an entrepreneur. As a senior impact investor, David had already challenged one team of entrepreneurs on this aspect by saying "All your numbers are great, but please don't forget that this is only hypothetical, as you still have to develop your product, then commercialize it [before having an impact]." He reiterated his comment to a solo entrepreneur who mixed actual with prospective impact, "How could you claim that you're presenting your actual impact if your product hasn't been commercialized?"

Impact investors saw the level of development of the theory of change, and the impact indicators, as mirroring the credibility of the self-reported prosocial intention. This appeared particularly clearly in the following assessment and the resulting conversation. Alberto, an impact investor, and Carolina, an external social impact advisor, challenged Beatrice on this aspect during her pitch. Chief among their concerns was that Beatrice provided no information about the social impact of the venture. Alberto started by asking:

"Beatrice, what about the social impact of the venture? Any thoughts about it?"

"Uh, well, I already told you, I wanna have a social impact."

"Look, that's great, this is what we do here! But do you have anything more

concrete? Who will benefit from your product? How would you measure the impact?"

"My product will improve life quality for people suffering from insomnia."

"Yes, we know this. But how would you like to measure the social impact of your product?"

Beatrice remained silent. It was Carolina's turn to take upon Alberto's points. Looking up from the document, she asked:

"Beatrice, it looks like you did not fill the theory of change framework, right?"

"I did my best .... I couldn't fill all the boxes."

"I like your idea very much, too. But could you please focus on the implications for the users? Let's start with your users. What can you tell us about them?"

[Silence]

"Beatrice, listen, I'm asking about how you measure the implication of the product for the users. By using which indicators?"

Beatrice's omission exasperated Carolina. Once Beatrice left, they highlighted her limited knowledge of social impact and forcefully condemned the absence of impact indicators. Carolina then sought Sofia's advice:

"What do think?" she asked, Sofia. "She sounds like it's the first time she heard the word social impact."

"Yes. I don't know. I don't know because she has been following the social impact training, so she must know."

"That's my point. Beatrice should have developed indicators. She should have an idea of the future social impact of her venture, among many other things," said Carolina, irritated.

"I agree with you Carolina, I agree. I have no clue," added Sofia, confused.

"What did she learn then? It's like she never heard anything about social impact ever," concluded Carolina.

Alberto found this aspect blatant too, signaling the loose credibility of her social mission. This was particularly shocking because it strongly contrasted with her eloquent claims during the pitch. Soon after the committee, Alberto and Carolina asked Santiago, her program manager, for more information about her commitment to the social impact training. "Well, in the same vein as her presentation at the committee," he said deceptively.

On a Wednesday afternoon, I joined Patrick to visit a team of entrepreneurs he was mentoring. He invited me to come, these "were interesting entrepreneurs" and were worth a visit for my research. While driving back to the office, I asked him why he found them "so interesting":

"Those are precisely the type of people I call opportunistic impact entrepreneurs."

I could feel a bit of frustration in his voice and asked for clarification:

"What do you mean?"

"They made up the social impact for us."

"How do you know?"

"They're easy to flag!"

"How?"

"Just look at how they understand social impact!"

"What do you mean?" I asked again.

"I asked these three guys. I asked them what social impact is, you remember."

"Yes, by the end of the meeting, right."

"Yes. They didn't answer. Honestly, how can they take care of their social impact if they don't even know what it is?"

During another investment committee, two impact investors discussed the market fit of a product a solo entrepreneur had pitched to us that morning. The entrepreneur wanted to develop a virtual care device. He had a technological background and spent most of his time talking about technical aspects of the product and how he aimed to develop them further with the investment money. While the two investors enthusiastically discussed how he could use the funding, Patrick interrupted the conversation to say, with uncharacteristic irritation,

"We shouldn't be losing our time wondering about the market for this product when this guy does not care about impact."

"Why?" asked one of the analysts.

"He hasn't said a word about impact indicators, nothing, no slide, no indicators, no [social impact] thesis."

"Well, he did a great pitch. I liked it," added the other analyst.

"Yes, he did a nice presentation. But he hasn't worked on that aspect [social impact] further than saying, 'Let's make this world a better place.'"

Impact metrics also provided the basis for a conversation about impact by looking into what should be measured and considered relevant. Luc, Patrick, and fellow investors viewed the awareness of what impact entailed and the level of development of the indicators created by the entrepreneurs as one dimension testifying to their promise's credibility. "If they don't care about impact, why would they spend time creating impact indicators?" Luc told me once.

If this holds true for those entrepreneurs who applied for funding without undertaking the acceleration program, the issue was far more complex for the entrepreneurs of the accelerated cohort, such as Beatrice. The reason lies in that they had been trained to develop a coherent theory of change and impact indicators. Further, they had developed a narrative bringing to the fore their prosocial intention. Under these circumstances, impact investors needed additional dimensions to ground their assessment, starting with the impact track record of the entrepreneurs.

## Impact Track Record

Impact investors connect specific aspects of an entrepreneur's track record to their prosocial intention and social mission. They invariably evaluate the entrepreneur's biography by scrutinizing their professional and personal experiences. They use the information, along with impact metrics, impact management, and impact prospect, to evaluate the credibility of their prosocial intention and social mission and, in this way, their promise to achieve social impact. Consider, for instance, the contrast between the biographies of Gerard, the entrepreneur Marc questioned in this chapter's opening, and Kilian, an entrepreneur who, like Jorge and Berta, is strongly socially oriented.

When Gerard pitched his venture, the investors applauded his humble attitude as an essential quality in an impact entrepreneur. It was not unusual for commercially oriented entrepreneurs to have a business career and, around 40, decide to quit and "to change their life." Impact investors viewed these entrepreneurs as highly capable of launching and developing a venture. In Gerard's case, there was a consensus on his business skills and financial metrics, with comments such as "He's got key people on board," "He knows a lot about product development," "His market need is bulletproof," and "He did an amazing job with the market research." Impact investors also appreciated that, as a consultant, he was used to long working days and "would be able to put the hours," as Sofia said. "This is vital for an entrepreneur. We all know this," she added convincingly to the room.

"Something that I like about him is that he has signed this contract with an automobile firm. That's great evidence that his project is interesting for other people, right?" asked Luis, a business angel.

"Yes, it is," answered Sofia.

"It's one of the most important skills for entrepreneurs," added Luc, for whom this aspect demonstrated his capability in identifying commercial partnerships. "It shows his skill in rallying people to his endeavor."

Along with Luc, a recently hired investment analyst named Luis was enthusiastic about Gerard's project and seemed especially impressed by his determination. Acknowledging Carolina's concerns, he tried to reassure her:

"This guy is very conservative. He will meet the objectives of the business plan, no doubt. And he managed teams at KMPG, so he knows what he's talking about. You can feel this when you listen to him talking. He sounds like a leader."

"I know," answered Carolina.

"So?"

"Please be careful with MBAs from LBS or Harvard...watch out with top experts. We need someone for a particular task, and those people usually don't have the right attitude."

Carolina was desperately calling for caution in approaching Gerard's business training. She insisted on scrutinizing his experience and skills in more detail instead of taking for granted that his training at a leading business school and his experience as a consultant would automatically turn him into a "great impact entrepreneur."

Beyond Carolina's concerns, half of the impact investors seemed satisfied enough to make an investment decision. Still, the assertion of Gerard's promise was not as straightforward. Most investors were suspicious of his abrupt decision to quit KMPG to launch a social enterprise because of a personal crisis and, apparently, a pressing ethical dilemma. If they were used to similar narratives from impact entrepreneurs, particularly those trained at Seal and who thus learned how to align with this convention of the field, several questions remained unanswered. "Why would an MBA graduate quit the security of full-time employment and a 200,000 yearly salary?" "Did he truly wake up one morning with a sudden desire to change the world?" "Will Gerard continue to develop his venture's social impact after the funding round?" "Would he resist pressure from commercial investors given his emerging success?" Marc warned other participants, "There is a cast of commercial entrepreneurs who are experts in pitching, winning prizes, and securing finance. It's all smoke and mirrors."

Kilian, a 47-year-old entrepreneur, did not belong to this cast. As such, he provides a contrasting example to Gerard. His pitch was terribly messy, even embarrassing for Santiago, his program manager, whose anxiety gradually grew as Kilian painfully went through his slides. Kilian belonged to those entrepreneurs wearing oversized white T-shirts and distressed jeans who had never entered a business school. He first worked in a small family business created by his father in his hometown. Then, in contrast to Gerard's stellar professional career, he worked as a commercial representative, driving across the country to meet local business owners. He had many day jobs without making them a career.

After a few months, Kilian launched a platform to connect job seekers with disabilities and prospective employers. In the room, Sofia was perhaps the most enthusiastic about the project, partly because she had closely followed Kilian's progression during the three months of the training.

Although Kilian's presentation was awful, she smiled at each of his slides, nodding enthusiastically. Once he left the room, she said, to testify to the credibility of his social goals and to emphasize his track record in the field,

"He has worked in the sector for two decades, he knows everyone. It's easy to see that, just look at the partnership he already secured although the venture isn't a venture yet, sort of. But this guy is convincing because he knows where the public administration fails, he has been working on that for ages."

Before this particular day, those who met Kilian during the three months of training had relentlessly praised his commitment to the social mission. Among other aspects, they applauded that, with limited financial resources, Kilian would fly to the city for the boot camp, sleeping on a friend's couch. He was passionate about what he did, and this passion was contagious. Playing in his favor, he also had an irresistible enthusiasm that put everyone at ease, and most of his interlocutors usually smiled with pleasure when he started explaining his idea.

Yet, passion was necessary but not sufficient for making an investment decision. This time, the burning question dividing impact investors centered on his capability of handling the commercial demand. Luc explained:

"He will be an incredible spokesperson and will convince everyone of the social mission, but he has no experience in managing someone, not even a company."

"Does he really have experience at all?" added Luis, sarcastically, to highlight Kilian's lack of business-related skills.

"Come on Luis," said Sofia. "He already told us where he worked!"

"Yes, but one of the risks is that he won't be able to use the funding to consolidate the business model and the team. Either we ask him to hire someone, or it's not clear to me how he will make it," further explained Luis.

This last sentence led to a complete change of expression on Sofia's part. She remained silent, and Carolina spoke up.

"We had entrepreneurs with MBAs, but who are not entrepreneurs at all, they didn't get what impact entrepreneurship means. Then, there are others who never went to a business school but who succeed … they may succeed even more than those stellar ex-executives at leading corporations. The training and professional experience is important, of course. But that's not everything."

These bits of the biographies of Gerard and Kilian reflect the existence of two dominant archetypes. As I said in Chap. 4, these archetypes do not fully reflect the whole spectrum of impact entrepreneurs. However, their analytical value lies in that they highlight a critical tension that shaped the decision-making process and that revolved around business skills versus prosocial intention. I almost invariably observed this tension as investors scrutinized the entrepreneurs' track records. More often than not, investors were satisfied with one aspect over the other. Some of them even believed that the two were incompatible. One way to address this issue for the entrepreneurs was to hire someone to take care of the demand they had not addressed, while they would help ensure that the two were aligned. Yet, at this stage of development, hiring was not an option given most entrepreneurs' limited financial resources. It also negatively impacted their credibility.

Patrick, Luc, Sofia, and others tended to solve this puzzle by prioritizing entrepreneurs with a solid business background but demonstrated interest in working out their social impact. A certain level of commitment to the social impact goals was necessary to develop an impact-related mission and, eventually, avoid mission drift at more advanced stages. They had to be convincing in their commitment although their experience and resulting skills centered on the commercial demand. As Matías did with Berta in Chap. 4, investors justified this decision by pointing out that the lack of a sustainable business model among socially oriented entrepreneurs would inevitably jeopardize their future social impact. In other words, it would make their efforts worth nothing, with negative implications for their investment.

## Impact Management

Impact investors also saw entrepreneurs' management decisions (i.e., participatory governance and employees' work conditions) and critical aspects of their personal life (i.e., the location of their office and the entrepreneur's lifestyle) as mirroring the credibility of their impact promise. In the first case, these dilemmas were easy to detect because they were publicly expressed and intensively debated. Personal life aspects, however, were harder to capture because most investors struggled to articulate them in interviews. Only by conducting observation could I see how they used them as a proxy to balance the self-reported prosocial intention with actual behavior.

Let me start with the story of Alvaro and Daniel. The two energetic, smiling entrepreneurs were in their 50s when they entered Seal to develop a community housing project addressing homelessness. The most energetic of the two, Alvaro, looked like a rock star with his hip jeans, black blazer, and moustache, and explained that they aspired to create a residence jointly hosting elderly and formerly unhoused people. The formerly unhoused people would take care of the facility in exchange for free housing during a defined period. At Seal, Alvaro and Daniel wanted to develop their business model and access potential partners. Friendly and motivated, "their project has much to like," said Sofia, who managed the work and inclusion cluster to which they belonged at Seal.

They had made solid progress during the training, established several collaborations, and pitched the project to the investment committee. On this particular morning, Thomas, a young investment analyst, picked up on the fact that the entrepreneurs' offices were located in one of the city's most expensive neighborhoods, to question their understanding of the needs of unhoused people. His skepticism became blatant when he questioned them in a deliberately provocative tone:

"That's great that you want to help homeless people, but how can you sense their real need?"

"Well, we spent some time with them and have talked to some associations," answered Alvaro.

"Talked with some associations?"

"Yes, we have developed the idea with them," added Daniel.

"I wonder why they would want to work in exchange for free housing. I mean, many homeless people would rather stay on the street than sleep at a housing facility. We know that from the surveys, right?"

"Yes," said Alvaro. He and Daniel looked surprised and were trying to decipher what Thomas meant to answer, but he cut them short in their reflection.

"So why would yours agree, specifically if you ask them to work?!"

There was a sudden and deadly silence in the room. Thomas was right in highlighting the lack of concrete evidence to demonstrate their market need. Specifically, the entrepreneurs knew little about how their primary beneficiaries felt about such a project. Thomas was truly irritated by the company's office location. He made this clear once the entrepreneurs had left the room by adopting a very caustic, almost cynical tone:

"These guys live and work in the richest neighborhood of the city. I'm sure they have no idea what life looks like in a poor neighborhood."

"Yes, that's also my feeling," said Lola. She then used the story of another entrepreneur, Jeiko, as a counterexample to emphasize the importance of demonstrating a prior relationship to the social issue at stake.

"Take Jeiko. He knows what he's talking about!" she said forcefully.

"How do they differ?" asked Thomas.

"He has been there. He has spent more than 15 years in the sector, doing street-level work, then working with the administration. He definitely knows what he's talking about because that's what he truly does."

The debates about entrepreneurs' management decisions also often related to the working conditions of their hires. Joel, a young entrepreneur who had successfully developed a geolocation device, explained to one investor who inquired about his employment strategy:

"I would mostly hire people on part-time contracts. I'm thinking about some internships in the first place, and part-time for those with work contracts."

"Why?" asked the investor, surprised.

"This way I could shrink costs as much as possible, right?" answered Joel.

The board of impact investors was shocked by how Joel approached hiring. Joel would later explain this aspect to me, saying he expected investors to support his decision to carefully reduce the costs given the early stage of the project. Andrea, a junior investment analyst, told Joel that he was wrong in his decision:

"Look Joel, the kinds of practices you use to hire people are not for impact entrepreneurs, you know."

"What do you mean?" asked Joel, confused.

"How could you pretend to improve people's quality of life if you underpay your workers? Don't you think this is contradictory?" asked Andrea.

"Hmm."

"Why create an impact enterprise if you contribute to precarious work instead of providing true alternatives?" continued Andrea in the nasty tone she sometimes used to express her exasperation.

Andrea's concerns were well-grounded. While in the process of writing this book in 2023, I met one evening with Marta, a former employee of Gerard. Since I stopped fieldwork in December 2018, the venture had grown tremendously to about 100 employees, out of whom Marta managed one of the client's segments. When we first met, in August 2021, she was at the inception of her contract. At that time, she was very enthusiastic about joining Gerard's venture. Two years later the situation had dramatically changed, and her original enthusiasm had vanished:

"So, how's your work there?"

"Well, I quit in May. It was too much for me."

"What? You seemed to like it there! What do you mean by too much?"

"I really liked it at first. But you remember, I had been working there for almost two years. I like it, I like the company. I like the idea behind it. But since last year it was just too much stress. I couldn't handle it. I was stressed all the time.

"Why? Too much work?"

"Oh yes. At the end of my contract, I was managing multiple customer segments. Alone. And I was making shit money, always at the same wage. More work, but same money."

"You were working long hours?"

"Yes, sometimes over the weekend as well. I just couldn't do everything."

"That sucks."

"Totally. The idea behind the company is great, that's true. And they are also very transparent. But can he [the founder] truly claim to be 'doing good'?"

"What do you mean?"

"When I worked there, people left every other week. It's unbelievable to see how often people left. I had a new colleague who joined last month. She stayed for two weeks, then she was gone! And instead of hiring more people, they give you more work for the same amount of money."

"How much?"

"Almost the minimum wage. No raise. Nothing. I was just too stressed and exhausted, and I quit. And then it took them ages to pay me the compensation."

"Why?"

"They told me my laptop had a scratch on the front. They took it out of my pay. 250 euros for a fucking scratch, when the computer was insured."

It was not unusual to hear entrepreneurs justify the work arrangements offered to their employees by pointing to their lack of financial resources. They also very often emphasized the passion that employees should have for their company and even used it as leverage regarding salaries. Likewise, I found that many entrepreneurs believed their employees should embrace the company's values and commit to the social mission. When explaining the challenge of hiring people while offering low wages, another entrepreneur told me, "We only want people who, we think, would truly love the company."

Gerard had opened new offices in additional cities, but Marta's working conditions hadn't improved. Chief among her frustration, perhaps, was Gerard's "hypocrisy" when he publicly claimed to achieve social goals and improve people's quality of life without disclosing that, at the same time, this came at the cost of employees' working conditions. In fact, in the meeting with Joel, Andrea asked, "How can you claim that you want to change the world when the working conditions you offer to people are miserable?" The entrepreneur nodded in silence, slightly taken aback by such directness.

As I was learning through my fieldwork experiences, another issue raising doubts about the credibility of impact entrepreneurs' promises was their self-estimated salaries. Patrick outlined this issue to me one morning as we were reviewing the business plan of a venture he had taken under his wing:

"I'm helping the entrepreneur to prepare for the investment committee next Friday. I've been working with him for a while, he's nice."

"Why do you like him?"

"He already went through the accelerator once, two years ago. And I also know his confounder. I met her at the fund I worked for."

"I interviewed him the other day," I said.

"Cool, how was it?"

"He was excited by the investment committee."

"I see that, the venture's great. I've invited some business angels from our network as well. He must get his pitch perfect first."

Patrick was checking for consistency between the information provided and the expectations of the board of investors.

At some point, he started staring intensely at his laptop. I could see that he had suddenly become nervous when reviewing the accuracy of the Excel cost and expense sheet, loudly complaining about the founder's salary:

"What's wrong?" I asked.

He didn't answer but continued to thoughtfully look at his computer screen for another minute. Then he turned to me, and explained:

"Look, Guillaume, I told him 15 times that he can't put his salary that high. 70k per year. Do you follow me?"

"No."

"Well, the venture is not operating yet, and he pretends to aim for the good of all. What else can I do!"

"What?"

"The investors will certainly call him a pretentious entrepreneur because of the salary. With good reason."

The behaviors described in these stories diverged from what investors expected from an impact entrepreneur. These divergences negatively shaped their subjective perception of the credibility of entrepreneurs' impact promises. As members of a moral community whose commitment to achieving social impact was a guiding field principle, investors adopted a moralizing attitude toward entrepreneurs when judging ventures' management. Further, they tried to judge the credibility of entrepreneurs' promises based on how the latter envisioned the future of their ventures.

## Impact Prospect

"So, how do you see the future of your venture?" Marc's question to entrepreneurs was almost conventional. Indeed, to appreciate how impact entrepreneurs envisioned their impact, investors probed their impact prospects. During their pitch, entrepreneurs had already presented some information clarifying these next steps, particularly how they would use the funding. Marc's question, however, targeted a broader issue, one that centered on how entrepreneurs would manage impact alongside commercial growth.

Inquiring about impact prospects was meant to ensure that the imaginaries developed by entrepreneurs about the future of their impact aligned with investors' expectations about the investment. Impact investors believed that these prospects would help them identify potential deviations between entrepreneurs' actual plans and their promises. Impact investors, thus, strived to apprehend how entrepreneurs viewed the midterm impact of their venture. And, as David liked to remind the entrepreneurs we listened to at investment committees, their impact was still in the making.

Marc's question hid a deeper concern about how entrepreneurs envisioned their impact, which was visible in the prices of products and services. Patrick, Luc, and others often related lower prices with the opportunity to strengthen the social impact of a venture by making the product accessible to a larger number of customers. Particularly, they were expecting the product to be available for underserved groups. This could be achieved, for instance, by having a low-cost product or by aligning the price according to the revenue of their clients. In other words, investors' understanding of impact was not limited to the benefits of using the product. They also expected entrepreneurs to provide products at lower prices to broaden the scope of the social impact of their project.

One morning at committee, Lucian, an impact investor specializing in health ventures, was particularly virulent about this aspect in his comments to a team of entrepreneurs. Once the founder had finished her pitch, he stared silently at her before taking a deep breath and explaining:

"Great product, important need. But it's still way too expensive. I agree, it's cheaper than competitors. [But] you won't reach many patients who need it badly but cannot pay the price. How will you lower the price?" Lucian looked inquiringly at the other impact investors sitting around the table, who nodded almost imperceptibly. Conscious of Lucian's piercing gaze behind his amiable smile, the founder was intensively thinking about an answer. Lucian reiterated, "How will you lower the price?"

When impact investors found that the initial price aligned with their expectations, they asked entrepreneurs how they would maintain this price over time. Specifically, they would wonder about how the entrepreneur would achieve this goal once the product reached the market. Overall, they always encouraged entrepreneurs to lower the prices as much as possible. Products and services had to be accessible to the broadest scope of people as evidence of their impact, they said.

Capturing how impact entrepreneurs envisioned the future of their venture was also eminently complex because most entrepreneurs did not know what this future would look like. Patrick articulated this point very nicely as the two of us shared a coffee in Seal's kitchen:

"What is very difficult for us is to know exactly how they see themselves in the future."

"Why?" I asked.

"Some of them don't even know, but for many, the future is selling the venture as soon as they have a good offer."

"Isn't what they're expected to do?" I asked again, naively.

"There is nothing wrong with selling their venture, but they should make sure that it won't jeopardize the future social impact. We invest for impact."

Thus, investors repeatedly asked questions such as, "Where do you see yourself in five years?" or "Would you sell the venture as soon as you have a decent offer?"

The case of Rosa reflected the importance of impact prospects for investors' decision-making process. After three months of intensive work at the accelerator, Rosa presented her brand-new impact thesis. Not surprisingly for someone who had just finished the acceleration program, she had to explain her social motivation. And so she began her pitch with a bold tale about her prosocial intention:

"I have always been worried about people's quality of life. That's why I studied biomedicine in the first place. I really wanted to dedicate my life to improving people's health. This has been one of my lifelong goals. In the last few years, I had the opportunity to achieve this goal by developing a new type of early-stage treatment with my colleague at the lab. The treatment we are developing speeds up the process and significantly lowers the probability of further disease development."

She then continued by thinking reflexively about what she had learned during the training at Seal:

"This journey has been incredibly insightful and challenging. I've grown both as a person and as a medical researcher. It has consolidated my goal to make people's lives better. As a researcher, it has been incredibly rewarding to learn about business and to develop new skills for creating my venture and expanding my social impact. This journey has been incredibly challenging, but I'm very happy about my progress and this learning process that will forever change how I approach my work as a medical researcher."

Rosa was quickly coming to an end and was asked about her prospects and what she would like to do:

"I will first try to sell the device to public and private hospitals. I believe this would be fairly easy ... I have a strong network with people at the hospitals because of the research we do at the lab."

"Then what?" asked Sofia. "You will still work there?"

"Then I will wait for an offer from a pharmaceutical firm. I would like to sell the venture within three or four years and move on."

This last sentence led to a complete change of expression on Luc's part as he grappled with what was contradictory to Rosa's opening social impact claim. He raised his hand energetically, jostling the table with his knees as he almost stood up from his chair, astonished. In a sarcastic tone, he was quick in pointing to an inherent contradiction in Rosa's plan:

"So, you told us you want to sell your venture to a pharmaceutical firm as soon as you have a decent proposition. This is your goal, right?"

"Yes," said Rosa, puzzled by his exasperation.

"Then, tell me how you will ensure they [the pharmaceutical firm] will care about your commitment to make an impact."

Luc's question resonated like a death sentence for Rosa because it implicitly threatened the immediate possibility of her receiving funding.

Weighting each of his words, he implicitly suggested that Rosa was "betraying" investors because of such a prospect for the venture. This is, in part, because of the contradiction with her self-reported prosocial intention and social mission, raising a critical problem for achieving impact in a way that aligned with the goals of the fund.

"So how would we know that our investment still has an impact after you leave?" Luc pointed out. "Why would these guys care about impact?"

Luc noted that her plan would inevitably shrink the social impact of the venture. This would have obvious negative implications for investors' expectations because of the explicit deviation between their goals and the actual plans of the entrepreneur. Rosa remained perplexed, and Luc finally broke the icy silence by concluding, "Would pharma care about social impact as much we do? Probably not!"

## The Role of Impact Promises

In a social world where impression management is the rule, it's unsurprising that impact entrepreneurs continuously use discursive strategies to make explicit their promises to achieve social impact. This is perhaps even more the case, I think, in settings like Seal. There, entrepreneurs are encouraged to create impact stories and convey a compelling social impact narrative when being socialized to impact entrepreneurship. It may be less apparent when entrepreneurs have not been previously accelerated or trained by intermediary organizations.

Yet, nowadays, not undertaking such socialization to impact entrepreneurship may be increasingly rare given the growth in popularity of these organizations and the crucial needs of entrepreneurs to access resources. Impact investors, then, do not only care about entrepreneurs sharing impact promises consistent with field standards. More importantly, they strive to evaluate the credibility of these promises during the decision making process. The real difficulty they face lies in distinguishing between what entrepreneurs say they will do and what they will actually do. For this reason, they waver, debate, and decide on the underpinning of their promise.

Accordingly, most of this chapter has been concerned with uncovering how impact investors critically examine entrepreneurs' impact promise. We have seen how they do so by critically moving beyond their self-reported prosocial intention and social mission to scrutinize their impact promise in a way that is both analytical and subjective. My argument is that this evaluation process enables impact investors to collectively construct a belief about the credibility of these promises, facilitating decision-making.

While trying to demystify the evaluation of early-stage impact enterprise, the concept of impact promise helps us to capture one unique aspect of this process, namely the assessment of the social missions and entrepreneurs' commitment to the latter at a very early stage. The concept revolves around the joint evaluation of four specific but interrelated aspects, reflecting an alignment of self-reported prosocial behavior, intention, and actual behavior. It brings to the fore the subjective perceptions of entrepreneurs' appraisals of social impact. Observable characteristics and self-reported prosocial intention, of course, matter for decision-making.[10] Nevertheless, this process is far more multi-faceted, complex, and nuanced.

To begin with, at the earliest stage, impact investors may not stop at these superficial aspects but may expect a specific social impact framing that matches role expectations.[11] However, as we have seen, they do not take entrepreneurs' tales about social impact at face value but scrutinize them by collecting evidence that entrepreneurs care about their social mission. Hence, if investors develop expectations that impact entrepreneurs should match the common definition of their role by displaying prosocial intention and role-congruent characteristics, they are also aware that self-reported prosocial intention and the impact promises may result from impression management strategies.

Just as important, the widespread belief among impact investors that the credibility of the impact promise is vital for entrepreneurs to achieve social goals reflects one crucial way they imbue the novel practice of impact investing with meaning. Everyone would agree that impact investing is an eminently risky endeavor shaped by radical uncertainty. Impact investors' commitment to this endeavor requires entrepreneurs to adhere to similar moral principles to align their goals. In their assessment, they build a belief about the credibility of the promises made by entrepreneurs by scrutinizing the four aspects of their past and present behavior examined in this chapter.

In addition, this journey into the experiences of the impact investors at Seal shows how much they view entrepreneurs as the critical force for

[10] Anglin et al. (2022), Kreutzer (2022), Lee and Huang (2018).

[11] See, for example, Anglin et al. (2022), Lee and Huang (2018), Molecke and Pinkse (2020).

achieving social impact in the challenging and extremely risky context shaping the creation and scaling of an impact enterprise but also, in most cases, its failure. This may sound trivial, but too often the contradictory nature of social and economic demands is brought to the fore to explain failure. By contrast, this chapter showed that impact investors believe that entrepreneurs' commitment to their social mission is a prerequisite for overcoming some of these challenges to achieve social impact. Resultingly, evaluating and developing credible prospects about entrepreneurs' aptitude to fulfill their promises is integral to investors' work.[12]

So, for impact enterprises at their earliest stage, I suggest four enabling dimensions of the entrepreneurial endeavor through which the credibility of these prospects is most likely to emerge. But this does not mean that this task is straightforward. The existence and growth of "opportunistic impact entrepreneurs" complicate this process. These entrepreneurs often enter impact entrepreneurship by creating meaningful opportunities for impact and attempting to convince others of their social goals. At the same time, precisely because of the lack of credibility of their promise, they raise suspicions that they are more inclined to focus on commercial profit. Consequently, impact investors view them as presenting a higher risk of mission drift. As Sofia did in Chap. 4, investors often pejoratively describe entrepreneurs' impact as "doubtful social impact."

Finally, this invitation into the nitty-gritty process of investors' assessment is also an opportunity to provide an alternative take on the role of impact measurement standards. These standards have been a core concern for scholars who noted their focus on activities or outcomes. In other words, indicators and frameworks measure *actual* social impact for ventures at advanced stages of development.[13] So far, so good. But what happens at very early stages when social impact has yet to be realized, as in the present case?

At Seal, early-stage impact investors care more about the promise made by entrepreneurs than their activities and outcomes in the pre-seed and seed stages. The reason is trivial. Indeed, at this stage entrepreneurs have no commercialized product yet, making product and market unavailable. Their unavailability, then, turns impact measurements into an assessment of how proposed activities may produce a social impact. Although impact

[12] See, for example, Huang and Pearce (2015), Mason et al. (2017), Maxwell and Lévesque (2014).

[13] See Maas and Grieco (2017), Molecke and Pinkse (2017, 2020).

indicators only inform about the potential future impact, entrepreneurs' awareness of these indicators and the related methodologies helps investors build credible expectations.

This is why, I think, some impact entrepreneurs may convince finance providers better than others who also show consistent and convincing metrics but whose promises to achieve social impact are judged to be less credible.

## Bibliography


Agrawal, A., & Hockerts, K. (2019). Impact Investing Strategy: Managing Conflicts between Impact Investor and Investee Social Enterprise. *Sustainability, 11*(15), Article 15.

Agrawal, A., & Hockerts, K. (2021). Impact Investing: Review and Research Agenda. *Journal of Small Business & Entrepreneurship, 33*(2), 153–181.

Anglin, A. H., Courtney, C., & Allison, T. H. (2022). Venturing for Others, Subject to Role Expectations? A Role Congruity Theory Approach to Social Venture Crowd Funding. *Entrepreneurship Theory and Practice, 46*(2), 421–448.

Barman, E. (2016). *Caring Capitalism: The Meaning and Measure of Social Value*. Cambridge University Press.

Cardon, M., Wincent, J., Singh, J., & Drnovsek, M. L. (2009). The Nature and Experience of Entrepreneurial Passion. *Academy of Management Review, 34*(3), 511–532.

Casasnovas, G., & Ferraro, F. (2022). Speciation in Nascent Markets: Collective Learning Through Cultural and Material Scaffolding. *Organization Studies, 43*(6), 829–860.

Feeney, L., Haines, G., & Riding, A. L. (1999). Private Investors' Investment Criteria: Insights from Qualitative Data. *Venture Capital, 1*(2), 121–145.

Grimes, M. (2010). Strategic Sensemaking within Funding Relationships: The Effects of Performance Measurement on Organizational Identity in the Social Sector. *Entrepreneurship Theory and Practice, 34*, 763–783.

Hehenberger, L., & Harling, A.-M. (2018). Moving Toward "Impact-Adjusted" Financial Returns: Closing Remarks. *American Journal of Evaluation, 39*(3), 408–412.

Hsu, D., Haynie, M., Simmons, S., & McKelvie, A. (2013). What Matters, Matters Differently: A Conjoint Analysis of the Decision Policies of Angel and Venture Capital Investors: Venture Capital. *Venture Capital, 16*(1), 1–25.

Huang, L. (2018). The Role of Investor Gut Feel in Managing Complexity and Extreme Risk. *Academy of Management Journal, 61*(5), 1821–1847.

Huang, L., & Knight, A. P. (2017). Resources and Relationships in Entrepreneurship: An Exchange Theory of the Development and Effects of the

Entrepreneur-Investor Relationship. *Academy of Management Review, 42*(1), 80–102.
Huang, L., & Pearce, J. L. (2015). Managing the Unknowable: The Effectiveness of Early-stage Investor Gut Feel in Entrepreneurial Investment Decisions. *Administrative Science Quarterly, 60*(4), 634–670.
Kreutzer, K. (2022). On the Discursive Construction of Social Entrepreneurship in Pitch Situations: The Intertextual Reproduction of Business and Social Discourse by Presenters and Their Audience. *Journal of Business Ethics, 179*(4), 1071–1090.
Lee, M., & Huang, L. (2018). Gender Bias, Social Impact Framing, and Evaluation of Entrepreneurial Ventures. *Organization Science, 29*(1), 1–16.
Maas, K., & Grieco, C. (2017). Distinguishing Game Changers from Boastful Charlatans: Which Social Enterprises Measure Their Impact? *Journal of Social Entrepreneurship, 8*(1), 110–128.
Mason, C., Botelho, T., & Zygmunt, J. (2017). Why Business Angels Reject Investment Opportunities: Is it Personal? *International Small Business Journal, 35*(5), 519–534.
Maxwell, A. L., Jeffrey, S. A., & Lévesque, M. (2011). Business Angel Early Stage Decision Making. *Journal of Business Venturing, 26*(2), 212–225.
Maxwell, A. L., & Lévesque, M. (2014). Trustworthiness: A Critical Ingredient for Entrepreneurs Seeking Investors. *Entrepreneurship Theory and Practice, 38*(5), 1057–1080.
Miller, T. L., & Wesley, C. L. (2010). Assessing Mission and Resources for Social Change: An Organizational Identity Perspective on Social Venture Capitalists' Decision Criteria. *Entrepreneurship Theory and Practice, 34*(4), 705–733.
Mitteness, C., Sudek, R., & Cardon, M. S. (2012). Angel Investor Characteristics that Determine Whether Perceived Passion Leads to Higher Evaluations of Funding Potential. *Journal of Business Venturing, 27*(5), 592–606.
Molecke, G., & Pinkse, J. (2017). Accountability for Social Impact: A Bricolage Perspective on Impact Measurement in Social Enterprises. *Journal of Business Venturing, 32*(5), 550–568.
Molecke, G., & Pinkse, J. (2020). Justifying Social Impact as a Form of Impression Management: Legitimacy Judgements of Social Enterprises' Impact Accounts. *British Journal of Management, 31*(2), 387–402.
Nicholls, A. (2009). "We Do Good Things Don't We?": Blended Value Accounting In Social Entrepreneurship. *Accounting, Organizations and Society, 34*, 755–769.
Nicholls, A. (2010). The Legitimacy of Social Entrepreneurship: Reflexive Isomorphism in a Pre–Paradigmatic Field. *Entrepreneurship Theory and Practice, 34*(4), 611–633.

Rawhouser, H., Cummings, M., & Newbert, S. L. (2019). Social Impact Measurement: Current Approaches and Future Directions for Social Entrepreneurship Research. *Entrepreneurship Theory and Practice, 43*(1), 82–115.

Reisman, J., Olazabal, V., & Hoffman, S. (2018). Putting the "Impact" in Impact Investing: The Rising Demand for Data and Evidence of Social Outcomes. *American Journal of Evaluation, 39*(3), 389–395.

Smith, W. K., Gonin, M., & Besharov, M. L. (2013). Managing Social-Business Tensions: A Review and Research Agenda for Social Enterprise. *Business Ethics Quarterly, 23*(3), 407–442.

Thirion, I., Reichert, P., Xhauflair, V., & De Jonck, J. (2022). From Fiduciary Duty to Impact Fidelity: Managerial Compensation in Impact Investing. *Journal of Business Ethics, 179*, 991–1010.

Vandebroek, T., Ferraro, F., Mascena, A., & Liechtenstein, H. (2020). Impact Quantification and Integration in Impact Investing. In R. Mir & A.-L. Fayard (Eds.), *The Routledge Companion to Anthropology and Business* (p. 97). Routledge.

CHAPTER 7

# The Making of Impact Entrepreneurship

In November 2023, six years have passed since our first meeting with Sofia. Seal has relocated to the northern part of the city, to a wealthy neighborhood close to the home of many multinational companies and venture capital funds. As I wait for Sofia to arrive for our lunch meeting, I'm struck by how much the décor of the restaurant has changed. Back in 2017, we used to go for lunch and chat about fieldwork at a casual restaurant close to the office. Today's restaurant, however, has an elegant ambiance with carefully designed décor, soft lighting, and luxurious furnishings. While reading my notes summarizing the information needed to update some sections of the book, I cannot but think of such a change as a signal of significant transformations.

"We have become two distinct organizations," starts Sofia to explain that they now operate the accelerator and the fund as distinct entities. "We run the acceleration program from the foundation. In January, it will be operated by a leading organization of the impact economy." Since 2013, the staff has accelerated 220 start-ups belonging to various industry clusters, she says, and created a new impact methodology. They have developed, structured, and strengthened their products to their corporate partners, and introduced more than 30 corporations to some of the world's social impact tenets. "And then we have the venture capital firm; we closed our first fund of 4.5 million in 2020. We already had three successful exits!"



G. Dumont, *Impact Work*,
https://doi.org/10.1007/978-3-031-64661-4_7

she adds, excited. "We launched the second fund in 2020 with 55 million. Not too bad, right?! And we're planning our third fund in 2025."

Building on this ethnographic journey into the day-to-day running of Seal, the book's core thesis is that impact emerges iteratively from a process of social engagement and negotiation among entrepreneurs, impact investors, corporate executives, mentors, and the accelerator's team members as they collaborate in the mundane processes of its production, what I name "impact work." Indeed, most of this book has been concerned with the practices and interactions among people holding different positions in the social world of impact entrepreneurship. At Seal, these people are socially engaged in the production of impact work. As such, exploring their daily practices and interactions illuminates many of the challenges faced by impact entrepreneurs and their collaborators. This book is also about an organization's attempts to create and promote a novel culture. This culture opens up a space where combining social and environmental impact with economic profit is desirable and, perhaps more importantly, possible.

Therefore, beyond the case of Seal, the book offers some insights into the role played by intermediary organizations in the development of novel organizational cultures. Through the different chapters, I have shown how the work performed at Seal leads to the production or appropriation of specific values, behaviors, and conventions that come together to constitute impact entrepreneurship. I have also shown how this work of intermediation contributes to creating impact entrepreneurs and impact aficionados who learn about the tenets of this new culture as well as negotiate them. Hence, in its main part, the book is about how an intermediary organization creates and shares bits of culture within and beyond its boundaries as well as about the dilemmas, hesitation, joy, and frustration of those engaged in this process. Only the empirical examination of how people produce impact work can enable us to critically question important assumptions about impact entrepreneurship and, more broadly, the fast-growing impact economy.

In other words, this book is about a culture in the making. A big part of this book has been focused on unearthing the activities through which people collaborate to ideate values, behaviors, and conventions of the culture of impact entrepreneurship. What is particularly interesting, and perhaps unique, is the diversity in goals, training, and personal and professional experience among those involved. Of course, the development of impact entrepreneurship finds inspiration in other organizational phenomena, such as commercial entrepreneurship, social entrepreneurship, and philanthropy. However, at the local level, different professional backgrounds tend to emphasize different aspects and values: an engineer the technical aspect of the product, a social worker the implications for people, a cardiologist the effects on the human body. In doing so, they borrow and adapt aspects that become foundational for developing their venture. Through their social engagement in impact work, they contribute, each in their own way, to defining what is deemed culturally acceptable in this social world.

What is perhaps the main characteristic of this phenomenon, and the feature that makes the concept of impact entrepreneurship of empirical and analytical value, is not only its location at the crossroads of market and non-market logics. It is, rather, the degree to which these logics are intertwined. Social entrepreneurship combines these logics but in ways that show important variations among entrepreneurs and social enterprises. Broadly speaking, a social enterprise must be economically *sustainable* while addressing a social mission, but the priority that people may give to one or another dimension varies. An impact enterprise, however, must be economically *profitable* in achieving its mission. The difference is not merely lexical. Impact or social enterprises can attract different types of collaborators and be launched by different types of entrepreneurs. Additionally, because impact enterprises are, by definition, profitable, the notion of social impact can hardly be apprehended without a reference to its profitability. Profitability, I believe, strongly contributes to making these enterprises attractive to a broader audience, reaching beyond the circle of impact aficionados. Further, it ultimately supports the development of impact entrepreneurship in a way that is probably more sustainable because it is more profitable than social entrepreneurship.

Next, this book has much to do with how people become socialized to this culture in the making. Behind popular narratives of people who are "born impact entrepreneurs," at stake here is a complex socialization process by which they learn the ropes of impact entrepreneurship. By signing up for Seal, some entrepreneurs undertake a genuinely transformative process through which they learn a novel cultural perspective and become impact entrepreneurs. Central to this transformation are numerous socialization activities, mechanisms, and actors, by which entrepreneurs gain the social knowledge and skills necessary to make sense of this culture and behave adequately. For instance, Seal shapes entrepreneurs' perceptions of desirable and undesirable behaviors, and the social impact and the investment committees certify the outputs of this process and the newly gained status. Whereby that people are not impact entrepreneurs *per se* may seem trivial, this book reveals they are carefully taught how to behave and think about impact entrepreneurship.

But this book also reveals that being socialized to impact entrepreneurship is not an uncomplicated look, listen, and learn process. The book advances some explanations for deviation. For instance, some entrepreneurs fail, often because their values and behaviors contrast with those expected from impact entrepreneurs. They may be urged to make severe adjustments to their behavior but reject these adjustments to remain in the traditional entrepreneurial field and its focus on profit-making. As they learn about impact entrepreneurship, they may be disappointed as they discover what it entails. They may find themselves puzzled and disconcerted by the fuzzy nature of many of its core concepts and principles. And, because they collaborate on almost every aspect of their entrepreneurial work with external stakeholders, entrepreneurs may be discouraged by these stakeholders from embracing impact entrepreneurship to, rather, develop a commercial venture. Exploring the tensions experienced by those involved in this socialization process is critical in order to understand the production of impact.

The idea that intermediary organizations play a critical role in constructing cultural referents such as those described in this book is not new. Intermediary organizations are central forces in creating and diffusing new cultural phenomena, and impact entrepreneurship is no exception. This book, however, offers a rare, highly detailed account of how this process unfolds by showing Seal's contribution to defining what counts as impact entrepreneurship versus what should be relegated to the field of traditional entrepreneurship, philanthropy, and the like. The book provides an inside look into how people working for these intermediary organizations define and share specific values, desirable behaviors, and interactional conventions. Of course, these values, behaviors, and conventions do not emerge from scratch, and I have shown how they are local appropriations of broader, general standards, picked up and adapted from other organizations and thought leaders across fields. Zooming into this melting pot tells us a lot about how people appropriate and negotiate existing knowledge about impact in ways that are meaningful locally. After all, a culture is, in part, a web of interpretations made meaningful by people.

In this book, I argue that social impact is produced by those engaged in networks of collaboration with different forms of social engagement. Most social impact research locates its source in individuals, the decision to achieve social impact through venture creation being the result of a personality trait and an eminently individual endeavor. Likewise, social impact becomes an inner quality of the venture. This book, however, portrays the production of impact in a very different light. First, it teaches us that impact is not inherent to people and organizations but socially constructed by people in the form of organizations. My aim, of course, has not been to eschew the role of entrepreneurs' traits completely. Certainly, some entrepreneurs may be more caring, generous, and altruistic than others. These others, however, can also develop an appetite for social impact. Alternatively, they may not develop this desire but aim to achieve social impact goals because it has become a commercial advantage with higher reputational gain. In short, people pursue impact for multiple reasons, which are worth exploring because they help explain the current manifestations of the phenomenon.

Additionally, but no less important, this book calls attention to the fundamentally collective nature of impact work. At the outset, everyone seems to agree on what social impact entails and the need to pursue it. Yet, this book reveals how much it is a negotiation process by uncovering how people collaborate in the performance of impact work. The people involved in these networks have different interests and goals, shaping their involvement and making their participation meaningful. The meaning they imbue in impact varies accordingly. Thus, theorizing about impact calls for acknowledging diversity in meanings and the role of the latter in enabling collaboration and crafting higher-level standards. This requires accounting for the social interactions in which people define and produce impact. Resultingly, it may be more insightful to uncover the polysemic nature of impact than to agree on a universal definition. Indeed, a universal definition would inevitably efface local meanings and, thus, would fail to explain the rationale guiding people's practices and interactions locally.

This is not to say, of course, that any investigation into the production of impact must be limited to exploring and theorizing local practices in a vacuum. Broader conventional referents undeniably inform these local practices but also unfold across different contexts with their similarities and particularities. Hence, it is to say that these local practices would enable comparing how people make sense of impact in different contexts. This, in turn, will allow us to trace similarities and divergences among them and explain the global dynamics underpinning the production of impact in a truly anthropological fashion. One clear ambition of this book, therefore, has been to offer an account of how impact work is produced in the case of Seal, which would enable comparison on a larger scale.

Finally, a lot of this book is about the promises people make about achieving specific imaginaries of the future. These imaginaries paint impact in a unique way and serve different functions for the development of impact entrepreneurship. First, impact imaginaries help those involved in the ideation, creation, and development of impact enterprises to define how the future of their venture—and thus its social and economic performance—will look. Impact imaginaries, therefore, are meant for impact entrepreneurs to organize and act. In elaborating these imaginaries, entrepreneurs create meaningful opportunities for a venture and spend much time and effort in creating social impact accounts and, more broadly, impact stories. In this task, they create images and scenes by evoking metaphors of one imagined future. Notably, the book shows that the fact that some of these stories are made from scratch is not fundamentally an issue if they align with the higher moral conventions governing impact entrepreneurship.

How entrepreneurs revise these stories to maintain or regain legitimacy raises expectations focused on understanding the venture characteristics and the future benefits for stakeholders. In impact entrepreneurship, most present activities are geared toward the future. Impact work, indeed, is fundamentally a future-oriented activity. Hence, sharing credible promises enables the creation of future imaginaries and is necessary to facilitate decision-making and, more broadly, collective action. This book also reveals the coexistence of different imaginaries of the future and the tensions they carry. First, these imaginaries may diverge because what makes the pursuit of impact meaningful for different people varies, resulting in the development of different future imaginaries. Second, these imaginaries may lack credibility. However, credibility is pivotal in enabling decision-making in a social world geared toward the future.[1] It is crucial to rethink past and present concerns in plausible, coherent, and acceptable ways for those involved. Therefore, the creation of credible impact imaginaries becomes one of the leading proxies through which people collaborate in and around the performance of impact work.

## Bibliography

Beckert, J. (2016). *Imagined Futures*. Harvard University Press.

[1] The work of Jens Beckert on the role of credibility in the creation of fictional expectations in economic action is particularly illustrative of this aspect. See, for instance, Beckert (2016).

# Appendix: Fieldwork at a Social Impact Accelerator

Starting a new fieldwork is always exhilarating. For several weeks over the course of 2017, I tried unsuccessfully to secure a field site for this study. I reached out and met with several accelerators' operating directors who concurred on the interesting nature of the research and sounded enthusiastic about it. Yet, having someone around documenting the day-to-day running of their organization was not an option. I understood. Who would like to have a perfect stranger documenting mentoring meetings with entrepreneurs or recording investment committees?

Luckily for me, Sofia approached this question differently. During a demo day at Seal in February 2017, I chased her through the corridor of the building. There, I pitched my project in 10 seconds and asked for a meeting. She agreed. A few weeks later, I found myself presenting my project at Seal's building. I had carefully ironed a shirt the night before and prepared an executive presentation of the project, which she found interesting. I spent a lot of time explaining that all this would be confidential and making clear that I wouldn't be bothering anyone. She thought it was fine but had to tell Jorge and Lola about it. The positive response came a few weeks later, with happiness and relief.

My first "official" day in the field was mingled with a certain apprehension. Sofia had asked me to come to the office on a Tuesday morning for her to introduce me to the staff. It was an ideal time of the year, she said.



G. Dumont, *Impact Work*,
https://doi.org/10.1007/978-3-031-64661-4

A new edition of the program was about to start, and I could begin my fieldwork by attending the upcoming boot camp starting next week. This way, I could closely follow the acceleration program from start to finish. "You will be able to see yourself how Seal transforms entrepreneurs," she said proudly and convincingly. "And it would be interesting for us to trace the evolution of the ventures," she added. As I would soon realize, Sofia, Lola, and Jorge knew they had an impact on entrepreneurs, but they seemed not to know exactly how. "You could help us on that," she noted. I nodded in silence, trying to figure how to.

But things turned out differently. On this day, I arrived earlier to have a coffee in front of the building and calm down. Still, I could feel the stress as I walked through the main hall of the building. Typically, you do not know anyone in the field setting. You have no clue about which role to adopt for others to understand your presence. What is clear, however, is that field participants will see you as an alien during these days, to say the least. Anticipating the need to motivate and explain my presence to different interlocutors, the day before, I had prepared a short introduction to myself and the research to be delivered to anyone I would meet. Hopefully, it would grow my confidence, I thought. I took the lift to the first floor, trying to convince myself I would do alright.

Seal's main office was hidden at the far right of the first floor. Turning left after the reception desk, you had to traverse the entire building by crossing the main room where the pitch sessions took place and navigating between meeting rooms with glass walls. This was intimidating because, depending on your arrival time, you could slightly disturb the action and have everyone staring at you. There was, then, a large terrace. The terrace was next to the main room, brightening up the space with natural light and creating a modern design. The glass walls allowed latecomers to see whose staff members were there having meetings and with whom. Yet, they could hardly avoid hiding their late arrival. Once at the right wing of this floor, the corridor ended with a large wooden door that always remained open except during closing hours.

It was 10 a.m. when I timidly knocked on this door to signal my presence. Looking inside, I explained that I had a meeting with Sofia. "Who are you?" It was Lola who then came through the door. Looking at me inquiringly, she added, "Sofia won't come today." I stood there, helpless. I felt totally lost and darkly pessimistic about the future of my fieldwork. She then asked about the purpose of our meeting. "Well, we agreed that I could conduct research here. She asked me to come this morning to meet with the staff and start," I said. Lola raised a quizzical eyebrow. "I haven't heard anything about this." After a few seconds that felt like an eternity, she started again, "We're about to have our weekly acceleration meeting with the program managers. Join us if you want."

## Questions, Setting, and Approach

"The meeting will be in this room," said Lola while showing me where to go. I turned back to look at the room, and through the glass wall, I could see Santiago, Nina, and Jessica sitting around the table and staring at me, intrigued. I believed they had witnessed my conversation with Lola, which made me even more uneasy. I mustered courage and pushed the door. I introduced myself as an anthropologist doing a research project. I sat next to Santiago, who smiled reassuringly while making some free space at the table for me to open my laptop. "So, you're an anthropologist, that's cool. What will you study here? What is your research question?" he asked, enthusiastic. I explained that I was interested in looking at how different groups of people contribute to new venture creation. I also explained that entrepreneurial stories were often promoted as individual stories, although they couldn't exist without the help of many people. So, I hoped to be able to look beyond the curtain of this popular view to more precisely trace out the role of these people.

I was not being broad on purpose. In fact, I could not be more precise because the analytical focus of my research was mainly unknown to me. As I explained to Sofia, first, and to Santiago, second, my ambition was to study the collective dimension of entrepreneurship. In typical ethnographic fashion, I did not start with a specific research question, a clear set of objectives and sub-objectives, or a hypothesis. This would allow me enough freedom to raise research questions alongside fieldwork development, I explained to Santiago. These questions would emerge iteratively as I came to better understand the field dynamics and people. I also explained that the experience gained alongside fieldwork development would naturally raise questions. Hence, they would be more likely to be relevant for people in the field.

Indeed, fieldwork is as much about the joys as the challenges of navigating organizational life. It is rather conventional for the people we conduct fieldwork with to dedicate a great deal of time during everyday interactions to sharing the difficulties inherent to the pursuit of their everyday work and life. But my task was not only to document and reproduce these in a mere descriptive fashion. Rather, it was to provide a different take on these questions enabled by my positioning as an ethnographer. I would spend a lot of time at Seal, but still belonged to a research institution whose goals differed from those of an accelerator.

Nina and Jessica looked skeptical. Santiago, however, seemed satisfied by my description of the project. "I see," he said before adding proudly, "Well, you're in the right place. This is very much what we do here at Seal. We connect entrepreneurs with people and help them to develop their venture." This was precisely why I believed that business accelerators provided a valuable setting for this research, I answered. Indeed, studying new venture creation ethnographically is particularly challenging. At the very early stage, entrepreneurs typically lack formal offices in which an ethnographer could conduct the substantial real-time observations at the heart of data collection.[1] Entrepreneurs often work for free for a long time until their businesses eventually take off, and they hold multiple jobs.[2] This precarious situation makes them hardly available to the ethnographer. The very nature of entrepreneurial work also makes it challenging to observe, given that much of it takes place behind a screen or in meeting rooms. Hence, being able to provide a behind-the-scenes look into "entrepreneurial action" requires either accessing in depth a single venture over a long time and accepting the high risk that this venture may eventually fail, or identifying a research setting that gathers multiple entrepreneurial teams.

Approaching this question with an interest in the collective dimension of entrepreneurship requires identifying a location where entrepreneurs interact with collaborators. Business accelerators provide just such a unique setting to ethnographers.[3] Created circa 2007 in the US, their explicit goal is to foster new venture creation and growth by delivering high-intensity training activities for entrepreneurial projects at the earliest stages of development. Toward this goal, accelerators gather in a single

[1] I find Elizabeth Briody and Alex Stewart (2019) to be overly critical about the possibility of using ethnography to study start-ups). They suggest that participation observation is useless in this context and should be replaced by other methods, such as interviews. As demonstrated in this book, however, if the challenges they highlighted are real for ethnographers, they can also be avoided by a careful choice of the setting, such as offered by accelerators.

[2] See, for instance, Carr et al. (2022), Folta et al. (2009), Lévesque and Stephan (2020).

[3] Elsewhere I develop this point in more detail by examining how this research setting has the potential to enable ethnographers to overcome several aspects of existing data and theorization of the venture creation process. See Dumont (2024).

space multiple entrepreneurs and ventures during a limited time. They hold functions previously held individually by different intermediaries, for instance, funding, information, knowledge, and market. These functions unfold through various activities during the program, including workshops, seminars, webinars, and individual mentoring. Actors of entrepreneurial ecosystems, including investors, policymakers, serial entrepreneurs, industrial leaders, and corporate executives, act as mentors.

In other words, a business accelerator is like a village. And as Clifford Geertz famously said, "Anthropologists do not study villages, they study in villages."[4] In other words, a business accelerator provides a setting to study different things, and these things connect to themes of broader interest. These themes, then, are explored by others in contexts different than the one of the primary fieldwork. Hence, gaining access to the backstage of entrepreneurial work by stepping into a business accelerator offers several practical advantages for ethnographers and the opportunity to explain broader patterns of practices and interactions among people.

"You're aware that we focus on social impact start-ups, right? What we do is different than what most business accelerators do!" I nodded in silence to Nina. In fact, I had not considered this focus when searching for business accelerators and trying to secure access. I was more concerned with identifying an accelerator providing physical training and gathering instead of a remote program. In addition, I was looking for a program with enough deal flow of ventures to collect data about multiple entrepreneurs simultaneously and trace differences in how the training shaped venture development. In other terms, that I ended up doing an ethnography of a social impact accelerator instead of a traditional business accelerator was accidental.

"Ethnography. What's that?" asked Jessica, one of the program managers. I sat thoughtfully for a few seconds, wondering how to summarize what ethnography entails. Nina did half of the job for me. She did consultancy work and used qualitative methods. "Well, it's doing fieldwork and being with people, observing them to explain what they do, right Guillaume?" I smiled, then answered, "Yes, we spend time with people in the field to document what they do. With this project, the ambition is to provide a firsthand account of what it feels like to work as an

[4] In other words, the locus of the study is not the focus of the study, and anthropologists study patterns in a specific location that others have being studying elsewhere. See Geertz (1973).

entrepreneur." I added, "As ethnographers, we're also interested in the meanings people imbue in their work." That talking about meaning was a bit obscure at that point. Acknowledging Santiago's intrigued face, I clarified, "We believe that this requires being with people instead of producing distant explanations based on a quantitative data basis." Santiago seemed pleased with this last sentence, particularly the fact that the ethnographer spends time observing people *in situ*. Here, I brought in Malinowski's seminal study in the Trobriand Islands[5] and the need for armchair anthropologists to get out of their office and share time with the people they write about to understand them in detail.

To my delight, Nina was very supportive of this approach. She added, "It's very important to explain how things work; it's not all about numbers. But it's also exhausting, right? Are you planning to stay with us for a while?" I did but had little idea of exactly how long. I said that it would depend on Sofia. Time was essential, I said, to build trustable relationships with people and, somehow, to become a member of the group. By saying that, I carefully explained that I had no pretense of becoming a full member but that only by long-term presence can one develop trustworthy bonds with people who, in return, set expectations about one's presence.

Jessica looked puzzled about the importance of developing relationships for data collection. I explained that these bonds enable ethnographers to gradually access the intimate bits of people's experiences and collect fine-grained and reliable data by taking field notes, conducting formal and informal interviews, and gathering secondary data.[6] To exemplify my point, I asked Santiago if he believed that he had the same relationship with Nina and Jessica today as on his first day at Seal. "No," he said, laughing. "It's a bit trivial, but you know each other better because you have been through similar experiences here at Seal, right? So the nature of your relationship has changed; you don't talk about the same things, and so forth." We all laughed.

## Participating and Observing

Participant observation is the hallmark of ethnographic research. It requires the ethnographer to become involved in the activities at the field site to vividly experience what work and life mean for the people under

[5] Malinowski (1922).

[6] Boellstorff et al. (2012), Hammersley and Atkinson (2007).

study. The extent to which ethnographers can participate in day-to-day activities ranges on a wide spectrum, but what is clear is that participant observation requires direct or indirect involvement in the scene.[7] This is fundamental, as we discussed with Santiago, for forging bonds within this setting, and the glorification of the view promoting researchers as flies on the wall, passively observing and documenting what is happening, vanishes. Who would tolerate the presence of a stranger remotely taking notes, hidden and silent in an obscure corner of a meeting room?

While this may seem trivial, there have long been concerns among organizational ethnographers about sharing bits of their presence with readers for fear that they would see this as contaminating the findings.[8] However, trying to be a fly on the wall would undoubtedly raise several pressing questions among the participants and arguably be experienced and depicted as intrusive. Further, any social group requires its members to participate in the group's interactions in one way or another. This, and other reasons, makes participation a natural and essential way to integrate the group always when it follows its inner dynamics.

"You can leave your stuff here and use this desk as long as you're with us," said Sofia a few days later when she finally showed up at the office. I found this reassuring. She legitimized my presence and provided me with a physical space from which I could progressively build a social role. I started meeting with each staff member personally to learn about themselves, their job, and their view on the entrepreneurs. In my second week, I attended the boot camp. This event was decisive for finding ways to actively participate in the staff activities. I started with preparing the room in the morning and cleaning up the space at the end of the day with the staff. A few weeks later, I was asked to design and teach a seminar on market research. Intimidated and excited about this opportunity, I prepared and delivered several modules on that topic. My involvement in this activity proved essential to building bonds Santiago, Nina and others, as I needed their help to prepare and teach the session. It was also a great way to connect with entrepreneurs and develop long-term relationships. For

[7] I develop this point in more detail in a methodological piece about immersion in organizational ethnography. See Dumont (2023a).

[8] While this aspect has been discussed at length in anthropology since the late 1970s, it has been taken up only recently by a few management scholars engaged in ethnographic research. I think particularly of the work of Michel Anteby (2013) at Harvard Business School that, because it was autoethnographic, called for such clarification. See also Langley and Klag (2019).

some, we continued working together on their market research after the training. After one year of fieldwork, I designed and ran a workshop for corporate partners to help them learn about early-stage entrepreneurship and the challenges entrepreneurs may face.

I tried my best to make myself useful by doing these and other activities because I was uneasy just sitting on a chair, silently listening and taking notes. But, more importantly, in doing so, I was growing expectations among the staff about my presence and showing that I could commit to the organization, albeit in a different way. This, I believed, was important because the cofounders asked it of all staff members. Further, it helped develop friendly relationships with some of them, which have continued until today, and also led to my being increasingly invited to staff activities such as the biannual team retreat taking place out of town.

Additionally, these activities provided opportunities for observing and documenting interactions and practices among different groups of people. For instance, I attended meetings between entrepreneurs and mentors, I participated in the selection committees during which corporate partners evaluated who would join the cohort, and I sat on the investment committees where entrepreneurs pitched their venture in the hopes of receiving funding. During these activities, I documented the interactions and introduced my research to these people relatively non-obtrusively. I took these encounters as an opportunity to follow up with interview requests once participants knew me.

By contrast with ethnographers who are already familiar with the research setting,[9] I came to impact entrepreneurship by chance, and my initial perspective was one of a total outsider, as revealed in the introduction of the book. Vernacular and highly popular terms such as "MVP," the "lean start-up methodology," or "business angel" sounded truly exotic to me. I had no initial interest in technological start-ups and innovation and, to be truly sincere, did not believe that any type of business could have an impact other than profit generation for a limited few.

I was not alone in this new endeavor. I quickly learned through my fieldwork experiences that some of the entrepreneurs were as much a novice as I was. Like them, I had to learn the ropes of impact entrepreneurship. Initially, I turned to the literature on the topic. On the advice of my

[9] Some ethnographers do start fieldwork with a long experience of the setting and its people as well as a high level of knowledge about the phenomenon. See, for instance, Dumont (2018), Mears (2011), Stephens (2020).

colleagues, I read some classic books for practitioners and textbooks to learn about the main concepts in the field. These readings were undoubtedly instructive, specifically for understanding the conversations I was hearing, and I learned the most about the practicalities of these concepts by attending the educational modules for entrepreneurs.

As I gradually developed a social role with staff members at Seal, I also spent time alongside four cohorts of a dozen entrepreneurs each. The boot camps offered a unique opportunity to meet the members of each cohort. Based on the relationships I built during these events, I then asked the entrepreneurs if I could attend their meetings with mentors and their visits to Seal's office. On some occasions, we communicated remotely about the work in progress. I visited their offices and working locations. I shadowed them at events where they pitched their ventures, joined their meetings with program managers, and spent time talking about their ventures.

Building a social role, however, is not a smooth process. In many instances, given my novice status, I was riddled with doubts about my aptitude for the job. Often, I felt illegitimate because of my limited entrepreneurial knowledge but also because I was not subjected to the same constraints as staff members, nor living the experience of the entrepreneurs. If my very presence in the field was initially made legitimate by Sofia's assessment of my research, I had to gain the trust of the staff from the bottom up. And, while Santiago raised both eyebrows to indicate a certain admiration knowing that I would dedicate my time to document what was happening at Seal, Jessica was more skeptical. "So you will be observing us, right?" she asked, clearly not enthusiastic about the idea.

A few weeks later, Sofia asked me to present my project to the staff during lunch. There, I spent much time explaining that I wouldn't study their work per se; rather, I was interested in analyzing how ventures develop during the program. The transformation undertaken was, of course, partly because of their work, but I was careful to put the focus on the ventures. That day, Sofia clarified this aspect to the staff much better than I: "You will study the entrepreneurs and help us understand why they evolve in one way or another, right Guillaume?" I nodded, smiling reassuringly.

I compiled most of the information in a field diary, constituting the core of the empirical material under analysis. Because superficial fieldnotes mean superficial data, the analytical opportunities they offer lie in the fine-grained nature of the descriptions of events, peoples, interactions, and practices. During fieldwork, I was lucky to be able to take many of my notes during the day, often in real time. This means that I reported dialogues accurately, often word for word. What made notetaking at Seal relatively unobtrusive was its conventional nature. During meetings, most participants were taking notes. In fact, Seal offered collaborators a notebook and a pen, and laptops were the most common working tool. I took notes every chance I could.

On some occasions, however, I purposely avoided notetaking in front of others. This was particularly the case when sensitive topics were discussed, when participants entered heated debates, or when I believed that someone was uneasy with the situation. In fact, on these occasions, no one was taking notes. Not only the sound of tapping on the keyboard would have been disruptive, but I also wanted the participants not to feel that their words and interactions were being recorded. When this happened, I typically took notes later during the day, sometimes by using an empty room at Seal's main office and, most of the time, at home.

A critical question for any notetaking activity is what to document. Given my ignorance about this type of organization and the activities in this setting, I started by taking notes about pretty much everything happening around me. At the beginning of fieldwork, one can rarely distinguish between what is essential and what is not. Attempting to document most aspects of the day-to-day running of the organization is how such understanding gradually develops and, with it, more focused notetaking.

My notes, therefore, gathered on descriptions and interpretations of what was happening and reflected my thoughts and feelings about what I was witnessing. For instance, during investment committees, I took descriptive notes on the content of the entrepreneurs' pitch, investors' questions, entrepreneurs' answers, individual evaluations of the entrepreneurs and ventures after the pitch, and reflective notes capturing my general view of the process. When available, I also consulted formal documents provided by the entrepreneurs before the pitch to complement my notes.

## Interviewing

During fieldwork, I recorded 68 semi-structured interviews. I found interviewing particularly useful for capturing individual experiences and representations in a context where much of the work observable to me was either taking place in a collective setting or alone in front of a screen, which Dominic Boyer has named "screenwork."[10] Among the different types of interviews available to me, I chose semi-structured interviews because they involve designing and using a guide covering several themes of interest, but are also flexible enough to work around these themes, identify aspects that I had not previously thought about, and develop these aspects further in real-time.

Scheduling interviewing, however, was particularly challenging. Most research participants had hectic schedules, particularly the corporate partners and the mentors, the latter volunteering their time for free at Seal. Many were usually happy to talk to me. Once the interview started, we typically spent between 60 and 90 minutes together. These interviews allowed for building relationships by meeting people in a different context. In fact, I insisted on visiting corporate partners at their offices or meeting with entrepreneurs at their favorite café. This was not only for their convenience; this way, it was easier for them to talk about their experience at Seal.

Participant observation helps make the best out of interviewing because it allows the ethnographer to conduct contextualized interviews. I had previously met most interviewees and gathered information about them through participant observation. This information fed the design of interview guides to maximize the depth of my data. It was also extremely useful to have shared memories and to use the events we attended together to exemplify specific points. Because I interviewed people gravitating around Seal but holding different roles, my guides shared key themes. Nevertheless, I often adapted the open-ended questions to the interviewee. I followed an iterative framework through which I improved them based on previously gathered data. This cyclical procedure increased reliability by identifying new themes and orienting upcoming data collection.

I began by interviewing Seal's staff members. As I mentioned, at the beginning of fieldwork, I tried to meet each of them individually with the ambition to learn about their role and initiate a relationship. I prioritized informal interviews because of my shifting role—from close colleague to interviewer back to colleague. During the first four months of the fieldwork, I conducted most of these interviews—namely long conversations in an intimate space based on a flexible guide I had prepared in advance. I found this procedure very useful for better understanding the organization, its explicit and implicit goals, the work tasks and roles of each

[10] Boyer (2013).

member, and their views on the challenges involved in their work. I could also easily ask additional questions in the following weeks to clarify some aspects. Later, during fieldwork, I also conducted seven recorded interviews with Jorge, Lola, Sofia, and some of the program managers. These interviews focused on the creation and growth of the Seal, the industrial partners, and the program's operational and strategic aspects.

I interviewed 14 entrepreneurs, centering my questions on their backgrounds, motivations, ideas, experiences at Seal, main challenges, and milestones. I captured how they learned new skills, implemented changes in their ventures, struggled, pivoted, secured funding, launched their MVP, and, importantly, gradually adopted the role of an impact entrepreneur by understanding its dual demands. For those willing to repeat, I interviewed them twice (middle and end of the program), asking about their progress and the benefits of participating. I asked them to draw a map of their network, identifying who was in their network and when they had spoken to them or received resources. While the number of entrepreneurs interviewed is obviously too low for an interview study, here, participant observation already provided rich information about their views during the informal moments we spent together.

Seven months into fieldwork, I began interviewing representatives of the corporate partners for a total of 15 interviews, including almost all the paying partners of Seal. Although I was not fundamentally interested in their role in the initial fieldwork stage, I gradually recognized their essential contribution to the program while shadowing entrepreneurs and attending the selection committee. These interviews were beneficial for gathering insights about their challenges in navigating their partnerships with Seal. They were also helpful in developing a critical view of the entrepreneurs and the acceleration activities. Of course, the representatives viewed me as primarily affiliated with Seal. Still, I found that many were eager to talk to me and open to sharing their views and criticism about the organization when I visited their offices.

Finally, by the middle of fieldwork, I started interviewing mentors, including serial entrepreneurs, policymakers, executives, business angels, investment analysts, industry experts, and members of the advisory board of the SIA. I waited to interview mentors once I better understood Seal and, specifically, the nature of the entrepreneurial work. The interviews focused on how they experienced their relationship with entrepreneurs, and I wanted to document mentoring meetings before starting the interviews. As for other respondents, I approached mentors based on earlier interactions during the program when I attended mentoring meetings or contacted them directly. When necessary, I was helped by Sofia and Lola, but also by Santiago and Nina, who facilitated contact information at my request and sometimes introduced me directly to mentors during events. I interviewed a total of 27 mentors.

## Analyzing

The analysis is a black box. Opening this black box requires several digressions from the dominant understanding of analysis as a task disconnected from data collection, highly procedural, and free of the researcher's interpretation. It forces us to acknowledge that this process is inherently iterative and inextricably connected, to data collection. More often than not, fieldwork starts without a clear research question, and it is only through the constant process of moving back and forth between our initial idea, current data, and emerging insights that relevant patterns and themes emerge because they are believed to be surprising or puzzling. These are then revisited repeatedly in light of the events, interactions, and practices documented in the field. These iterations and the resulting insights feed into data collection by orienting participant observation and interviews. Indeed, one key strength of ethnography is that these insights gradually enable the narrowing of data collection as ethnographers consolidate their ethnographic understandings.

In other words, nothing is more necessary for comprehending what analysis entails than acknowledging the perpetual interplay between data and insights. As best demonstrated by the case of the impact investors discussed in Chap. 6, insights are constantly revised by triangulating them and moving beyond the curtain of people's discourses *or* actions. Alongside fieldwork progression, I became aware of the importance for impact entrepreneurs to create compelling social impact accounts to convince others of their social impact intentions. I had been in the field for about one year but had not anticipated this aspect, nor were investors openly talking about it initially. However, I documented their doubts about the credibility of the accounts offered by entrepreneurs. Credibility was important for impact investors, but they could not explain what made a credible account. As I participated in investment committees, I further investigated this question by centering my sights on identifying the implicit evaluation standards they use to judge entrepreneurs' accounts. I also asked investors about these standards, their importance, and their affordances on some occasions and revisited them as I was still collecting data.

Opening the black box of the analysis process requires acknowledging its collective dimension. The analysis is typically depicted as the researcher analyzing a database alone before presenting the results of the analysis to others who would judge their robustness. In fact, critical to the analytical work is sharing emerging insights with research participants and colleagues alongside fieldwork progression. The importance of sharing these insights while in the field is clear. Indeed, the construction of a social role through participant observation should ideally lead to deep embeddedness of the researcher into the field dynamics and the construction of solid and intimate bonds with its inhabitants. As a result, the researcher commits to participants' beliefs as a necessary means toward integration and tends to adhere to these beliefs. This mechanism carries negative implications for taking the necessary analytical distance,[11] with the risk to become native and naturalize their view and perspective.[12]

Yet, one of the goals of the ethnographic approach is to provide empirically grounded explanations of what goes on in a specific location.[13] For instance, I remember very well one conversation with a colleague in the middle of the fieldwork. One morning in his office, I was praising how unique Seal's work was and eloquently describing my research participants as fighting against all odds to make this world a better place. Amused, he picked up his laptop and showed me the website of the Ashoka Foundation. "Read this," he told me. On the main page, I read some similar statements to those made by Jorge to the entrepreneurs on the first day of the boot camp, making me realize that I had not even started thinking analytically about them.

If the steps described above are often labeled preliminary analysis, they critically pave the way for a more formal analysis after fieldwork. After 15 months, I gradually reduced my presence at Seal to attending selected events, primarily the social impact and investment committees, for the

[11] See Favret-Saada (1977) for an insightful example of why commitment to participants' beliefs is key to accessing and explaining different social realities.

[12] See Karen Ho's (2012) very insightful methodological commentary discussing how she experienced this process during her ethnography of Wall Street. In particular, she reveals how she had to move from traders' beliefs about their practices to start acknowledging the role of their socialization in the explanations they provided her about their practices.

[13] See Olivier de Sardan (1995) on the pitfalls of "going native" and, this way, reproducing and celebrating the beliefs and habits reigning at the field site.

remaining four months. By January 2019, I had spent 18 months in the field and collected considerable data with the different groups of interest. Volume, of course, is not the test for quality in data production. More importantly, I had spent a considerable amount of time thinking about the significance of this data, specifically during these last four months when I lessened my field presence and "knew" my data quite well.

I left the country a few months later to start a professorship position abroad. To be frank, I seriously missed the exhilaration of my days at Seal. Specifically, the ever-changing workdays and the friendly relationships I had developed with some staff members and the opportunity it offered to me to meet new people weekly. I only gradually began to experience my exit from the field as a relief. Collecting data daily is tiresome. Additionally, the geographical distance was necessary to detach myself from the field. Also, by exchanging about my fieldwork with my new colleagues in the working environment provided by a business school, I started to approach the insights generated during fieldwork through a different lens. Many of my colleagues worked on organizational and entrepreneurial processes, and they opened me to a new world of concepts and theories.

These new influences have been vital in refining the findings from my initial analysis. In particular, an essential aspect of the formal analysis revolves around working through the data by reading and writing. I guess this is not truly surprising, as ethnography is as much about writing as it is about fieldwork. Among the themes identified as relevant, some will lead to the preparation of a research article or a book. Therefore, preparing the article requires identifying appropriate segments of the data to be analyzed with this theme in mind, leading to early drafts of the findings. These drafts would then be shared and commented on by colleagues, allowing me to revisit some of these themes and complement my data. This may lead to the emergence of new themes or refining existing ones to better match the data until a final version of the manuscript is submitted. In other words, the process of writing articles is one way to break down the immense volume of data by identifying exciting themes to be developed independently.

Ethnography as an approach offers unique opportunities for triangulation. It enables strengthening the quality of the analysis because data about the same event can be produced through the combination of different methodological tools. Certainly, this is also the case with mixed methods studies. However, articulating participant observation and semi-structured interviews is unique in increasing the data's depth and the interpretations' reliability.[14] For instance, by observing mentors during their interactions with entrepreneurs, and by later interviewing them about these interactions, I was able not only to document their actual behavior and collect their descriptions of this behavior. I could help them articulate aspects that might not be revealed using one tool or another. This was particularly important because the observational context of the interaction between the mentors and the entrepreneurs powerfully shapes their actions.

Ethnographers are much more likely to attend to multivocality and, therefore, collect data with different groups of stakeholders. The reason lies in that fieldwork, by design, is a space where the ethnographer interacts with these groups as they participate in everyday interactions.[15] This characteristic of the ethnographic approach enables gathering different perspectives about the same event as well as contrasting these perspectives. Ultimately, this allowed for revisiting most themes that emerged during the fieldwork. This is particularly important when the goal is to unearth the meanings people imbue in their actions, and their diversity, to offer comprehensive explanations for the practices and behaviors documented in the field.[16]

## Limitations

When I knocked on Seal's door for my first day of fieldwork, I was totally ignorant about entrepreneurship in general and impact entrepreneurship more specifically. Although Seal was located within a 15-minute bike ride from my apartment, I had to learn the language and the conventions orchestrating impact entrepreneurship, as well as to gain technical knowledge to understand the "how to" of this social world. As is often the case, not being already accustomed to the environment, I believed, provided me with a fresh view of the practices and interactions I was witnessing.

[14] See Becker and Geer (1957), Jerolmack and Khan (2014).

[15] I develop this point in more detail in Dumont (2024).

[16] Becker and Geer (1957) questioned the value of using semi-structured interviews alone several decades ago. Their discussion has been continued recently by opponents (Jerolmack & Khan, 2014) and proponents (Lamont & Swidler, 2014) of the use of interview. In my view, the crux of the discussion is not on agreeing on which methodological tool is better than the other. Instead, it is in acknowledging that, beyond their benefits and limitations, it is only in their articulation that we can fully unleash their potential.

However, it also profoundly shaped the content of the data I collected. Certainly, a researcher with a deep understanding of the entrepreneurial process would have focused on more technical aspects of the tasks performed at Seal. Similarly, someone with knowledge of social impact methodology might have focused more on how social impact was constructed and measured. Someone knowledgeable about organizational dynamics might have collected data about hybridity and how distinct organizational logic coexisted at Seal. I spent considerable time learning about impact entrepreneurship while conducting fieldwork and have thus implicitly collected data reflecting my progress during this learning process. Yet, given that most of my research participants were walking into a new experience as much as I was, I believe that my original ignorance was also a strength to be able to capture and document their struggles with impact entrepreneurship as they learned on the go.

As I came to the end of writing this account, I realized that, in many instances, I tended to focus more on the struggles and challenges of those I was observing than on their excitement and exhilaration, which also carry the ideation and development of an impact enterprise. I believe one reason lies in the choice of the setting. Indeed, by definition, a business accelerator is an organization relentlessly challenging entrepreneurs and collaborators on many fronts until, eventually, celebrating their progress by the end of the program during a demo day.

Another reason, probably, lies in the over-glorification of the work of impact entrepreneurs who engage in pursuing social or environmental goals instead of being exclusively focused on profit or the high praise around choosing entrepreneurship as a career. However, like their counterparts, early-stage impact entrepreneurs are likely to experience fast failure and are full of doubts about their choices. Further, as we have seen in this book, not all impact entrepreneurs nor all their collaborators share a fervor for achieving social impact goals. Overall, inconsistencies and contradictions are interesting because they help identify the challenges people face in their everyday organizational practices and interactions.

How generalizable are the insights provided in this book? Several reasons make me believe that many of these insights are not idiosyncratic to Seal as a particular unit of observation. Chief among these reasons is that ethnography enables the generalization of processes.[17] Applied to the

[17] Tony Watson (2001) provides a very insightful example of this potential in his ethnographic work on managers.

present work, this means that other people probably experience similar challenges in various contexts. Further, they may solve these challenges in similar or different ways according to the characteristics of these contexts. Second, ethnography also fundamentally enables the identification of heterogeneity within the phenomenon under study. In fact, the chapters of this book unearth the existence of a wide array of perspectives about impact. These perspectives shape the manufacturing of impact through the production of impact work. That the different people inhabiting this book imbue "impact" with different meanings is essential in that it suggests that this is likely to be the case elsewhere, particularly given that the field is in the making. Third, because of the close involvement in the field, the detailed account provided here can inform the practices of anyone entering this type of organization. In fact, I have wrestled with practices and events that other social scientists have identified in other locations. Fourth, the design of the accelerator and the long-term nature of the ethnographic approach enable the study of a relatively large number of ventures with similar characteristics. Fifth, the organizational features of Seal are similar, in many respects, to a great deal of business accelerators elsewhere. Hence, if some problems and questions raised by my fieldwork are undoubtedly field-specific, others are more likely to be detected in different settings.

In sum, the aim of this book is not to generalize about the larger population of impact entrepreneurs and impact aficionados in general, nor to offer general statements about the situations I have documented at Seal. Instead, it is to identify some of the processes to which segments of this population could be subjected, to provide a dense description of these processes, and to theorize about them in a way that would help explain practices and interactions unfolding elsewhere, among those inhabiting the social world of impact entrepreneurship.

## Bibliography

Adler, P., & Adler, P. (1987). *Membership Roles in Field Research.* Sage.

Aldrich, H. E., & Ruef, M. (2018). Unicorns, Gazelles, and Other Distractions on the Way to Understanding Real Entrepreneurship in the United States. *Academy of Management Perspectives, 32*(4), 458–472.

Anteby, M. (2013). Relaxing the Taboo on Telling Our Own Stories: Upholding Professional Distance and Personal Involvement. *Organization Science, 24*(4), 1277–1290.

Appadurai, A. (1986). Introduction: Commodities and the Politics of Value. In *The Social Life of Things* (pp. 3–63). Cambridge University Press.
Bacq, S., & Alt, E. (2018). Feeling Capable and Valued: A Prosocial Perspective on the Link Between Empathy and Social Entrepreneurial Intentions. *Journal of Business Venturing, 33*(3), 333–350. https://doi.org/10.1016/j.jbusvent.2018.01.004
Bandinelli, C., & Arvidsson, A. (2013). Brand Yourself a Changemaker! *Journal of Macromarketing, 33*(1), 67–71.
Becker, H. S., & Geer, B. (1957). Participant Observation and Interviewing: A Comparison. *Human Organization, 16*, 28–32.
Boellstroff, T., Nardi, B., Pearce, C., & Taylor, T. L. (2012). *Ethnography and Virtual Worlds: A Handbook of Method*. Princeton University Press.
Boyer, D. (2013). *The Life Informatic: Newsmaking in the Digital Era*. Cornell University Press.
Briody, E. K., & Stewart, A. (2019). Entrepreneurship: A Challenging, Fruitful Domain for Ethnography. *Journal of Business Anthropology, 8*(2), Article 2.
Carr, J. C., Marshall, D. R., Michaelis, T. L., Pollack, J. M., & Sheats, L. (2022). The Role of Work-to-venture Role Conflict on Hybrid Entrepreneurs' Transition into Entrepreneurship. *Journal of Small Business Management, 0*(0), 1–24.
Dees, J. G. (1998). *The Meaning of Social Entrepreneurship*. Comments and Suggestions Contributed from the Social Entrepreneurship Funders Working Group.
Dewey, J. (1939). *Theory of Valuation* (Vols. 2, 4). University of Chicago Press.
Dumont, G. (2018). *Grimpeur professionnel: Le travail créateur sur le marché du sponsoring*. Paris: Editions de l'Ecole des Hautes Etudes en Sciences Sociales.
Dumont, G. (2023a). Immersion in Organizational Ethnography: Four Methodological Requirements to Immerse Oneself in the Field. *Organizational Research Methods, 26*(3), 441–458.
Dumont, G. (2024). Fulfilling the Process Promise in New Venture Creation Research: The Ethnography/Accelerator Approach. *Strategic Entrepreneurship Journal*, Online first. https://doi.org/10.1002/sej.1494
Ebrahim, A., & Rangan, V. K. (2014). What Impact? A Framework for Measuring the Scale and Scope of Social Performance. *California Management Review, 56*(3), 118–141. https://doi.org/10.1525/cmr.2014.56.3.118
Emerson, J. (2003). The Blended Value Proposition: Integrating Social and Financial Returns. *California Management Review, 45*(4), 35–51. https://doi.org/10.2307/41166187
Emerson, R. M., Fretz, R. I., & Shaw, L. L. (2011). *Writing Ethnographic Fieldnotes*. University of Chicago Press.
Favret-Saada, J. (1977). *Les Mots, la Mort, Us Sorts. La sorcellerie dans le Bocage*. Gallimard.

Folta, T. B., Delmar, F., & Wennberg, K. (2009). Hybrid Entrepreneurship. *Management Science, 56*(2), 253–269.

Geertz, C. (1973). *The Interpretation Of Cultures.* Basic Books.

Goffman, E. (1959). *The Presentation of Self in Everyday Life.* Doubleday.

Hammersley, M., & Atkinson, P. (2007). *Ethnography. Principles in practice* 3rd edn Sage.

Ho, K. (2012). "Studying Up" Wall Street: Reflections on Theory and Methodology. In L. Aguiar & C. Schneider (Eds.), *Researching Amongst Elites: Challenges and Opportunities in Studying Up* (pp. 29–48). Routledge.

Jerolmack, C., & Khan, S. (2014). Talk is Cheap: Ethnography and the Attitudinal Fallacy. *Sociological Methods & Research, 43*(2), 178–209.

Lamont, M., & Swidler, A. (2014). Methodological Pluralism and the Possibilities and Limits of Interviewing. *Qualitative Sociology, 37*(2), 153–171.

Langley, A., & Klag, M. (2019). Being Where? Navigating the Involvement Paradox in Qualitative Research Accounts. *Organizational Research Methods, 22*(2), 515–538.

Lévesque, M., & Stephan, U. (2020). It's Time We Talk About Time in Entrepreneurship. *Entrepreneurship Theory and Practice, 44*(2), 163–184.

Mair, J., & Martí, I. (2006). Social Entrepreneurship Research: A Source of Explanation, Prediction, and Delight. *Journal of World Business, 41*(1), 36–44.

Malinowski, B. (1922). *Argonauts of the Western Pacific: An Account of Native Enterprise and Adventure in the Archipelagoes of Melanesian New Guinea.* Routledge.

Mears, A. (2011). *Pricing Beauty: The Making of a Fashion Model.* University of California Press.

Moeran, B. (2005). *The Business of Ethnography.* Berg Publishers.

Moeran, B. (2007). *Ethnography at Work (New).* Berg Publishers.

Moeran, B., & Christensen, B. (Eds.). (2013). *Exploring Creativity: Evaluative Practices in Innovation, Design, and the Arts.* Cambridge University Press.

Montgomery, A., Dacin, P., & Dacin, T. (2012). Collective Social Entrepreneurship: Collaboratively Shaping Social Good. *Journal of Business Ethics, 111*, 375–388.

Olivier de Sardan, J.-P. (1995). La politique du terrain. Sur la production des données en anthropologie. *Enquête. Archives de la revue Enquête, 1*, 71–109.

Patriotta, G., Gond, J.-P., & Schultz, F. (2011). Maintaining Legitimacy: Controversies, Orders of Worth, and Public Justifications: Maintaining Legitimacy. *Journal of Management Studies, 48*(8), 1804–1836.

Reinecke, J., Van Bommel, K., & Spicer, A. (2017). *When orders of worth clash: Negotiating legitimacy in situations of moral multiplexity.* In C. Cloutier, J.-P. Gond, & B. Leca (Eds.), *Justification, Evaluation and Critique in the Study of Organizations, Research in the Sociology of Organizations, 52*, pp. 3–72. Emerald Group Publishing Limited.

Schumpeter, J. (1911). *The Theory of Economic Development*. Harvard University Press.
Stephens, J. P. (2020). How the Show Goes On: Using the Aesthetic Experience of Collective Performance to Adapt while Coordinating. *Administrative Science Quarterly*, *66*(6), 1–41.
Vatin, F. (2013). Introduction. In F. Vatin (Ed.), Evaluer et valoriser: Une sociologie économique de la mesure(édition revue et augmentée, pp. 17–37). Presses Universitaires du Mirail.
Watson, T. (2001). *In Search of Management: Culture, Chaos and Control in Managerial Work*. Thomson Learning.

# Index[1]



[1] Note: Page numbers followed by ‘n’ refer to notes.



G. Dumont, *Impact Work*,
https://doi.org/10.1007/978-3-031-64661-4

## I



## L



## M

SPRINGER NATURE

# GPSR Compliance

*The European Union's (EU) General Product Safety Regulation (GPSR) is a set of rules that requires consumer products to be safe and our obligations to ensure this.*

*If you have any concerns about our products, you can contact us on ProductSafety@springernature.com*

In case Publisher is established outside the EU, the EU authorized representative is:

Springer Nature Customer Service Center GmbH
Europaplatz 3
69115 Heidelberg, Germany

The manufacturer's authorised representative in the EU is Springer Nature Customer Service Centre GmbH, Europaplatz 3, 69115 Heidelberg, Germany. If you have any concerns regarding our products, please contact ProductSafety@springernature.com

Printed and bound by CPI Group (UK) Ltd, Croydon, CR0 4YY

30/09/2026

02225583-0002